My true/ legendary story with the Green Man & Beyond sapiens' wisdom, ultimate meaning and fixed destiny

My true/ legendary story with the Green Man & Beyond sapiens` wisdom, ultimate meaning and fixed destiny

Benjamin Katz

Library of Congress Control Number:		2020913138
ISBN:	Hardcover	978-1-9845-8881-4
	Softcover	978-1-9845-8880-7
	eBook	978-1-9845-8879-1

Print information available on the last page.

Rev. date: 07/21/2020

To order additional copies of this book, contact:
Xlibris
1-888-795-4274
www.Xlibris.com
Orders@Xlibris.com
812060

ACKNOWLEDGMENTS

I wish to thank Shai Gabay and Susan Sclipcea for their essential contribution to this manuscript. The two had given me very useful feedback on the final process of assembling the manuscript. I wish to thank my sister, Ziva, for making the beautiful paper clips, which adorn the front and back cover of the books, and brother, Menachem Katz, for contributing his drawings, which you will find in book 1.

Book 1

My True/Legendary Story with the Green Man

PART I

Childhood – the days of absorbing and receiving the blessed nutrient

In the beginning

Somehow somebody created a lighted tunnel for him, and it should lead him somewhere.

Abraham was born in Palestine shortly after WWII ended and three months after the atomic bombs were dropped on Hiroshima and Nagasaki, which had forced Japan to capitulate. There lived at that time many Arabs and just over half a million Jews in Palestine, which was under British rule.

Abraham did not know—for how could he know?—that he was born immediately after the Holocaust, the worst human massacre ever, the worst Jewish genocide in history, and the biggest disaster for his parents and their families, friends, and peers. They had lost all family members from the areas where they had lived for generations in Poland, Ukraine, and elsewhere in Europe. His childhood was overshadowed by these atrocities and the Great War in 1947–1948 against Arabs, which resulted in the kibbutz destruction and many dead friends and members of his parents.

That also meant that he grew up with a story about justice, who triumphed over evil as seven Arab countries conspired to destroy the new state, Israel, and the story of how the kibbutz members had fought for their cause just as the Russians fought for Stalingrad. The battle on his kibbutz had become a myth of the struggle for the new state, Israel. All these things he did not know yet, but these events set their marks in his innocent child soul and helped later on to shape his relationship to the human world and insights into human nature.

Before the war erupted in 1947, the kibbutz was surrounded by Arab villages and caravans on the way to Jaffa and back to Gaza passed by. In the ever-trot and quiet like a distant dream, they moved through the desert while the camel's silver bells tinkled: ling, long, ling, long. It is life's eternal song.

He was barely three years when Egyptian forces encircled the kibbutz and bombarded it from the surrounding hills. The carnage was huge, and the bombs hit the children houses shortly after the children had—in the cover of darkness—been evacuated. This evacuation he had some reminiscence. He remembered the violent sobbing as parents, who had to stay back in the kibbutz to defend it, waved goodbye to their children.

His mother lifted him to a woman, who took him into the darkness of an armored personnel carrier, where she put him on a cold and hard metal bench.

It was pitch-dark, and he could not see anything, only hear sniffling children around her, who were scolded if they cried loudly. His legs were too short to reach the floor, so his feet dangled in the air. He was afraid of falling into the dark abyss and of the weeping adults outside, and he wanted to cry, but he should not as his mother told him.

They had to cross the Arab lines, and therefore, they had to be quiet. The cars with the kids started moving with extinguished lights, and there was someone who held his hand in the darkness. He thought that this row of cars looked like a camel caravan, only without the bells ringing ling, long, ling, long. The only sound that could be heard was the motor humming.

Some children sniffled quietly, but the engine humming sound blurred their sobbing. He wondered who it could be that held his hand. A female voice close to his ear asked him in a whisper if he was afraid, and he replied, "No, but I love light . . ."

He hesitated a moment and said, "Yes, I'm afraid of the big bad wolf."

The woman whispered that there were no wolves nearby, only wild dogs and small coyotes in the fields. He replied, "There is a wolf in the kibbutz! There is a man named Wolf."

She laughed softly and said that although the man was called Wolf, he was not a real wolf. But Abraham insisted that there was also another wolf in the kibbutz.

"Where is he?" she asked.

He answered her with a rhyme, which he had learned by heart: "If you will go out there, the wolf will eat you with skin and hair!"

"Well, this wolf comes from fairy tales, not from real life!" she said.

"Sweet Abraham, you know what you can do to get all the wolves in the world to disappear? You just sing the song I taught you a few days ago." And now he knew who she was. It was Ruth, who cared for them in the children's house. And she began to sing in his ear.

> *Through the darkness of night, we bear our burning torches.*
> *They light up our way so we will not topple.*
> *So come to us and turn on your light, and the wolves will flee away into the dark night . . .*

"You know that wolves are afraid of torches and flames and the light which they spread around them? Try to sing it so you can suddenly see the light."

He began to sing the song, and suddenly, there was light everywhere; burning torches danced in the darkness like the grains in a wheat field when the wind blows through them, and now he was not afraid anymore. But then he remembered the deer in the fields had neither fire nor torches and could be in danger.

"What about the deer?" he asked. "Where do they get the light and fire against the wolves?"

"You can sing the song about them, so I light torches for them while you sing," suggested Ruth.

He began hesitantly, "What do the deer do at night?"

"They close their big eyes and stretch their long legs so they can sleep in the night," sang Ruth.

"Who does keep guard to protect their sweet dreams at night?" he sang on.

"The lighted white moon in the sky is their best guard. It smiles to them in their hiding place and whispers to them, 'Be quiet now. It is now time to sleep. It is night!'" Ruth replied.

"What do the deer dream at night?"

"They dream that they play with fine tiny glass marbles with the elephants and that they win all the competitions."

"Who does wake them up in the morning after the night?" sang Abraham.

"Neither an elephant nor a monkey, a dog, a rabbit, a peacock, or a hare."

"It's the sun's rays that wake them up from their sleep at night," he concluded the song.

"There, you can see for yourself!" said Ruth to him. "At night, it is the light from the moon that protects them, and in the day, it is the light from the sun that protects them from the wolves. It is like having torches with blazing fire. Can you see it for yourself?"

Abraham nodded eagerly. Yes, he could see it for himself.

He suddenly felt happy in this pitch darkness, in the growling wagon because he knew how the deer were constantly protected by the light so that the wolves could not eat them.

"When we come home again, can we play with the deer with our marbles?" he asked.

"Yes, we do it when we get back home," he heard her say as she kissed him on the cheek. And then he fell asleep.

It was the night the children houses were razed by the Egyptian artillery, but Abraham slept soundly in the armored car that brought the kibbutz children northward while he dreamed of deer, which held the burning torches with their front legs and hid the fine glass beads in their mouth because they do not have any pockets to put them in.

The day after, he woke up in a small bed in a large house, with the other children around him in their small beds. They cried a bit, and he asked where they were living now.

"We have traveled to a foreign country!" a big boy said to him. One girl asked if her parents could find her in this foreign country when they came to pick her up.

"They will neither come today nor tomorrow. They may never come again. They must fight against the evil Arabs," said the big boy before he turned around and walked out.

Abraham and the others lay in their beds and wept until they had to get up and eat their first breakfast in "the new foreign country."

THE LIGHTED TUNNEL

The first thing he saw when he came out of the house was a lighted tunnel opening in front of him, which flashed between the dusty trees on the other side of the square, just behind an empty water basin. A glimmering ray of light penetrated the leaves and beamed at the tunnel exit while some voice whispered, "Let the light of torches rise and shine and show you how to harness darkness and spread light!" And the light burst forth and filled the tunnel with fluid of gold.

He stood on the stone steps to the big house belonging to a rich Arab man, who left it when the war had started, and the light flowed down the stairs, down his bare feet, and to the dusty path. From the edges of the circular pool filled with clear water that lay in the middle of the dusty square, small bright dots of light like colorful diamonds flashed and sparkled. He walked gingerly down the stairs, along the dusty road, and over to the grove, which enclosed the lighted tunnel. His little legs trudged through the deep, soft, and warm dust. The sunlight heat penetrated down to the dust and burned his toes, so he jumped a few times out to the roadside, where the undergrowth and the hard crust were cooler to walk on.

He heard a woman's voice behind his back far, far away. "Abraham, where are you going?" But he went directly inside the lighted tunnel, so he could not listen to her or to the rest of the world. For now, he listened only to himself. And yet he imagined that soon, within a moment, he would hear the heavy, regular steps behind him—this encroaching world—and that a panting, breathless woman would pick him and carry him back to the house, which was filled with coolness, deep shadows, and ordinariness.

But nothing happened, perhaps because he was invisible in the light tunnel.

He jumped from one tuft of grass to another and could feel that he was going out on a great journey. Suddenly, he stood in a large clearing, which he vaguely recognized. In one corner stood three white-painted wooden houses, surrounded by large eucalyptus trees that shaded the flowing golden light. In the shadows at the entrance to one of the houses stood a small bed, and he knew immediately that something was strange about it. In the bed lay a boy under a light blanket with his head resting on two large white pillows and with big brown eyes that followed Abraham with a suspicious gaze.

He was not sure if he knew the boy. It seemed to him that his mother had once told him about a boy who could not get out of bed.

"Why can't he get out of bed? Does he have no legs to walk on?" he asked his mother.

"Yes, he has two legs," his mother said, laughing, "but he is sick, so he is too weak to go."

What did it mean to lie in bed and to be too weak? He did not understand it. When he woke up in the morning, he jumped just out of bed as easy as a light feather. He approached the boy who watched him gloomily and concentrated and became frightened by his tired old man's expression.

The boy leaned on his elbows and looked at him while he coughed violently. They looked at each other for a while without saying anything. The boy would soon die, but neither of them knew yet.

"Who are you?" asked the boy.

"Abraham," he whispered.

"Why do you whisper? Are you sick in your throat?" the boy asked with a terrible laughter.

Abraham did not answer but just kept staring at him, knowing that the light from the tunnel protected him.

"Who are your parents?" the boy interrogated. "What's the name of your father and mother?"

This question Abraham could not answer. He knew his father as a father and his mother as a mother, and his father was also a great hero who fought somewhere else, and that was about all he knew. He looked at the sick boy and grimaced.

"Can you whistle?" the boy asked him.

He tried to whistle but failed. Now the boy smiled, and his face looked like a bird of prey. Abraham came to think of the birds of prey his father had once in a cage and one day had escaped and flew away.

"Have you seen a big black bird of prey?" he asked the boy.

"I have seen many. It's the big birds that catch small mice and other small animals. They can catch a pup or a kid. I have a picture where you can see them all," the sick boy replied.

"I have a great bird of prey, which my father had caught and put in a cage, and we have an ancient tortoise which may be four hundred years old, and we also have a monkey and a brown bear, not a teddy bear," boasted Abraham.

"You're lying!" the boy shouted suddenly. "You don't have a monkey or a bear! The monkeys live in the zoo and in Africa, and the brown bears are living in America. Those we have not here, you idiot."

"I have a monkey, and it is so big." Abraham showed it with his hands.

"You are full of lies. Get out of here!" shouted the boy excitedly.

"Why do you cough all the time? You do not look like a real child," said Abraham.

"Go your way! You're full of lies! Go away!"

Abraham was angry that the boy did not believe that he had a monkey and a bear.

He turned to the boy and shouted, "You are full of lies! I will go out and catch more monkeys and bears, and you will not be allowed to see them!" He turned his back on the sick child and went back to the hot, dusty path and toward the lighted tunnel.

Sometime later—and he did not know how long—he was told by some older children that the adults had thrown the sick boy into the trash can.

He had been coughing a lot and made lots of rotten carrot-colored poo, and finally, he died and was thrown into a large garbage can. Now he was gone, and therefore, he would never get to know that Abraham actually had a monkey and a bear.

Abraham stood in the sun on the sidewalk with horse's harness on him and helped play the horse role as the small children should always be horses, and he was wondering what the coughing boy was doing down in the trash can. He wondered what he was eating and drinking down there. He decided to ask his mother what a little boy was doing in a garbage can in the middle of the night and when he would get up again and go home.

He saw the hungry cats that run in and out of garbage cans, but he was not sure if the boy could also do it. He was not angry with the boy anymore, and he thought it was bad for him that he just had to get down into the garbage can without his father and mother or other children he could play with. It could not be much fun, although maybe he played just a kind of hide-and-seek.

And then he forgot the boy, for the lighted tunnel could not stop there, where eerie haze and pain prevailed.

The light was warm and like liquid gold, and it lit a small enchanted world, far from the horrors of war, sorrow, and death. He saw small and large turtles crossing an unknown track toward eternity, for they were incredibly old and could not die. He ran up and down the soft, warm sand hills. He saw fantastic flowers blossom and wild tulips in purple and deep red, which waved to him as beautiful peacock tails. From the top of the big house, the children launched up to the sky large colorful kites. They flew higher and higher through the bright blue sky over the green plantations of orange trees and right up to the moon. A few of them did not come back like the boy who shat carrot-colored poo in his bed. They flew away like migratory birds that travel farther after the winter, and he thought it might be sad to go so far away without having its kite parents with them. Now and then, little Abraham could feel a stab in the heart at the thought of the things and the people who disappeared and did not come back but what it meant in relation to all the light that flowed from the tunnel and brought new exciting experiences and people from afar.

There was a dark-skinned old woman from Mexico on a wicker chair while the sun was going down, and the day took on violet and orange hues. She sat under the big eucalyptus and seemed to daydream, or maybe she was engulfed by the slow and lazy clouds, which marched over the pool. She was very old, perhaps as old as a turtle, and it was the first time he saw an old man. In the kibbutz, there were only young people and children, for all the grandparents died in Polish ghettos and death camps, his mother had told him.

In the books, he saw pictures of old people. They had round, rosy cheeks and smiling lips and large, long silver beard. But the woman from Mexico was small and wrinkled and had hunchback. She opened her mouth, and he was gripped by fear when he saw the deep black hole opened up. He stood at a safe distance and heard her breathe deeply and noisily.

Now he knew that she would soon die and be thrown into the trash can, perhaps down to the little boy. As a tired migratory bird, she came from a distant place to land on a wicker chair among the eucalyptus trees to die or migrate once again in the display of the violet and orange evening sky. But she did not have to end in a bin in Mexico if they have such a thing up there.

When darkness enshrouds her, he thought, *she will rise up from her chair and fly up against the dark sky. She would soar up there like a small defenseless migratory bird and fly far away.* He felt sad that she had to fly alone, without a father, a mother and good friends, all by herself to Mexico.

In the evening, just before going to bed, the children were speaking on dying. Nachama, a girl from his group, told him that when you die, you are away, and then they bury you in the ground, and you lie there, absolutely quiet.

"Do you lie there all the time? And what about the garbage can?" he asked.

"Man is not buried down in the trash because he will get to smell disgusting, but when you get into the ground, you are there!" she said firmly.

"And what do you eat and drink there?"

"You don't eat and drink down there, you fool!" she replied. "A man who dies does nothing. A man only lies there."

During this night, many of the children shed tears when they came to bed, and he did too. But David gathered them around his bed and told that what Nachama had told them was not right, for a man could be to another person when he died, or animal, maybe a dog or a goose, and others were born again.

At night, he had a nightmare. In the dream, he lay under the ground covered with fine, loose soil. He jumped out of the hole and brushed the dirt and dust off him while he shouted, "I'm not dead!" But then he began with his comrades to go in a single line down toward a green and fertile meadow, and all the children were turned into geese. It must be death, he thought. Behind them walked a woman from the kibbutz, whom he knew well. She held a long, thin stick in her hand as she hurried them up. He thought that they were going to a lush meadow, where they could play.

Time passed, and the light was not as gold and warm and liquid as before. He began to see other things in life. There was something that was hidden beyond the lighted tunnel.

And the day came when the lighted tunnel was penetrated by time.

He was out for a walk in nature, along with some other children. Suddenly, they saw a woman from the kibbutz run to the adult who cared for them and excitedly whispered something to her. Both began crying while they called a boy named David to come to them. Afterward, they, the children, were told that David's mother had died in the night.

David had listened impatiently, and although they had tried to hold him, he wrenched himself free and ran after a white fluttering butterfly.

At the funeral, which was the first one the children participated in, he saw the grown-ups weeping bitterly while David ran humming around. Abraham looked at his friend and then at his own mother, who was crying. He saw the people let the coffin slip down into the deep hole in the ground, and he knew suddenly that it was true that the dead were left there, deep down in the earth. And even if they woke up and knocked on the coffin lid, who would be able to hear their cries and see their tears?

A shadow began to show its contours over by the entrance to the lighted tunnel. If this is how it is, then there is not only light but also frightening darkness in this world. Then what about the turtles and eternity? What happens to them? Don't they live forever? When he could not answer the questions, he began to sing, and the song led him back to the lighted tunnel, which warmly caressed him in its glow.

ENCOUNTERING THE EVOLVING BUSTAN

A gardener who plants his Bustan must water and fertilize it. This is something all children who grew up in nature know, and in addition, he should plant fruit trees so that they can beat deep roots and suck nourishment without compromising the neighboring trees and catch the light effortlessly. But the gardener must also weed the weeds if he is to get his Bustan to thrive and flourish, provide shade, delight the eye, and give the man his fruits. But there is also another secret goal for Bustan, which is visible only to the initiated.

From time, the gardener must heal all felling diseased trees, and sometimes he must cut down trees to make room for new and young trees. All these tasks are carried out by a good gardener in tune with the changing seasons and circumstances.

Abraham's kibbutz had been razed to the ground during the war, and he had only a vague recollection of how it had been before. He remembered that he rode on a big, brown, and scary donkey while his father went beside him and held on to him, and he could remember the sound of sloshing water in the Arab clay pots, which he had been drinking.

He also remembered the night when he and the other children in the children's house were awakened by the noise of an airplane, and he was able to see how it threw something down on a house nearby and how the darkness was suddenly illuminated by a powerful flash of light, followed by a huge blast. Then he remembered the glimpse of the nocturnal evacuation of the children and the adults' desperate crying when they saw their children leave the surrounded kibbutz. But then again, the lighted tunnel popped up and removed all horror and pain.

His father came to visit them during the war two truces. He arrived as a desert wind in his jeep and always dusty beyond recognition and was immediately surrounded by his mother and the other grown-ups, while Abraham was sitting on his mother's arm in the middle of the tumult and waited patiently for his father, wanting to see him. He waited for this sweaty and bearded man, who had been foreign to him, who would come over and kiss him on the cheek with his prickly beard and lift him into the sky, so high that he was almost dizzy and scared, and then drag him down toward his face so they could rub noses. He was tense every time the strange man showed up, and each time, he hoped that he had something exciting to him. Once he got a can of pineapple in sweet juice and a can of corn, and another time, it was steak canned from a country called America. He also got some Jordanian coins with the king's portrait, which was so great that he wanted to go and see the king face-to-face.

But of all the wonderful small gifts he had received from his father, he liked best the small round candies, which could change color. When he got a package of them, he ran to his hiding place in dense bushes, and there, surrounded by whispering eucalyptus trees, he took a candy forward. He took it in his mouth and forgot the world around him. The quivering and vibrating air danced around him, and the yellowish horizon merged with the light blue mountains, while he kept the candy on the tip of the tongue. There he sat, the evening shadows began to spread around while darkness was tiptoeing and he could hear his mother call him. But he did not answer so long as he had a candy in his mouth.

A candy could last a long time, for he took his time to consider the fantastic colors along the way turned up: red and orange, purple that turned into Marengo, fresh grass green that became sunny yellow and eventually melt in angelic white. While he licked it, he thought of the bearded man and his mother, who said, "Now run off and play with the other children. We will soon get you."

But that day he would not play with the other children because he would not share his sweets. Occasionally, they found yet his hiding place, and he had to swap some of the sweets for a small, fine glass bead with butterfly wings inside or for a triangular stamp, like the big kids thought was very expensive.

Suddenly, the war ended, and then they were driven home again.

His father continued as a senior officer in the newly formed army the government hurriedly had built up. The kibbutz was still surrounded by a large black barbed wire fence, and the area was full of anti-tank obstacles and landmines, which occasionally exploded in the fields when a dog or a fox ran over them, and there were some members from the kibbutz, who lost their legs as they hit them with their tractor. He was afraid of the big stray dogs that roamed close to the houses and sometimes had the kids help their own dogs in the fight against the starving dogs from the abandoned Arab villages.

He was angry with his mother and father and would not obey them but ran away. He could crawl through the barbed wire and come out to the open fields, among the stray dogs and the exploding mines. His mother yelled at him and ran after him, but he was so good at running that she could not catch him, calling a male neighbor to chase him and grab him. His father was in the army, so he had nothing to fear from that quarter. Through the heat haze, he could see the yellowish parched land in front of them. Desert wind brought the stabbing and piercing grit with it. It blew a day or two and then headed south and stopped, after which a devouring Hamsin (very hot days) broke out. The air was quivering hot, heavy, and suffocating, and at night, it felt as if the darkness was engulfed in an invisible and corrosive fire.

The summer was hard, and Hamsin felt endless. It was perhaps for this reason that his first meeting with the Bustan seemed so overwhelming for him. He was almost four years old when his father came one early morning and woke him in the children's home and helped him get dressed and brush his teeth. And the two drove in the jeep. It was the first time Abraham was allowed to sit beside his father in this smashing, gasping machine, and he kept firmly in his father's trousers. When they had gone a long way through the scorched fields in the fresh morning air, they hit a dusty road.

"Behind the hills there," his father said, showing with his hand, "a big sea is lying as I have told you about." He asked, "Shall we travel to the big blue sea?"

There had to be great excitement out there with gold ships and boats that glided over the calm blue water surface with small sailors in blue and white sailor jerseys, all children, who pulled a large snorting and laughing whale. The rope was fastened, and they pulled and pulled.

"Not today! Today we cannot reach it, but I want to show you something else that is very beautiful. I am sure that you will think about it. It is a

Bustan, an Arab garden with fruit trees, vegetables, and spices," his father said.

Abraham wanted so much to see the blue sea. He could splash in small blue waves, the round smiling waves laughing, playing with one another, and disappearing in the gold-plated horizon. He could imagine a boat sailing out in the horizon, on which there were young sailors who slept soundly while the east wind drove their boat further and further away, right there where the sea disappears in the horizon. He thought on how they could find back if they did not soon wake up. Now drove his father against a low chain of round hills. He noticed that the landscape had changed while he had dreamed away to the blue sea.

The hills were covered with blood red, lemon yellow, and white flowers, and there were so many of them that it looked like a huge blanket.

"See, Father!" he cried, elated. "See all the flowers there!"

His father smiled at him. "Take care! I stop now the car!" He braked suddenly in front of a large stone block between the white limestone debris. All of a sudden, he saw the most beautiful blanket of colorful flowers he had ever seen. His eyes, accustomed to the desert gray and yellow colors and its barren nakedness, could not be satisfied by the colors of this giant floral mosaic.

"Come, my son! We must tread the hill!" shouted his father and started to go up with large, measured steps. Abraham started running after him. He caught up with his father halfway and continued past him. When he reached the top of the hill, it was as if a bolt of lightning struck him. He gasped so loud that his father looked at him anxiously. On the slope to the west was still a thick carpet of glowing red and purple anemones, and a little further away, behind a low cactus fence with red ripe, pungent fruits, lay the Bustan.

Many years later, as a young man, he saw the film about Kaspar Hauser, telling about a boy who spent his first sixteen years in a deep, dark cellar or cave. Somebody took care of him and taught him rudimentary language. One dark night, he was carried away by this mysterious man and brought up on top of a hill. Morning broke out, and he saw for the first time in his life the sun rise and colorful creation/miracles: green lush fields that flashed in the sun, golden yellow cornfields, forest with its green trees, and clear blue sky. This was similar for the experience Abraham had had with his father at the entrance to the Bustan.

The Bustan was cradled in gentle sunlight as an indescribably beautiful mosaic of all shades of green, bloodred pomegranates, red-hot poppies, almond trees, white and pink flowers, and vines with bunches of green and red grapes, lemon trees, orange trees, and mulberry trees with deep red, juicy, and fragrant fruits, all enveloped in a sense of intoxicating fragrance. He heard the soporific hum of bees, and the world went merry-go-round. He closed his eyes and pressed his small fists against the eyelids. When the movement stopped, he opened his eyes again, and now he saw a number of ancient, gnarled, and wrinkled olive trees that stood by themselves. The world around him stood still; it trembled a little bit still, but the dizzying movement had stopped.

He moved his eyes to the north, where the cactus fence framed three magnificent mulberry trees with branches heavy with pink, black-red, and white-yellow juicy berries. He saw a man looking at them from an arbor close to a well surrounded by small white stones. The man spread his arms out and greeted warmly his father as he gently tucked behind his father. They embraced and then his father pushed him toward the man who looked at him with his piercing black eyes and patted him on the head as he laughed, saying, "Your Abraham looks like my little grandson, Akram. They resemble each other like two drops of water from the same well," he said.

The two men quickly became engrossed in conversation. Their voices became softer and more distant, and instead, he heard the sound of birds singing and chirping like in a blurred dream. When he was about to give in to the gentle whisper of the trees, Naim, his father's friend, came to him. "You, Abraham, my friend's friend, and therefore, you have to climb up in my trees and eat all you want, but stay far away from the well, for it is deep and dangerous!"

Abraham's father looked at him and said, "We sit in the arbor, and remember, my son, you can taste it all, but beware that your stomach does not crack or that the branches do not break and take care now when you climb! You know where we are."

"You can climb the tree, Abraham, and call me if anything happens. Is it okay? " asked Naim and patted him gently in the neck, and Abraham nodded.

He ran down a small slope and to the almond trees, where he stood for a moment and listened, and he heard his father's muffled voice.

He stood in a small clearing, trying to decide which direction he should go. First, he sat at the irrigation canal and took some water with both hands and tasted it. It tasted fresh, and he got down on all fours and drank the shimmering waters. Then he stood and looked around and saw a small sparrow, which jumped from the grass by the almond trees. He could look at its downy feathers that it was very young and thought that it had to be thirsty, so he decided to catch it and get it to drink of the cool water. He moved cautiously toward it, as he had learned to do with the white doves, which landed often by the square close to the kibbutz water tower, but every time he approached the bird, it hopped away while with some clumsy attempts, it tried to get on wings.

He followed it, and a little before they came right up to one of sycamores, the bird spread its wings and flew hesitantly up against the tree's lower branches. He looked up in the large old mulberry tree and decided to climb after the sparrow, but at the same time, he saw a lot of red, pink, and white yellow berries lying on the ground filled up with maturity and sweet juice. A large flock of black ants was trying to drag some of them away, and the sight preoccupied him so much that he forgot about his little bird. He looked attentively at the ants, which fought hard to push and pull the big berries off place. He saw a hole in the ground where their column came, and he lifted a big juicy berry, carried it to the entrance, and pushed it into the hole.

A sweet scent filled his nostrils. He sucked on his fingers. The taste was intoxicatingly sweet. He came to think of his favorite candies that changed color. He lifted a thick berry from the dusty ground, blew dust from it, and tasted it slowly. He took another berry, this time a white-yellow berry, and it also tasted great. He took the fruit out of the mouth and looked long at it; it did not change color, which he had hoped for, yet he threw himself into the berries and decided to eat as much as he could do without a stomachache.

A large berry from the tree fell down on his forehead, and he looked up and saw the throng of beautiful berries that hung just above him. He came back to think of the thirsty sparrow sitting precariously on a branch farther up the tree, and he decided to climb to help the bird down. He got hold of a branch and pulled himself up against it. His legs were fighting in the empty air to reach the branch, and after a major effort, he succeeded in beating his legs around the branch and rise. From there, it was not difficult to reach the tree's crown. He sat on a thick branch and headed out carefully after the bird, which gave a small sharp peep from its throat and flew down to the ground. Just before it hit the ground, it flew up again and disappeared among the olive trees. He thought that a bird of prey or a cat easily could snatch such a precarious flying young sparrow and was sad that such destiny awaited his sparrow. He noticed that the garden became very silent.

He could not hear his father or Naim, the gurgling water, or the buzzing of the bees or birds singing. The deep silence, sunbeams, painted colorful mosaics among the leaves, and his drowsy state made his eyes heavy and tired.

He rubbed his eyes to eliminate fatigue, but now he watched the sunbeams weaving a gold wire among the branches. He followed attentively the golden thread to a thick, gnarled branch that he decided to climb over and straighten out. He climbed carefully on the branch while he tried with his small hands to straighten the branch up. He was about to lose his balance of overwork when he heard a clear voice. "What are you doing up there, Abraham?" It was a lively and cheerful voice that came from the tree's foot, and he turned his gaze downward and saw a strange man under the tree in a bright green robe. The man smiled at him.

"The branch is crooked and will break," stammered Abraham. "I try to straighten it out. Otherwise, it will break."

"Well," the man said, chuckling, "you try to straighten up a crooked branch when the whole world is crooked and warped?"

"Yes," Abraham said softly without understanding the meaning as he watched attentively the man near the foot of the tree. *I wonder if he had seen how greedily I had eaten the berries,* he thought. He wiped out the juice from the corners of his mouth and chin.

"So you will save the branch!" observed the man. "Let it break down. There are too many heavy berries hanging on it!" Then he was silent for a moment while he seemed deep in thought. "Yes! It will break down . . .," he murmured. "And what do you do with a tree that bears too much fruit, so it is destroying itself? Should it be saved?"

He looked at Abraham, who did not know what to say. The man's face lit up, and he was present again. "And what do you want, Abraham?"

"I want this orchard!" he replied promptly.

"It is a good wish," the man said with a smile.

Now Abraham began to wonder how the man knew his name. Was he Naim's friend?

"Are you Naim's friend?" he asked. "Do you work here?"

"No," the man replied. "Naim has worked this Bustan for many years, but he has to leave it soon. Maybe you can nurture your own Bustan when you will grow up, which may come to resemble in a way this one, but you're going to work hard for it, for a Bustan should always be changed and transformed. Are you sure this is what you want?" asked the man as he looked tenderly at him.

Abraham nodded quietly and looked at the man, but he could not understand how a Bustan may be constantly changing and transforming. Suddenly, he noticed that the silence disappeared, and the garden came to life again.

"Do you know, Abraham, how to care for an orchard like this? Look around and see how many different fruit trees do exist here side by side in harmony with each other."

"Yes," answered Abraham. "A man must water the trees. Otherwise, they die of thirst."

"It's true!" The man nodded. "But is there more to do?"

"My father fertilizes the trees. He takes some dried chicken manure from a big bag and spreads a bit of it around them, and then he waters them."

"Yes, for the trees must also have nourishment, and you know, Abraham, what they need apart from water and nutrients?"

Abraham looked at the man and said nothing. He did not know it but would not admit it to the stranger, whose robe gleaming bright green in the sun amazed him. *Where does the green light come from?* he wondered.

The man smiled at him. "In an evolving Bustan, you should ensure adequate distance between the trees so they do not atrophy, and only the strongest will survive. Keep on planting new and healthy trees. It's the first thing you need to remember.

"The second is that a gardener must weed in his Bustan. He must remove suckers and weeds so the trees will not be stifled and that he will have to do this all the time.

"The third is that the trees become sick and old like people. They should be cared for when they are ill, or they must be felled when they become incurably sick so you can plant a new, even better tree instead." He sighed. "Yes, a gardener must also fell trees that cannot survive and risk spreading disease in the garden. Do you think you can remember it all, for only by doing it all together, you get a Bustan like this?"

Abraham looked solemnly at him and nodded.

The Green Man smiled and repeated his word. Then he said, "I've got to go now, but we will meet again. Do you think you will recognize me when we meet?"

"What is your name?" Abraham asked.

"Why do you wish to know it?"

"For if I know your name, I will remember you."

"It is just the same." The man sighed, saying, "I have no name . . . and many names. Call me the Green Man, all right? You will remember me one day without knowing me by right name, I'm sure. You are a wise boy. So goodbye to you and see you another time." He waved, turned, and went.

It looked as if he floated first across the cactus fence and was soaked up by the sunrays before he completely disappeared. Abraham peered out over the horizon to capture the man's character through the incandescent light that flowed violently against him, but the luminous green glow was gone. He quickly jumped down from the branch and ran to the cactus fence where the man had disappeared a moment ago.

Again, he peered out over the horizon and on all sides, but the blinding light now enveloped the entire landscape, so he could not see anything. He began to run toward the small entrance at the fence but stumbled and fell. He had beaten his knees until they bled but stood anyway and ran to the arbor while he yelled at his father with tearful voice.

"What has happened to you, my friend?" asked his father and looked in wonder at the bleeding knee while Naim came hurrying with a pitcher of water in his hand.

"Sit down, Abraham. I cleanse your wounds. It's nothing to talk about, and you will hardly notice it," Naim said as he carefully washed the bleeding knee.

His father found in his military bag a military bandage, and Abraham was now occupied by the white gauze, which they laid on the wounds and stopped to snuffle.

"Where did you fall, son?" asked his father.

"There." He pointed toward the cactus fence. "There, where the man with the bright green clothes disappeared," he stammered.

"What man?" both asked at the same time.

"He stood there under the tree and spoke to me as I sat on the branch. He promised me a Bustan, and then he disappeared over the fence. I ran after him, but suddenly, he was away."

21

"What did he ask you about?" Naim asked urgently. His eyes were dilated and his face gray as ash.

"He asked what was it that I wanted, and I said an orchard as you have, Naim, and then he said that I can get something alike if I will work properly for it, and so . . . he talked about a garden which always changes, and then he said farewell and that I should not forget him because he would come again."

"When did you see him the first time?" Naim asked.

"He suddenly stood under the mulberry tree and spoke to me. I did not see him coming."

"He stood there and talked to you," repeated Naim and walked toward the tree, where he laid himself down on all four and started sniffing around.

Abraham followed his father to the mulberry tree. "I do not see any track," said his father. "Naim, my friend, there are no footprints. The boy fantasized. The war has made him a fantast."

Naim began to follow an invisible track.

"What in hell are you doing, man? The boy daydreamed, and you believe him. There has not been anyone here. Only light wind was passing by. The boy has a lively fantasy." His father said, laughing. Naim stood and looked at his father with a stern glance.

"It is something you do not understand, my friend. There was someone here, but we cannot see him, if he does not wish to be seen. He will only be seen by those he chooses to talk to. Your son was blessed today, Nachum, but you don't understand it!"

His father looked searching and confused at the old Bedouin, whose life he had saved during the war and because of his connections had been allowed to retain its old Bustan.

"Yes, your son," muttered Naim, "was granted today the visit of the all-powerful, insightful teacher of the age. He leaves no trace, but I know he has been here today."

"I do not know what you're talking about," said Abraham's father in a hard tone. "Naim, you are my friend, and a person shall live in his own faith, but do not fill my boy's head with nonsense."

"What is it you do not understand, my friend?" said Naim with a quivering voice. "You do not understand what it means that he, the Khidr (the secret teacher according to Sufi sources), appeared in front of your son today? This means that my time is running out and the same for this

Bustan . . . but the torch must be delivered to a person who will entertain a new Bustan, and your son has today been blessed as the one to bring it into life one day!"

Naim went to Abraham and laid his heavy hand on his head. He looked for a moment at his friend and then gently lifted the boy and kissed him on both cheeks before he slowly turned to all four corners of the world while he muttered something in Arabic.

"What do you say, Naim?" his father asked.

"I proclaim that your son has been given new life today, Nachum. The corn in the fields sprout today, and harvesting people's songs will now fill his heart. He will create another Bustan for us humans."

"With this prophetic power, may you tell me also what will happen to us in the future, Naim?" His father smiled laboriously.

Naim put Abraham gently back on the dark topsoil next to the irrigation channel while a silvery tear ran down his brown cheek. "I can only see into the future when the veil lifts itself up as it happened today in the form of a blessing. And I can see that you and your people are going to destroy this Bustan when I will not be here anymore. But your son will lead the way to a new Bustan for a better and more enduring one than this one, and it comforts my old heart!"

"What is this nonsense all about?" his father cried. "I gave you the documents from the authorities granting you the permission to possess and preserve this Bustan for the next twenty years. Didn't I?"

"Yes, my friend. I have not forgotten this, but you come from an effective and noisy world that does not have peace of mind and wisdom, and therefore, you turn everything into money, profit, and greed and, in this process, destroys everything. You will see! They will destroy this Bustan . . . but your son will show us the way to a new Bustan for better people than you and us when the time comes!"

"And where did you come from, Naim?" His father laughed hoarsely. "From the great invisible worlds, where the future is determined?"

"No, but the veil of time was lifted up today so I could glimpse into the future." Naim smiled. He turned to Abraham and, with a solemn expression on his brown face, said, "Remember, Abraham, that there was a man with green robe under the mulberry tree today, and he was for you the Green Man! He comes again when he promises it, so do not be discouraged, and wait patiently for him because he will surely come again!"

Pesach feast

He was happy, very happy; it was springtime, and they should celebrate Pesach. Abraham got his neat blue pants, and his mother filled his pockets with nuts and showed him how he could break them.

For Pesach, kibbutz families and their friends and guests gathered on long tables in the dining room. Their kibbutz was not as high up in Pesach religious ceremonies but more in the meaning behind Pesach story, the history of the Jewish slaves emancipating themselves from slavery and migrating toward the "promised land" as free people.

They ate however in eight days the party lasted, only unleavened bread, matzo. Abraham's father claimed that it was stone-aged diet that they ate in these days—lots of vegetables, nuts, meat, and fish. On the first evening, Seder, they ate too bitter herbs and green herbs, which they dipped in salt, egg, and a puree of apples, nuts, and cinnamon, which was to create the illusion of the clay, as slaves in Egypt sled with, and they placed a Seder dish on the table with those things as well as a burned lamb bone.

The salt water symbolized the slaves' tears; the bitter herbs, the bitterness of slavery; and the green herbs and egg, spring and rebirth. And they read from Haggadah, the story of the Exodus, in the kibbutz version. Abraham loved the story and its exotic scent but was also very concerned about the drama of moving from bondage to freedom; for him, Pesach was the yearning and aspirations to, and struggle for, freedom, where they celebrated not only that the Jews were free people now but also as a reminder for himself of the duty to work for the freedom of all people in the world.

He loved to hear Moshe, a kibbutz member with a beautiful baritone singing on the podium the traditional song among others on Moses, who struck the water out of the rock when the Jews wandered in the desert and were close to die of thirst. He closed his eyes and listened, enchanted to Moshe's velvety baritone that filled the dining room with its magical tale.

"And Moses smote the rock so that water came leaping forward. And the water filled up the water vessel, by a miracle, a great miracle."

The culmination of the celebration occurred when the kibbutz large choir went to the podium and loudly and polyphonically sang a song that made him shudder. "Get up you wanderers of the desert." He was as enchanted by the song's magic:

> *Arise, wanderers in the desert.*
> *The road is long and the war is not over,*
> *You have walked a long time.*
> *But before you come to your destination,*
> *a long and wide road is awaiting you.*

40 years of wandering in the mountains and in the sand
sea will cost the lives of six hundred thousand of your brothers.
Do not let their corpses hold you back
for those who died, in bondage they died.
Let us walk past them!
Let them lie there and rot
along with their slaves' belongings
which they took with them
from Egypt, the slavery land.
Let us forget the slaves
who could not uproot the slavery from their hearts,
who could not live without their daily onion, garlic and
meat.
Maybe the desert wind will today or tomorrow
cover them with sand or they will be prey for the vultures.

He thought while listening to the choir singing it that it must be so; a journey away from slavery and toward a promised land is bound to great suffering and cost many lives and that six hundred thousand slaves lives was the price for the many who became free people as the case was with his parents, who had left East Europe in 1936 to fight for a Jewish homeland, and the price for establishing the state of Israel, a refuge for the Jewish people, was staggering yet necessary, six million Jews who lost their lives under Second World War. Otherwise, the nations of the world would not allow such state to be established, he was told.

The first of Maj

They stood in a long line on the football field, children front and the adults behind, all in white shirts and blue shorts. Abraham listened with his comrades under a blazing sun to long speeches as party leaders held for the adults, and he felt both drowsy and dizzy. After the first speaker came another speaker, and they went on and on indefinitely. He became impatient and began shifting weight from one leg to the other. The air quivered with heat, and he only waited for the time all of them would sing the "International," and then the `International` tractor would come from the dusty field to the scene.

He was pleased to see the "International" this time really moving, gasping and coughing up against the dining hall at its tracks to lead them to the final victory over the fat, greedy, and complacent capitalists who shamelessly exploited the working class in the big cities, which he, his father, and all the kibbutz members and children also belonged to.

He could not remember all the words but thought that the song was great and electrifying, and the magic event occurred finally, at long last, when three accordion players played for, and four hundred people sang the song with solemn and full voices.

> *Arise ye workers from your slumbers*
> *Arise ye prisoners of want*
> *For reason in revolt now thunders*
> *And at last ends the age of cant.*
> *Away with all your superstitions*
> *Servile masses arise, arise*

We'll change henceforth the old tradition
And spurn the dust to win the prize.

Refrain:
So comrades, come rally
And the last fight let us face
The International unites the human race.

No more deluded by reaction
On tyrants only we'll make war
The soldiers too will take strike action
They'll break ranks and fight no more
And if those cannibals keep trying
To sacrifice us to their pride
They soon shall hear the bullets flying
We'll shoot the generals on our own side.

No savior from on high delivers
No faith have we in prince or peer
Our own right hand the chains must shiver
Chains of hatred, greed and fear
the thieves will out with their booty
And give to all a happier lot.
Each at the forge must do their duty
and we'll strike while the iron is hot.

During the song, he wondered what it meant to be condemned, how the kibbutz members became a slave army, and who suppressed them.

Now he remembered that his father had told him that the kibbutz was the proletarians, not slaves, that they fought against the great capitalists who would oppress them as slaves and that the International would lead them into this decisive battle, but where was this International that was supposed to lead them? The song was over, he thought in panic, and the International had not showed up yet.

Abraham peered toward the kibbutz garage, which some of its back was visible through the eucalyptus trees, and waited for the red-painted tractor, called International, to come rolling, coughing, and snorting, but why did it not come? It would lead them to the nearby religious kibbutz, where they, the proletarians, would start the revolution against the blinded God believers who would not let diaspora mentality vanish and could not live one day without praying to their god who, according to his father, was a mere figure of the imagination and the opium of the people.

He also thought about mammon. What did it look like? He believed that a lot of large gold coins piled up in a dark basement or scattered all over the floor in a deep cave was mammon and that on top of all this gold sat a fat capitalist and looked at them with greedy eyes.

When the ceremony was over and the tractor did not show up, he went to his mother and asked why the International would not come and lead them to the war against the capitalists.

"What kind of International tractor are you talking about?" asked his mother.

"I talk about the red caterpillar in the garage!" he said. "Father can just start it and drive it out. I saw it yesterday in the garage."

"Why should it come up now?" his mother asked, bewildered.

"This International shall lead us to a revolution!" he replied.

"How does it look like?" asked his mother, smiling.

"I said it before. It's the red tractor with caterpillars, which stands in the garage. We can put a big machine gun up on it, for it will frighten the capitalists and make them run away."

His mother began to laugh uncontrollably. He started crying and beating her with his small fists, and then she stopped laughing and gave him a hug. He stopped sniffing, and she explained to him that the tractor was not the right International. The right International was an association of proletarians in the world who would gather and march against the enemy. It was the right International.

On the evening before he was sent to the children's house, his mother read a story for him about a girl named Sleeping Beauty, who had fallen asleep and slept for one hundred years and only woke up when she was kissed by a prince. "Can you sleep so long without eating and drinking?" he asked.

"No, I cannot, but the story is not a real story. It's an adventure, where you tell something that is not true to say something else that can be true," said his mother.

"Why? Can't you just say what it really means?" he asked.

"I can also sometimes, but in a fairy tale, there is always something more to understand than what is being said, something you have to imagine and understand. In Sleeping Beauty, it is about a beautiful young woman who is brought to life by a handsome prince. I think that the hidden point was that many people sleep throughout their lives but hope that someone will get them to wake up and feel alive. It does not happen in life!"

"Why will they rather sleep?" he asked. "They can play. They can travel,work and have fun . . . instead of sleeping . . ."

"It is because they are afraid that they cannot do well in life, and they are afraid of making mistakes if they try to do something that they want, and then they will fail. So they dream their lives away."

"Dream life away?"

"Yes, Abraham. They fantasize, for example, that there will come a prince and help them to have a better life. That was what our parents had done in Russia. They dreamed that God would save them from the Nazis. One should never daydream. We fight instead!"

"It is too hard stuff for him," muttered his father, who was sitting with a newspaper.

"I don't think so," replied his mother defiantly. "We can teach him to dream less and instead do something without waiting for miracles. It's the difference between us and the others. We create and struggle to change, and they talk and talk for no avail."

"Is Stalin also a man who does things without talking so much?" he asked his father.

"Yes. Without him and the Red Army, the world would have been lost to Hitler," said his father gravely.

"Why do you confuse his mind with Hitler and Stalin?" his mother asked angrily.

"I don't confuse him at all. I say to him that there are people who daydream and that there are people who accomplish meaningful things, and there are those who just live their lives, and then there are those who accomplishes things like us. The final words on Stalin's huge impact on the world we live in have not been yet said," concluded his father.

"You and the sun of all nations, Stalin!" his mother hissed. "You go too far! Abraham needs some concrete examples so he can relate to and not some sinister mass murderer as a model."

"Can't you stop arguing!" shouted Abraham.

"Yes!" replied his mother. "Tomorrow we will read about some great people for you. If you want to be great, you have to know how to become one!"

"Can children become great people?" he asked.

"No!" said his father. "But they can possess abilities and creative power, which can cause them to become great one day if they will work hard for it."

"I will work for it!" said Abraham. "I will cultivate the most beautiful Bustan on earth . . . I have promised him!"

"He really still believes in his fantasy," growled his father.

Abraham thought that he could be both a gardener in a Bustan of his own and a prince simultaneously. It might be the only explanation for why greatness and heroism enticed him so much.

To the stars with Laika

Abraham got his scientific interest when he was about nine years old. As some might remember, in 1957, the Russians sent a dog named Laika into space.

It was the first time a living being was sent out in space, and the children in the kibbutz were very excited about it. Now Russia was not only the mother of the socialistic nations but also the room's father. They looked up at the sky at night, hoping to get a glimpse of Laika. Sometimes they could hear her barking among the stars, and a good friend claimed he had some of Laika's droppings hit him on the head; further investigation showed that the droppings came from a flying sparrow.

Following detailed discussions, some of the children who had some knowledge of rocket motors, ballistic missiles, engines to live up to the communist challenge sent a kibbutz cat into space in their own self-designed rocket.

Abraham and a buddy started to read about how to build a rocket and managed to steal a substance called carbide, which, together with water, was to be used as fuel in the rocket motor. From the kitchen store, they picked two large empty cans that had contained olives and pickles.

Then they went in search of spaceship candidates. They started to lure four cats with some chicken heads from the henhouse. The first was quickly disqualified because it was too big and heavy compared with the rocket thrusting capability. The other seemed to them to be rather dull-witted and without any sense of technical insight, and the third was also a bit strange, which was not surprising since on a closer inspection, it was revealed that it was, in fact, a hedgehog. The last cat belonged to the school principal and was called Ben-Gurion by Israel's first prime minister, and they agreed that both those factors made it suitable as their cosmonaut, and when Ben-Gurion even did not protest much, they set on the project. They washed the big olive can and put on its floor rags so that it was ready as Ben-Gurion's bedroom, dining room, and dashboard. In the other can, the carbide substance was placed next to a bowl of water so they could mix them together when the countdown started. Small holes were made in the can from which the fumes and the gases could come out. They drilled also a small hole in the bottom of the can to the fuse, which was a clothesline from the laundry that got soaked up in kerosene from a tractor in the field. Now everything was almost ready for the countdown. Despite Ben-Gurion's last-minute protests, they placed it in the olive can, mixed carbide substance with the water, set fire to the fuse, and watched intensely how the little fire tongue approached slowly the cucumber can.

Abraham could feel his heart pounding with excitement when the fire reached the primer can, and the rocket flew up into space. Everything worked perfectly and smoothly. When the rocket reached the window height of their one-floor house, the rocket's first stage, cucumber can, fell down and set fire to the grass on a small dry field. The olive can was rising upward toward the open space in what seemed to him as supersonic speed, but when it reached as high as the ridge of the one-story house, it became obvious that it had lost steam, and Abraham began to doubt whether it could break free from gravity. And sure enough, when it came a little farther up the roof, an explosion took place, not as big as the first but more stinky, and their spaceship crash-landed on the roof next to the water tank.

Astronaut Ben-Gurion came out of its can fresh and hearty, looked a little contemptuously at the children, stretched its back out, and then went down the drainpipe and back to earth. The children looked at each other, shrugged, and went home.

The aftermath of space travel was an earful of the kibbutz firefighter who had to go out and put out the fire and did not have much left over for the aspiring scientists and their ambitions. The headmaster was also a bit upset when he found out that Ben-Gurion had lost interest in mouse hunting and instead constantly was looking for pickles and cucumbers.

For Abraham, this project was the end of his career as a rocket scientist and expert. But after this space experiment, he decided that this was the very first daring step he took on his way for creating one day his Bustan. He knew already then that he would need much courage, stamina, endurance, and wild creativity to accomplish this particular feat.

Dark night: Akram comes to the kibbutz

Abraham's father had told him that his friend Arif, who was Naim's son, would visit them with his son, Akram. In the afternoon, Abraham ran to the water tower, waiting for them there. After a long wait, he saw a cloud of dust that whirled toward the kibbutz and when it reached the well and then turned into a dozen riders on their camels in traditional Bedouin garments, armed with machine guns and long chains with cartridges dangling down their shoulders. When they came to the pine grove, they stopped the large animals and made them kneel and lie down on all fours, after which they were welcomed by the assembled kibbutz members. They belonged to a unit, which served as scouts in the army, and they were invited together with Arif and his son to the kibbutz to join the Chanukah celebration.

The children were eager to sit on the back of these camels and stood in a long line to be taken up on the camels' back by their masters. Shortly afterward, a jeep suddenly stopped behind them, and an officer and a small black curly boy with almond eyes and delicate features jumped out of the car. Abraham's father and the officer, who had black mustache and burning eyes, embraced each other. Abraham already knew that he was a high-ranking officer, like his father, but it was the first time he presented himself and his little son to Abraham. The son was a little younger than Abraham, and he spoke Hebrew with some hesitation and a slight accent.

"Why does he talk that way?" Abraham whispered to his father.

"He is a Bedouin, and his father is too, and their mother tongue is Arabic," he replied and smiled at the boy and his father. The boy was not afraid or shy and went straight toward Abraham. He followed Abraham over to the grove, where they played all afternoon with the other children. Later on in the evening, Akram, Abraham, and his group comrades dressed themselves in white, and with lighted candles in their hands and singing, they entered the classroom, where their parents and families were awaiting them.

Their female teacher warned them once again not to get too close to one another because of the lighted candles. The electric light was turned off, and in the darkness, which descended, they went into the dark class in a long line with their lighted candles in their hands and were singing.

"We have come to chase the darkness away with lights and fire in our hands! Each of us carries a little light candle, but together, we bring warmth and compassion."

And then they trampled emphatically with their feet a few times on the floor, so did Akram too, and with shining eyes, they shouted together, "Away with you, darkness! Away with you darkness! Away with you fear! Give place for the bright light for us to steer!"

And when they repeated this rhyme could Akram sing it with a loud, clear voice. Abraham patted him on the shoulder because he was impressed of how quickly Akram learned the song and because this song often gave Abraham hope and courage during the dark nights when the kids in the children's house in their beds could hear the hyenas' plaintive howls from the nearby fields.

When the party was over, Akram was allowed to sleep together with the other children in the children's house. They had to wait long in their beds before the adults went home, and when silence had finally fallen, the children slipped out of their beds, put their blankets on the floor, and sat and talked together to harden themselves against the fear of darkness.

The full moon sailed up the starry sky, and long silver rays shone through the window and down on them. Abraham drew a domino game forward, and they gazed long at dominoes luminescent phosphor spots in the moonlight. That night, Abraham taught Akram to play dominoes and showed him how the dominoes could topple one another when put side by side in a long line.

The two boys whispered not to wake the two girls, who also slept in the room, and they vowed that they would stay awake all night.

"Are you afraid of darkness?" Abraham asked his new friend.

"Only a little bit! I am used to it, for where we live, there is dark all around the settlement. We have no electric light as you have. We have some battery-driven lamps. We don't used to sleep together with girls before we get married with them."

"Why don't you do it?"

"It is because we behave in a different way towards women."

"Girls interfere in everything, but at least so when they are asleep. Otherwise, they are noisy when they talk. They do not remember to whisper secrets as us boys. They cannot run very long or quickly, and one should always wait for them and help them because we should be equal, the grown-ups say," whispered Abraham.

"They urinate also strangely—they squat when they do that," said Akram.

"There was a time when we were playing father, mother, and children, and then David urinated on Pnina lying on her back there. She was completely wet and hooted. So we do not bother more," Abraham said to his friend.

"I once saw a man near the clan well who did it with a donkey. He shouted after me, and I was so scared. It was very frightening," said Akram.

"I know a terrible song, an eerie song that is best to sing at night, so you really become scary," Abraham said.

"So sing it. I am not afraid of songs," said Akram and looked at him.

"But what if you get scared?" Abraham asked empathetically.

"When we are together, I am not really afraid," whispered Akram.

"Good, but if it gets too scary, then say stop to me!" whispered Abraham back.

"Sing it," repeated Akram.

Abraham looked attentively at him and started with a quivering voice.

> *Dark night, dark night, the wind whispers*
> *Dark night, dark night, the trees creak*
> *Dark night, dark night, the stars blink*
> *Sleep soundly, my child, turn off your light*
> *Sleep, my child, turn off your light.*

Abraham lay in the darkness and thought of the last lines of the song, when Akram remarked, "It's not at all scary. It's just a lullaby."

"Vent just a moment. The sinister part comes soon," whispered Abraham.

> Dark night, dark night, you're sleepy and dizzy
> Dark night, dark night, on the way to your door
> Dark night, dark night, armed to the teeth
> Three evil riders who have their vice errand.
> Sleep soundly, my child, who have their errand?

"What do you think, Abraham, the evil riders are thinking about? What do they intend to do?" Akram asked."Evil people always have evil thoughts," whispered Abraham.

"I get goose bumps of this song."

"Now the end of this song comes closer. Don't get scared," said Abraham and peered under their beds.

> Dark night, dark night, one of them was the predator
> devoured by a beast
> Dark night, dark night, the second one fell by the sword.
> Sleep well, my son, since the third one forgot your name
> And cannot find your door.
> Dark night, dark night, the wind blows
> Dark night, dark night, treetops are humming.
> Dark night, what are you waiting for?
> Do you sleep while the road is free of danger?
> Wake up, come free as the road is free!

They sat quietly for a long time.

"It was good that he had forgotten our name," said Akram, "but it would be even better if he died. It would be safer for us, but what kind of people these horsemen are?"

"They are evil people, killers riding on horses," replied Abraham.

"And where do they go to?"

"It is quite clear. They ride home to us or other good people when we all are asleep."

"Now I am a little scared," said Akram with trembling voice. "There was one night when I was little, my father was sitting outside our home and kept guard with a submachine gun because there were some evil people who wanted to harm us. Maybe they were these horsemen."

"Did they come to your place?"

"No! They were afraid of my father. He is a good sharpshooter . . . This song is bad," said Akram angrily. "How can we know if the last horseman completely forgot our names or whether he will suddenly remember them?"

"Man could kill him," said Abraham.

"Do you know what?" said Akram "I think my father is chasing this kind of evil riders. All murderers and robbers are afraid of him, for he finds them always. I have heard it from many people from our tribe. Tomorrow I will tell him about the last rider. He'll find him. Do not be afraid!"

And so they sat with their blankets on the cold stone floor without being able to sleep while they waited for the morning to come so they could see the sun come up and would stand in all its glory and gobble the black darkness away.

KIDNAPPING

Abraham was coming out of the kibbutz's perimeter and moving toward the fields, and on his way, he thought of *Gulliver's Travels*. He had just finished the book and was especially moved by the chapter where Gulliver, after his ship had sank, was washed up on foreign beach. While he lay unconscious, there came the dwarfs out of their cities and pinned him down to the ground with ropes so he could not move.

His father told him again that great people could accomplish many great things in the world, if they were not all the time prevented by narrow-minded people. Abraham thought that he meant dwarfs, who would not accept that others created greater things than they themselves were able to make. There were three dwarfs like men in the kibbutz, and he asked his father if they were acting like that.

"No!" his father replied promptly. "For the first, they are not real dwarfs, and for the second, they are also Socialists. Socialists are no narrow-minded people with dwarf souls."

"But you have said that souls do not exist!" Abraham protested.

"It's also true!" his father admitted. "Capitalists have a greedy ideology. This faith in profit, consumption, and greed makes them mentally dwarfs." His father tried with another explanation, though it did not convince Abraham, but he said nothing, knowing his father's impatience.

Abraham wondered what he would do if he landed in a dwarf country, where they would hold him down unless he served their purpose and were just as greedy as them.

He thought about how easy it was to control a giant like Gulliver, if there were many dwarfs; they only had to tie him down and get him to do what they wanted, but Abraham would never accept this; he would fight them before they could have a chance of binding him tightly and making him obey. "Never give up. Fight always shrewd, cunning, and dirty and wait until you can win the battle," he repeated his father's motto. "In war, you must take advantage of all available means, even also the dirty ones," he repeated to himself what his father had told him.

He crawled into a deep ditch, which was used as a waste dumping place for the kibbutz. He was nearly eight years, and he was looking for old magazines of *National Geographic* because he loved the stories of past Emperies like Rome, Athens, Babylon, and Egypt. He liked to watch the pictures on their wars, heroic deeds, royal crowns, and daily life, and he was possessed by the Roman soldiers and their generals, the ancient sailors, and the Greek philosophers, who walked between the marble-plated temples in the shade of pine trees in a breathtaking landscape. He went around among the scattered junk, where you also find metal containers with little shaving cream, old pictures, broken glasses, and maybe some coins that someone had come to throw out. This time he found an old picture book, which he decided to take with him.

Suddenly, he heard a noise and saw a large unshaven young boy who was standing at the edge of the ditch and watched him. He held a short dagger in his right hand and a thick stick from a pine tree on the left. He was flabby with a small protruding belly, and his face was round, sweaty, and bloated with a mouth that was half open and was filled with white foam that flowed down his lips. He had a thick, black, and curly hair and was dressed in long black pants, pink cotton shirt, and sandals.

He looked like someone from *National Geographic*, thought Abraham, a eunuch or a fat emperor, like Nero perhaps. He stepped into the ditch without saying a word and lashed out at Abraham with the hand that held the dagger. Abraham stepped back and looked at him.

"What are you doing here?" he asked in a hoarse, trembling voice.

"I am looking for some missing lambs," Abraham lied to him.

"You will not find them in these piles of junk," the boy said. "But I know where they are. Come, I will show you where they hide!" he said and grabbed Abraham's arm while he grimaced.

"But my mother said that I should not go with strangers," said Abraham and tried to free his wrist from the boy's grip.

"Am I a stranger? I'm like you, a child, but just a little older." Abraham so looked precariously at him. He had never met anyone like him before.

"Do you think that we find the lambs there?" Abraham asked, pointing to the mountains in the east.

"I've just come from there and saw them halfway." The boy pointed with the stick. "I came from the village over there, and there were some sheep and lambs grazing in the fields. I'll show you where they hide."

I will have to run away, thought Abraham. *The boy is stronger than I am, but he is also fat and flabby, so maybe I can outrun him.* The boy took hold of Abraham's arm with one hand while he raised his stick in the air with the other. The dagger he had he pushed down between his pants and the shirt.

"Do not look at me, sinful Isaac," he hissed suddenly.

"I am not Isaac, and why should I not look at you?"

Abraham was aware that the boy mistook him for someone else and that something was dangerous about the whole situation.

"My name is Abraham and not Isaac," he stammered.

"No, you are a little cheater! I am Abraham, your father, and you are Isaak!" shouted the boy suddenly.

It occurred to Abraham that the boy was crazy and looked upon him as Isaac, which were to be sacrificed by his father Abraham to God. Cold sweat began to run down his back. The boy was raving mad, like the people he had once seen on the streets of Ashkelon City. They looked scary and screaming, yelling and spitting, and his mother had told him that they could be dangerous. He had to figure out how to get away from the crazy guy.

"Stop looking at me, Isaac," the boy cried.

"Why?" asked Abraham, frightened but also insistent.

"Because there are horns growing right now on my forehead in the twilight, and you may not see them grow!" he shouted.

"What kind of horns you talk about? I look in the other direction and not at you," stammered Abraham.

"It is God's horns! They grow in the middle of my brow, but you must not see them because you are sinful."

"No, I have not sinned!" Abraham said.

"You are the sacrificed lamb," the boy said forcefully.

"No, I'm Abraham," Abraham said.

The boy forced him to take the lead and pushed him up the slope. They walked for a long time across the fields toward the east without stopping while the sun went down over the sea behind the hills, and Abraham felt fatigue spreading in his body. His legs ached, and he was thirsty, his head throbbed, but he did anyway noticed that the boy pulled a little on the left leg and that his breathing was heavy and hassle. He began to cry quietly.

"Why do you cry, Isaac?"

"I am not Isaac, and I'm tired and thirsty, and you squeeze my arm. I told you that I will not run away!"

"If you just come with me without resistance, I'll stop holding you so hard . . . Is it a deal? For I am your father!"

"Yes!" Abraham said. "Who are you?" asked Abraham.

"I am Abraham, your father, and God gave me a mission and said to me what I need to do it to get his blessing."

Abraham began devising an escape plan to get away from the crazy guy. He thought that he would exhaust him and then outwit him. He just had to wait for the right time when he could kick him hard on the left leg and in his balls and then run away into the darkness. If he could get away with taking the stick or the dagger from him while he winced in pain, he would also be able to protect himself against the wild dogs on the way home.

"You are going too fast!" Abraham said to him.

"We have to reach the place before it gets dark," the boy replied.

Suddenly, some black crows flew over them, and it got the boy to cover his sweaty and swollen face with his elbows while he began to growl.

"What do you say?" Abraham asked.

"Black crows are bad omens! I have to protect myself against their poison, so I ask for my father God to protect me!" he shouted. "Bi, bi, bi, salt, salt, salt. Let me sacrifice Isaac to you, my Lord."

Abraham's heart galloped away. It was getting darker and cooler, and now the moon rose slowly through some light clouds. Abraham noticed that the boy again started to wheeze and now almost limped. For a while, Abraham walked beside him, almost as if in a dream, while prairie wolves were howling in the distance. He could see some shadows resembling people, or maybe they were coyotes who passed by in the distance. They looked like rapid-moving shadows on the fields during the moon's blue light, and further away, the fields seemed to have turned into a river of flowing silver with deep blue spots.

Suddenly, a figure of a man appeared out of the shadows and walked beside him, signaling him to be quite. His robe shone as bright green grass, and he moved silently and almost without touching the ground. He came close to Abraham and leaned toward him and whispered, "Be ready to execute your plan in a moment. If you kick him in the balls, he will fall down, and then you will take his stick and hit him hard on both legs and one time on his head before you run away!"

"Shall I hit him on his head?" whispered Abraham.

"Yes," said the Green Man promptly. "If you wish to be a gardener in an evolving Bustan, you are also the garden's guardian. Now do as I say!"

Abraham nodded.

"And if the wild dogs persecute you, so hit them hard with the stock, and if they still do not allow you to go home, climb up the nearest tree and wait there till daybreak, and remember to hit the boy hard on the lame leg and face without hesitation or mercy! He is crazy and dangerous and wants to kill you!" whispered the Green Man before he disappeared into the shadows of the night.

They continued into the nearby cemetery, where the boy sat on a tombstone while he was gasping for air deeply.

"It is now! It must be done before Satan comes from the dark and mixes!" said the boy and loosened his grip on Abraham, and just at that moment, Abraham kicked him twice hard in the crotch. The boy screamed, writhed, and fell while the stick rolled along the ground. Abraham was quick to pick it, and in a lightning quick movement, he struck with all his force the boy on the lame leg and knee. The boy uttered another scream, and Abraham swung back the stick and beat him this time on the second leg and twice in the head and then again on his hand, so he lost the dagger. The boy was now disarmed on the ground, and Abraham hurried away with the stick and dagger in his hands.

When he reached the edge of the grove, he saw a green glow and a glimpse of the Green Man, who pointed the direction to the kibbutz and the way home.

"Do not be afraid. I'm watching you until you reach home. You've promised me to create an evolving Bustan!" He laughed gently, and Abraham noticed how all fear disappeared while he ran home through the silver-bathed fields, and the dusty way was shrouded with a stream of moonlight and green flashes.

Festival of Lights—Chanukah

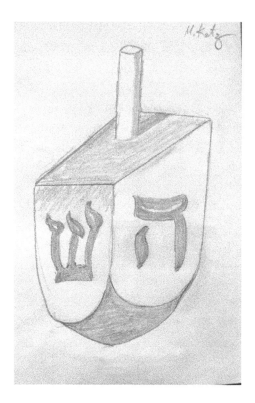

The winter was rainy and stormy, and the kibbutz dusty roads transformed quickly into thick mud traps, so the tractors that had tracks constantly had to pull the other tractor out of the mud when they got stuck in the mud pool.

At that time, a band of Palestinians from Gaza attacked a kibbutz nearby, killing and wounding many people, after which the Israeli armed forces avenged the attack by killing seventy people from Gaza, and so the conflict rolled on and on.

Abraham's father told him that this conflict would continue for a long time, maybe one hundred years, because the Israelis would not give up the areas they had conquered during the war, which the Arabs had lost, and the Arabs would not give up their dream of going back to their old places.

"So the war will continue?" Abraham asked his father.

"Yes! We must realize that we will live on our swords for a long time," he said.

His mother, who overheard the conversation, exclaimed, "Why on earth you tell a ten-year-old boy that the war will continue indefinitely? What are these murky perspectives you draw for him? He is a child, so let him enjoy his childhood!"

"I tell him about our reality, and I will not fool him with a tale of paradise on earth. He might as well learn that people are not able to establish peace on earth and that there is no reason to trust them. What did the Second World War has taught us? We were about to disappear from the face of the earth, while other nations were either indifferent or played their cynical game. We must be the strongest in all conflicts, and the others should fear us. That's what I will teach my son!"

"Do you need to emphasize this day and night? And I wonder if you have not already made your point. See him, Shika, David, and Akram run around with their wooden swords and their bows and arrows and constantly play war. Enough is enough! We have the right to a peaceful life once in a while," cried his mother.

His father gave her a light hug, and she turned and walked sobbing into the apartment.

Abraham looked puzzling at his father and asked what it was that made her sad.

"The girl from your class who has been sick for a long time died today, and your mother has just visited her family. Her friend Miriam died last year, and the girl from your class was also named Miriam. I think it is therefore."

Abraham breathed deeply. He did not know that his classmate had been so ill, and now another funeral again. He had learned to cope with it when adults died, but he thought it was unbearable when death hit children and young people.

After the girl's funeral, they were supposed to hold three mourning days, but then it was fortunately Chanukah for eight days, and it was this holyday he liked best after Pesach because it was a festival of lights in the middle of the winter darkness and because they celebrated the happening of a miracle, and he was fascinated by miracles caused by the invisible hand of both nature and man.

Abraham knew the story of Chanukah by heart. Man celebrated an event that took place around the year 165 BC, when Israel was occupied by the Greeks, whose leader was called Antiochus Epiphanes, who forbade Jews to read and study the Torah and to lead a religious life.

Judah Maccabi led a rebellion, where the Jews managed to free the country from Greek oppression and to recapture the temple, which had been desecrated and filled with Greek statues of gods. Worse still, the Greeks had left the flame that always should burn in the temple as a reminder of God's eternal covenant with the Jews, which went out. But the Jews were lucky. They found a spare container with enough oil for one day and sent scouts to find more oil, but they were delayed and did not come back after eight days, but a miracle occurred, so the oil that was meant for a day burned in all eight days.

Abraham loved to revive Chanukah story along with Akram and the other children. They were playing that they were fighting in the mountains with spears, bows and arrows, and swords against the heavily armed Greek soldiers, and he was delirious when the big boys chose him as Maccabaeus. In the rain and mud, the two armed forces battled back and forth until the Maccabees finally took the temple, which was marked with a chalk circle on the ground and lit the lamp again.

When his mother came to fetch him and Akram home for tea and cake at four o'clock, the two boys, elated and happy, were covered with mud from head to toe, but it meant nothing. The fight had been riveting and was ended fairly, and he had forgotten all about the death and grief of the girl from his group. It was there he almost intuitively found out that when he was fighting for a just and great cause, world's sorrow vanished out of his mind.

THE GREAT PEOPLE
IN HISTORY

Abraham's father asked him one day if he knew the word "sublimation."

"Our whole project is based on the idea of sublimation," said his father and explained to him that the kibbutz is based on the idea that you listen to an energy called libido, which is the energy that makes all animals wish to procreate, but the kibbutz members channeled it toward the higher goal as to build a kibbutz and a new life for the Jewish people. It was this sublimated libido of the people that made the creation of Israel possible. "It is the energy that refines the people and improves the world!" his father explained.

"And what happens to the fertility of man when you sublimate the libido? How do you get children?" Abraham asked.

"You can still make children. It's like bees make honey from the flower nectar while life in the hive continues, and they constantly get new bees. You move just some of the libido energy to another area where you can work for some other goals such as improving the world and man instead of using all the energy to make new babies," said his father.

"Is it only us in the kibbutzim who can sublimate like this?"

"No! This is done in many kibbutzim and in Russia and in China and in many other countries. Where the proletariat controls the historical events, they sublimate in order to become better humans."

"Did Stalin do it?"

"Of course, he did it. He worked only for the revolution and for a better society. He is a symbol and an ideal for all of us. But in the capitalist countries, people live just to live well and consume as much as they can, and they believe in greed and God!"

"And God cannot sublimate them?" Abraham asked.

"Not at all! God exists after all only in the believers' imagination, and they fill themselves with illusions about life after death instead of focusing on making this world a better place to live for all of us," concluded his father.

"Why do they do that? It's ridiculous!" he exclaimed.

"They do it because there are many people who find it easier to disappear into a fantasy or wishful thinking than to work hard in order to realize an ideal. 'Mundus vult dicipi' is a Latin proverb that means that people will be deceived because they wish to be deceived. So people are deceiving themselves and others. They do this all the time, but since they often believe their own lie stories, they forget that they are deceiving themselves," his father concluded.

"What did you call this in Latin?" asked Abraham.

"Mundus vult dicipi: the world wants to be deceived, and therefore, it is being cheated."

"Mundus vult dicipi . . . Mundus vult dicipi," Abraham repeated these magical words.

As some girls from his group began to develop small breasts, their teacher told them about the changes that would happen in them, both girls and boys, and how the sublimation of their instincts would help them to be better youngsters and afterward adults contributing socialists. Although boys and girls still went in the common bath together and continued to sleep together in the same bedrooms, they had to prepare for a life with impulse control, for what was a real socialist without self-control and the will to delay the need for love and procreation? To postpone needs and desires and to channel the libido at large and life-affirming goals, Abraham took this very seriously because he then would be able to accomplish much greater things than the common capitalist young people who were controlled by their desires. He practiced postponing his needs and built up a steely character by putting a piece of chocolate that they got once a week in front of him, fasten his eyes on it, and waited at least three hours before he ate it, and besides, he trained hard in all sports to be strong and persevering.

He wanted to be a great orator like Demostones or Trotsky, so he went on practicing speeches with two smooth stones in his mouth. This was the way he trained his voice to the day when the great and significant events would be an inseparable part of his life. "Through hardships to stars" his father always said was a noble ambition. He explained it, and Abraham swore to himself that it was the path he would try to follow.

Arif and the Story of the Sand

The time flew by, and after the sixth grade, Abraham and his group moved to a school that stood on a small hill outside the kibbutz. At that time, it was arranged that Akram would move permanently to his class and stay up to the age of eighteen. Akram promised Abraham that they should go on adventures together and that he would teach him how to shoot with a semiautomatic rifle; they would scout, camouflage themselves, and he, Akram, would teach him how to read tracks in the sand and would also show him how his tribe lived and how they bred horses.

One afternoon in midsummer, Akram's father, Arif, came with his son and a few suitcases with clothes and other necessities to his parents' house. Arif asked his parents whether he could talk with Abraham alone while Akram stayed together with them.

They drove in Arif's jeep toward the hills in the east. The roads were dusty, and the jeep bounced, so Abraham had to hold the seat in front not to be thrown out of the jeep. When they reached the hills, Arif stopped the car, and they walked toward a small bush, where Arif asked Abraham to sit.

"Abraham," he said to him, "soon, you will be adult according to your traditions. Is it true, Abraham? Next year, your family will celebrate your Bar Mitzvah!"

"I do not know! As you know, we do not believe in God!" said Abraham.

"You do it your way, your father told me, and you do not have to believe in God in order to mark the transition from childhood to adolescence. We also do this on our way!"

Abraham fell silent.

"God or not, you belong not only to your kibbutz or to your people but to all of us. This is what my father, Naim, told you and me ten years ago before he died."

"What do you mean by that?" Abraham asked.

"I just think that there are many Jews and Arabs and Bedouins and people from England, USA, France, and many other countries that are in the group they are born into and grew up in even if they move to another place, but it is not so with all people. There are some people who have a larger wingspan and have been blessed to go beyond the ordinary human narrow sense of belonging. They are there for humanity as a whole and belong to its dreams and aspirations . . .

"My father gave you a sign, and the Green Man blessed you and chose you to be the gardener in an evolving Bustan, which nature is not yet revealed. It is a great honor but also a heavy and frustrating commitment as you don't get the fruits of your work to either see or taste," continued Arif.

"Why is it a heavy and frustrating duty? Your father both tended and saw the fruit trees and tasted their fruits. Why not me?" protested Abraham.

"It is because the Green Man talked with you on another Bustan, a transforming one, and you are going to deal with people, not fruit trees . . . and as the human heart can quickly be corrupted by vanity, megalomania, and distorted notions, you are coming to fight hard to pursue this goal. Therefore, you should, like Musa, whom you call Moses, do it without expecting any personal gain, fame, or others' admiration. Moses died before he could enter the Promised Land. He had trouble with his people, which you have read about, and he was sometimes disappointed and angry, but he undertook yet his obligation, and it made him a great man. He could have left his obligation, but he chose to persevere and carry out its mission. There is no other way for them who can create an evolving Bustan for humans."

Arif fell silent for a while, and then he looked at the bewildered and disoriented Abraham and added, "I will continue with this talk because I know that you will one day understand what I say now!" He smiled sadly.

"You can still choose to live a life like the great majority of people without such burden! People's lives are not important beyond their biological span, even though they deny it. The life I am talking about is a completely different one from the ordinary life. It is transforming people and their lives and social intercourse and leaves enduring mark on where the journey of advanced intelligent-like us- will bring us to ."

"I do not understand what you are talking about, Arif!" said Abraham.

"What is it that you do not understand? Ordinary life is like reading children's adventure throughout people's lives without ever accomplishing something significant and enduring for the sake of all the evolving humanity, but life can become a transformative and evolving journey for all of us when some of us receive the grace to lead the way. It is not everyone who has the opportunity to choose such endeavor, but the ones who have been blessed by the Green Man have this opportunity. Do you understand this now?" Abraham nodded hesitantly.

"Man can choose to run away from his destiny, for we are not entirely in the hands of determined fate. We can choose sometimes . . . But if you choose to pursue escapism, convenience, craving for gratification, laziness, or fear, you choose to refrain from taking on a responsibility that is greater than any personal ambition. So when it involves a responsibility for the whole humanity, one needs a blessing in order to start on such mission. Do you understand me now?"

"Not completely, Arif!" Abraham said with a quivering voice.

"I'll explain it to you little by little. Today I start with a tale," Arif said.

He patted Abraham on the cheek, squatted, and began to tell.

"Old people report that after Allah the Great had created the world and the people who would live in it, he had two lumps of clay left. Of the first one, he created a camel and with the other one, a palm tree with sweet dates. On their way in the desert, thought Allah, people would be able to search for the evolving Bustan of humanity, which they are blind for, spoiled by affluence and comfort. Allah was wise and knew that people who are well fed and fat lack incentives to create and attend an evolving Bustan, which constitutes the oases in our infinite evolving journey we may follow. We need the desert, tell the elderly, for its quietness, peace, and longing for transforming orchard and evolving travel.

"Allah seeks out in the desert, when the world's noise and inconvenience becomes too overwhelming, and we feel that Allah's desert is the place where this journey can materialize, not on affluent, rich soil. If Allah leaves the noisy world, with its confused and constantly hectic and defocused seeking people, in order to rest under a palm tree, or in a beautiful hidden oasis, let us learn from it. And this is Abraham, our hidden history, mankind's endless journey through time, where they constantly have managed to transform themselves and their world. Although most people in this noisy, confusing, and overstimulating world have forgotten it, it is still their history and destiny, and we are here to remind them about it.

"The endless desert, the universe, and nature, you must remember, Abraham, are totally indifferent regarding our lives, and we are the only ones to grant this ultimate meaning to our lives. Allah gave us the potentiality to perform this miracle, to show how we can break the constraints of life and evolve further and further. The Green Man leaves us with the message: 'God creates and leave us alone!' The rest we have to accomplish by ourselves. And the evolving Bustan is a crucial roadmap in this effort . . ." Arif paused.

"Do you dream of something special, Abraham?" he asked suddenly.

"I cannot quite remember," whispered Abraham.

"You probably dream about girls. You do that, and Akram does it, and it is quite normal." Arif laughed and was silent for a moment.

"What do you dream about?" asked Abraham, blushing.

"In your age, I dreamed also about girls and what boys can do to them, but luckily, I took charge of my dreams, so now I dream about a river, desert, sand, and a gentle wind full of waterdrops."

"I don't understand! Why do you dream such a strange dream!" Abraham inquired. "Can you elaborate?"

"Sure!" Arif said.

"There was a river that flowed through different landscapes, and each time it met an obstacle, it forced its way by sheer force. But one day it came to a landscape that it could not penetrate or pass by, and therefore, it could not continue its course.

"Then it heard a voice. 'If you continue to press on as usual, you end up as a quagmire or a mud pool.'

"'But in such a way, I have always dealt with all difficulties on my way,' the river said. 'What should I do instead?'

"'You can let the warm wind sucks you up and carry you over the desert and the mountains and then let you fall down as rain and start a new life,' whispered the voice.

"'I can't do this since I will lose myself!' said the river.

"'You will only lose a part of yourself that is causing you problems, but your core will follow, and it is the most important,' whispered the voice.

"And after much hesitation did the river just that and realized that rebirth can only occur along this way," Arif concluded his story. "To create and nurture an evolving Bustan, habitual and customary ideas won't work. The humans of today will have to transform themselves. This is the only way they can avoid becoming a 'quagmire' and nothing else. Do you get me now, young man?"

Abraham watched him intensely and nodded. "Yes! I think I begin to follow your thinking, Arif! It took me some time to understand it, but now I can start to follow it . . ."

LAST MEETING WITH THE BUSTAN

From the kibbutz's large red-painted iron gate, twisted to the west was a wide, dusty road around the graveyard, where all those who died in the war were buried. The dusty way ploughed through the cornfields on the big orchard of almond trees on the small round hills in the horizon. There was autumn in the air, and the dust on the road was soft and warm.

Now he ran toward the arbor, where the guard kept looking for unauthorized guests who tried to steal almonds and watermelons. Two months before, the scent of the blooming almond flower could reach all the way to his room at night, when the west wind from the sea stroked the landscape. After school and the compulsory three hours of work in the fields or in the cowshed, he took his precious Adidas shoes on and ran along the road past these thousands and thousands of fragrant, graceful trees on the way to his destination.

Sweaty and out of breath, he ran up the winding road while he admired the view despite the fact that there was something disturbing in this uniform landscape. The many trees that stood in long, straight rows as tightly disciplined soldiers and sumptuous unit felt completely wrong, but he did not know why. Soon, the farmworkers from the nearby cities would arrive, eager to shake the almonds into the cloth covers that which were spread out under the trees. The guard with his big dog, his rifle over his shoulder, and his salt cartridges in a glittering belt around the waist was also there. Abraham and the guard knew each other well as he often ran past the hut. Even the vicious dog now could like the boy and contented himself with some controlled growling at the sight of him.

He slowed down when the dog approached with wagging tail. Amin stood outside the arbor in the process of repairing the south flank of the hut with some old white-yellow flour sacks.

He yelled at the dog, which came rushing, and sniffed at him while he stroked it gently on the neck and back. It was big and black, a cross that resembled a German shepherd and a Doberman. It was proud and majestic in its ritualized movements, assertive, and war experienced. One day he saw it fight with two dogs at once, and it was as slick and stupendous as Jack London's "wolfhound" when it was at loggerheads with the surrounding dogs.

They went toward Amin, the dog in front, and he was moving behind. He shook hands with the tough, sinewy Bedouin and was welcomed into the hut, where there was shade and cool. He saw the steaming water jars, with the precious drops of refreshing water. Since he was a little kid, he had been fascinated by these clay pots, and he thought that the water there was the best you could get.

In the corner of the hut, there were lying a couple of big ripe watermelons and an elongated ammunition box made of wood, and beside the mattress, his eyes and nose caught some fragrant and warm Arabic flatbread that Amin had just taken from the oven. Next to it, on a white plastic plate lay three fresh onion and some hard-boiled eggs, and then there was a large glass with black olives. Amin belonged to Arif and Akram El Uzaiel tribe from the northern part of the Negev desert.

Abraham breathed deeply while the sweat on his face and shoulders slowly began to cool.

"Do you come from the cowshed today, Abraham?" asked Amin, smiling.

He smiled back and muttered, "Can you smell it?"

The man patted him on the shoulders.

"This smell comes from Allah's blessed perfumery. Want to taste the watermelon?"

He nodded, and Amin bent down after a big butcher knife that lay under the mattress.

"Amin," he asked, "can a camel fall in love with a human? In my cowshed, there is a cow that has fallen in love with me. Do not laugh at me! Don't you believe me? It's true, although I do not have much sense of how a cow falls in love with a human. Those workers I work with are laughing at me all the time. Have you bewitched her, they keep asking me? When she sees me come up against the stall, she runs up to me and wants me to pet and scratch its head and between the shoulder blades. She licks my hands with its rough tongue and looks so sad at me with its big, gentle eyes that it hurts. It must be an expression of love, although many believe that cows can't really attach themselves to people, such as dogs do."

"I do not think that you can expect love from a camel, but it obeys you," Amin said, giving him a big, juicy, and red slice of watermelon.

"And what about you?" Abraham asked.

"I'm not thirsty yet, but you may well eat it. They are delicious right now."

He put his teeth into the juicy, ripe fruit, so the juice ran down his cheeks and chin and onto his gray sweating and dusty undershirt.

The dog looked at him with an expectant gaze, and its eyes were almost golden colored by the strong sunlight.

Amin sighed deeply and looked at him. "You run very well, Abraham! There was a time when I could run in the same manner. Like a wolf. I could run away from our camp and to the well, a distance of, yes, ten to fifteen kilometers, fill water containers, and run home again. We have good runners in our tribe, boys at your age, twelve to fourteen years. They want to run a race with you when you come to visit. When your father was responsible for us in the Negev Desert after the Great War, he was also good at running. We ran even in a race, which he had arranged, but times have changed, you know, and from tomorrow, you do not have permission any longer to run on this road through the almond trees, said my boss. You have to find another place to run."

"What does that mean, Amin? Do you think that I steal?"

"Do you think that I suspect you, my friend's friend, as to steal? Do you consider me as a shallow person?" the Bedouin raised his voice in anger.

"No," answered Abraham, while the dog raised his head and looked at them.

"Do you see, my friend! You have been able to visit the Bustan all these years, my friend. You were able to visit your Bustan all the years I've been here, but you cannot anymore. Boss prohibits this."

"But why does he prohibit?" asked Abraham with anger in his voice.

"Tomorrow morning, the bulldozers will start razing the Bustan and all the area around it. The boss and his thick buddies from Tel Aviv believe that the Bustan is good for nothing today. It is a waste of good, fertile soil. That is how he thinks."

"Good for nothing? What kind of idiot is he?" shouted Abraham tearfully. "What does this obese swine know about what is useful? His kinds have gradually destroyed everything beautiful because it is good for nothing. Look at this uniform landscape around us, and now my Bustan?"

"Abraham, the Bustan is not yours as the soil here is neither yours nor your kibbutz. It now belongs to the state, which rents it out at will for Mammon's sake."

"Yes, but it is mine, no matter what you think!" Abraham shouted. The dog stood but lay immediately down again as Amin called it to order.

He patted Abraham on the shoulder and said, "Abraham, you are a young boy with a violent temper, fiery, I would almost call it. No one can wear an old Bustan on his back all alone! You can plant it, cultivate it, enjoy its fruits and shade until the day it is time to die out, but it can always be yours in your heart. When the time comes, you will be able to cultivate a different Bustan but not similar to the one here!

Don´t cry!Amin said, his voice breaking as he clasped Abraham on his head while the boy was weeping silently, "But though!

But you know very well that everything we humans have here on earth is transitory." He tried to console the boy.

"Yes, I know, but why does it have continue like this?" Abraham sobbed. "Why do stupid and greedy people accelerate it? Can't they just leave it alone? Do they lack land? What are they lacking? Tell me."

"This is how people become ugly when time is money," said Amin and looked at him.

"Greed feeds up more greed. Their bottomless greed they cover with fine words about the progress of colonizing the desolate land, to make it flourish with thousands of flowers. All the filth and the rubbish I have heard ad nauseam, and now they will flatten my Bustan," he added with tears in his eyes.

Amin glanced at the dusty road on which the hot air was corrugated in soft, transparent dance movements. *Everything about time is money in the new world,* thought the Bedouin. *The air dances in the heat, and it restores my childhood dreams and adventures, and here stands a boy with a broken heart because of a Bustan. And he sees things in the dancing air that was there and that were my precious, but which have now faded away as if by magic, leaving only dump heartache. He sees things that should be here, but they are first to come many years from now. My tears have long since dried up, and this young boy who does not yet know the brutal demands of life has to build up a shell, a solid shell around his heart if he wishes one day to establish the real Bustan. He must understand that he will have to transcend our reality if he wishes to establish an enduring Bustan. A Bustan in our reality will flourish and wither and flourish again as long as human stupidity is enduring.*

He looked around. The dog lay on his back and rubbed in an attempt to get rid of his fleas. A cloud of dust rose in the arbor, and the Bedouin kicked his dog in the belly, which hurriedly rolled to the entrance with a plaintive howl.

Abraham felt the dry dust in his throat. *The dog,* he thought, *is like many people, a slave most of the time but can become a terrible tyrant. What the hell! The dog does not concern me. They will cover my Bustan with soil and plant on it even more of their almond trees in long, straight rows. My childhood country, what are they doing to you? All the mysterious, enigmatic, unpredictable, and untamed places in you, they cover away under their effective products.*

"May I get some water?" asked Abraham. Amin handed him the big clay pot, and he bowed back and drank greedily of the cool water before he put it gently back and stood.

"Sit down now, Abraham," said Amin. "The sun is high up in the sky. It is too strong yet, and I have something for you!"

"From whom?"

"From Arif, the pathfinder!"

"Ha, Arif!" *Did he say anything about this? Could he not prevent it?* he thought bitterly.

"Arif asked me to greet you and say that just as a child grows from living solely on the milk and gets used to solid food, so you must also grow up. You must develop a new Bustan, and your Bustan is not this one. It served as a guide of what was to come so you could see it for your inner eyes. That's what Arif would tell you," said Amin.

"What can I use it for?" Abraham stammered.

"Arif has said that this Bustan shall die like everything else human, but he gave you an image of the transformative, evolving Bustan, which you have first to create within yourself, and once you will give birth to it, it will not die because it is constantly transforming! Do you understand?"

"Do I understand?" asked Abraham, slightly annoyed.

"Yes! I understand it well and you too, but you do not know yet. One day you will not only understand it but also do what it takes to create it!"

"If he and you understand it, so I will probably do it too one day," Abraham said.

"You will understand it in due time. You were granted a blessing, and the blessing is in line with Zaman, Makvam, and Ikhvam, which means the right time, the right place, and the right people, and they are not included in our constellations! But you will know when the right constellation is there," said Amin.

"What are you saying?" asked Abraham and looked at him.

"I say that just at the right time, in the right place, and with the right people can evolving Bustan be brought to life. You will be there on the day when the constellation is present. It was the Green Man who saw it," said Amin.

Abraham looked at his hands and began to cry again, and Amin held him.

"Please sit down and calm down before you run further."

"No, thanks, Amin. I would like to see the garden for the last time, for I will not come again."

"You are angry, my friend," said the Bedouin. "I can remember the day when we let our sheep and goats graze around here after the Great War, and I also remember the man Naim, who owned the Bustan and tended it, and one day he just disappeared without a trace. Your father and Arif and his son, Akram, were looking after him for a long time. The best of our people and pathfinders among us were looking after him. But Arif said to your father, 'It is no good to keep on searching for where he went, only invisible track lead, and you will not see them. He died the best death a man can die.'

"'What do you mean by that?' your father asked. 'A man cannot just disappear without a trace?'

"'I believe that there is no trace of your friend and my father, and that was not committed a crime. I can promise you that Naim was much loved and appreciated by all.'

"And your father looked at him for a long time and muttered, 'Have I heard this before?'

"And Arif held him and said, "Yes, and the first time you would not believe it.'"

"Why are you telling me this?" Abraham asked.

Amin was silent for long time, gazing at the dancing hot air. He gazed at the light blue mountains in the east, which seemed to dance in the hot air. "So you do remember Naim, my friend. You were so little at the time when the Green Man came by. You say it is the last time you come here, so I say goodbye to you now. I also remember all that disappeared, but I am not to get angry, worried, or sad by anything that is temporary."

"At my home, in the kibbutz, there is no one who is interested in my Bustan. My father calls it my obsession. He doubts whether it ever happened," said Abraham.

"When one is focused on changing everything in nature, as to make the earth's breathing turn upside down, such one has not the mind to remember what he sees and is visible for the endowed," said the Bedouin. "Only Allah the Great knows where all this leads. Maybe people's self-destruction will lead to a new epoch? Only the almighty knows the direction of the evolving human caravan." Amin stood and walked toward Abraham and hugged him softly.

"Remember, Abraham, to act resolutely at the right time, right place, and with the right people. Otherwise, your life will be wasted in sheer ordinariness. The blessing should not be wasted on such life."

Again, Abraham felt how grief welled up in him. He waved to the Bedouin and started running on the dirt way. He kept on running. He did not look back. When he came up on top of a hill, he stopped. The Arbor, Amin, and the dog were gone. He went through scattered debris and rocks and tried to tame his thoughts. *Why will they not remember? They are about to change it all, building ugly houses, demolishing all the old, eradicating the free country life, camel caravans, sheep and goats' bells, and the wandering nomads.* He felt that all what he cherished and remembered was sentenced to just be swept away as something he had dreamed. But he knew that what he remembered was a true reality pushed aside in front of his eyes by another vulgar, presumptuous, and noisy one.

He looked up at the hills. The world around him began to spin around like a carousel. *What is happening to me?* he thought.

Little by little, the carousel slackened and finally stood still. He was still dizzy and sat on a large white limestone and lay then on the parched earth. He did not know where he was and when he came to himself again. He woke up as the sun was going down in the west. He got up and resumed its course, and when he reached the Bustan, he could feel the cool salty breeze that came from afar, from the Mediterranean Sea.

Sweaty and out of breath, he lay on the fertile, warm earth of the Bustan. He closed his eyes, and then it came back. The world began to spin but this time more slowly. It was as if his head rose above his body and floated freely, so he could see the azure sea as a giant whirling. He felt pain in the neck. He opened his eyes, and there stood his Bustan in its splendor, endearing and completely quiet.

Man, oh man, what's happening to you? he thought. *All the plants, trees, and flowers in straight, long, disciplined rows: almond trees; the kibbutz cottonfields with their sweet, intoxicating, toxic pesticide odor; and wheat fields. The land is swallowed, flattened, cultivated, but its soul is gone. People are so effective in their actions, and their hearts are so effective, but is there a soul in an effective heart? Why can't they see the soul in a Bustan?*

It was true what Amin had said that all things passed away and that one must not bind himself too much to the perishable, but he had also said that an evolving Bustan don't die as it keeps evolving and transforming. It was a comforting thought and balm for the crushing pain that would not entirely disappear, but knowing that Bustan could not die comforted him and gave him hope.

"But can you live without this Bustan?" Abraham asked himself. "I can, I must, I have to. I will run out of this Bustan and into an everlasting and transforming new Bustan. But I will take my farewell by going between the trees, shrubs, and irrigation canals with the flowing fresh and cool, silvery water. I wonder if there is another Bustan out in the future which will accept me and where I can feel at home as this one."

The sun baked on his forehead and brought him back to reality. He stood and looked around. Under an old fig tree earth was soft, and there was shade. The reddish green succulent figs hanged from low branches. He wanted to savor them one more time to remember their sweetness, to remember everything. He plucked a few pieces and lay down under the tree.

The coolness of the shady haven mingled with the salty sea breeze. He filled his nostrils with the air, closed his eyes, and tasted the figs. He ate slowly and let the sweet juicy pulp fill his mouth and taste buds, and recollections of an indescribably wonderful feeling surfaced from his early childhood.

He could feel the storm inside him now was subsiding. For a moment, it felt as if he had slipped into the crystal clear sleep. He heard a dear old lullaby, and his consciousness merged with the ballad gentle rocking rhythm. At the same time, he felt wide awake, and he heard very clearly a quiet, velvety, and enchanting voice that spoke to him.

It felt like a warm wind that grazed his face in a gentle caress.

"Abraham, oh, Abraham, please stay here, stay here, and put their blind ignorance behind you. They will never get rid of it. They are lost and don't know it . . ."

"Who are you, and why are you speaking to me?" he muttered, first dazed but became terrified and cried, "Who are you?"

He glimpsed behind closed eyelids almost like in a dream something that writhed along the crooked branch above him while almost hypnotic threw his head back and forth and hissed. Abraham opened his eyes and saw the yellow-green lines of the snake that slowly slid toward him. He remembered a sentence from a textbook: "A poisonous snake does not attack unless it becomes provoked," but the snake continued moving toward him. Then he heard a terrible, desperate scream. Where did it come from? The snake stopped and looked at him in astonishment. A strong gust of wind rustled suddenly through the Bustan, so it shook and rattled in the leaves. Abraham fled without knowing where. Only when he was far away from the tree he stopped and turned around and saw now the big snake hung down from the branch just above the place where he had been lying a moment ago. He thought he could see the snake grinning, and he continued running as fast as his legs could carry him, and only when he reached the hills he dared to stop to catch up his breath. The sun's last rays gilded the landscape around him, and he was not sure if what he had experienced in the Bustan had actually taken place or whether it was something that belonged in a secret universe, with no visible clues that Naim had disappeared into it. When he ran toward the kibbutz fields, away from the Bustan and the hills that kept it safe for a long time, he felt a slight breeze that cooled his sweaty forehead. The disappearing sunrays mixed with velvety colors and the scent of the wheat and sweet whispers, which came from somewhere invisible for him. When he went through the gate of the kibbutz, the sweet murmuring disappeared, and the world became pitch-black.

He walked into the cone of the electric light from the projector at the fence and was overwhelmed by the feeling of having left something behind him and asked, tired and resigned himself, "What is that I've lost there?" And then he knew it was his childhood that ended there, and he could not see what was to come instead, or where the road now would lead him to, and how he would ever find an evolving Bustan to work for and dwell in.

PART II

Adolescence – the days of gestation of the blessed nutrient

If a human doesn't try to improve the human world and just lives his/her own ordinary life, he/she ignores the essential of being a human.

—BK

THE VEIL FALLS

Abraham read the following:

"To Jews discussed for about 120 years ago the Jewish problem, which was a dilemma between being people without a country and nationhood or fight for national home in Palestine, and as good Jews are used to be, they disagreed. One focused on the existing Jews who settled down in America and elsewhere and who lived with their culture and common language, Yiddish. The other was advocating, creating a Jewish national home in Palestine, and reviving the Hebrew language. When they could not agree, one of them said, 'All right, let us agree to share it all between us two. You take all what already exists of Jewish life, and I take that which does not yet exist. With other words, all the real and concrete must be yours, and all the aspirations, dreams, and efforts to create such reality will be mine! The land of Israel and a modern Hebrew language does not exist yet, so I take them.'

"And he thought regarding the moral of it. Both the state of Israel and modern Hebrew languages became realities, so it is more meaningful to nurture a viable vision than to accept passively the existing. Without a great vision of the future and fighting spirit to turn dreams into realities, stagnation is the destiny of those who cling themselves to the present alone. Historical development and progress are always being driven by aspirations, dreams, and active, goal-oriented efforts," he concluded.

The lush green meadow

Days disappear, and time is short,
and years pass by almost unnoticed!
Beauty blooms up and withers away
*while I daydream without doing a thing . . .*They were preparing for a large theater, where almost all the school's more than one hundred students participated. The play was called **the lush green meadow** and focused on the black Americans interpretations of the stories in the Old Testament. There were scenes from the stories of Adam and Eve and the serpent in paradise, Cain and Abel, Noah`s ' Ark, Moses who led the Israelites from bondage to the Promised Land, and several other stories. Abraham was offered the role of Moses and went enthusiastically into learning the texts by heart. Akram and Abraham had also been chosen as angels in the gospel chore, which was added to this play. When Abraham did not play his role, the two of them dressed out with white garments and white wings.

Abraham saw it playing this piece as a great opportunity to learn English and was very excited about the gospel texts and songs. He spent many nights rehearsing his role as the reluctant Moses as God had chosen and assigned to him the mission of leading the Israelites to the Promised Land.

He was greatly moved by the scene where Moses led his people out of Egypt for forty long years, wandering in the wilderness, knowing that all the people who had lived under slavery, including Moses himself, were to die in the desert. He got tears in his eyes and had to make an effort not to break into tears when the choir sang.

When Israel was in Egypt's land. Let my people go.
Oppressed so hard, they couldn't stand. Let my people go.
Go down, Moses, way down in Egypt's land. Tell old
Pharaoh to let my people go.
Thus spoke the Lord, Ball Moses said, Let my people go. If
not, I'll smite your firstborn dead. Let my people go.
Go down, Moses . . .
The Lord told Moses what to do. Let my people go.
To lead the children of Israel through.
Let my people go. Go down, Moses . . .

When Moses, who was Abraham, died on the scene, Abraham ran backstage and changed into an angel costume and was ready for the next scene, where Akram as Joshua lead the Israelites seven times around the walls of Jericho as they blew their trumpets until the walls collapsed.

There he stood, erect and solemn among the group of tenor singers, and saw his friend continue his mission and conquer the land from their local residents. It was obvious to him that this was the right thing to do, and he sang in a loud voice and enthusiasm with the song, *Joshua fit the battle of Jericho, Jericho, Jericho.*
Joshua fit the battle of Jericho, and the walls came tumbling down. Hallelujah.
You can talk about the men of Gideon. You can talk about the men of Saul.
But there're none like good old Josha at the battle of Jericho
Up to the walls of Jericho with sword drawn in his hand
Go blow the horns, Josha cried. The battle is in my hands.

The play was so successful that they came to play it more times for full houses for audience of nearby kibbutzim.

When they played for the last time, Arif came and saw it. He applauded enthusiastically when the play was over and invited Akram and Abraham to ice cream and soda in Ashkelon city as thanks for their achievement.

"It takes a half hour to drive there, and your parents allowed me, Abraham, to take you with us as tomorrow is Saturday, so you can sleep long," muttered Arif.

On the way, Arif asked Abraham if he knew where Moses had excelled and where he had failed.

The question confused Abraham, but he replied, "Moses pulled the passive, distrustful, and slave marked Israelites together, and in forty years through the desert up to the Promised Land, he made them to one brave-hearted people. I can only see his great achievement: the completion of a great mission. I don't see failure!"

"In his act, there are both great achievement and a failure too," said Arif.

"He responded to an imperative to deliver his people from slavery to liberty and lead them to the Promised Land, knowing that he would not be allowed to set foot on it. He met resistance among his people, and yet he accomplished his mission. But where had he failed?" Arif asked again.

"Why do you think that he failed at all?" asked Abraham.

"When the Israelites had settled in the Promised Land, it took only a short time before they started to behave like all the other people around them. They were in conflict with each other. They cheated and lied and did not manage to put the legacy of the slave mentality behind them and thus undermined through their behavior themselves as the chosen folk and Moses's great achievement."

"But Moses died before he came into the Promised Land, so it could not be his guilt or fault!" Abraham protested.

"Yes. It was his responsibility. He should have known that forty years were not enough as to erase the slave mentality in people and get people to transform them fundamentally," insisted Arif.

"Who have said that they should transform themselves? God gave him the task of bringing them there . . ."

"Wandering in the desert toward a Promised Land must be understood as a long battle in order to complete a transformative process! That's just how it is for. Otherwise, it is a waste of huge effort, if people don't transform . . .

"And you, my son! You played as Joshua so skillfully and impressive. What a company I am together with here, Moses leading his people into a Promised Land and Joshua who conquers it!" Arif smiled.

They drove to the old Arab quarter in the city of Ashkelon, where some of Arif's acquaintances had a café, which kept open at night. There, they drank light beer and was served a lavish meal with all sorts of delicacies from the Orient and amused themselves with the people who flocked around Arif, offering them small glasses of arrack.

It was almost five in the morning when the first sunrays broke through the café windows, and Arif rose, heavy and a little drunk, and led them out to the jeep.

"You drive us back to the kibbutz, Akram!" he said to his thirteen-year-old son. "I can't drive right now."

Akram took the wheel and turned out to be an experienced driver.

"Where did you learn to drive?" asked Abraham, amazed.

"My father started to teach me for more than three years ago. Where we live, it is easy to learn to drive. It's like riding on a horse or a camel, and this is something one Bedouin boy of good family should be able to!" Akram said.

Arif muttered with his eyes closed while he stretched out beside Akram, "The sun is about to rise up, and the stars are fading . . . No, falling down . . . Can you sing the song 'My Lord, What a Morning' from the play? It is so beautiful."

Abraham and Akram smiled to each other and sang the song in two voices several times as the sun rose and the stars faded, and happy smile spread across Arif's face.

> *My Lord, what a morning / My Lord, what a morning / My Lord, what a morning / when the stars begin to fall.*
>
> *You'll hear the trumpet sound / to wake the nation's underground / looking to my God's right hand / when the stars begin to fall.*
>
> *You'll hear the sinner moan / to wake the nation's underground / looking to my God's right hand / when the stars begin to fall*

The sunlight caressed the awakening world, and the cool breeze caressed their foreheads, and they kept singing gospel songs while the most breathtaking dawn was born in front of their eyes and while Arif was deep asleep.

GILI

He came to their school from the city at the age of fourteen. His mother died few years ago, and his father, a scientist in Weitzman Institute, decided to give him kibbutz spirit and life approach. Gili had a younger sister who stayed at home. Gili, Akram, and Abraham made in all secrecy a treaty, one for all and all for one, and blended their blood together to empower it.

When Gili became fifteen years old, his father gave him a silver Hercules telescope of 30 x 15 on a black polished metal tripod. He was allowed to have it in the school as it could be used in teaching. He was allowed to use it to his own observations from the water tower on Friday and Saturday night. The first Saturday evening, he invited Abraham to come up with him. The water tower was fifteen meters high, and access to the roof was done by an outside metal ladder without railings that were built into the wall. Abraham, suffering from acrophobia, climbed convulsively up the ladder while he stared at the wall twenty centimeters ahead. He dared not look up or down, just stared straight ahead, and with fear in the heart and a step at a time, he continued toward the top of the water tower. He cursed the builder who had taken to build the ladder and swore to himself that it would be his first and last trip on the ladder. He had agreed to it because he would not appear as a coward to Gili, who looked up to him because of his courage, social skills, and thinking capacity, and this reputation he did not want to squander.

Climbing up the ladder made him think about all the other things he was afraid of such as walking alone in the dark in the fields, where he always made sure to arm himself with a thick stick, and he was also afraid to dance ballroom dancing. Akram was an excellent dancer with good sense of rhythm that threw out both couples dancing as the Arabic chain dance, which he always led the way. He had tried to teach Abraham couple dance, but his legs would not quite follow rhythm, so he gave up but not without a pang of envy toward his friend.

While Abraham climbed upward, he could suddenly smell smoke from the nearby grove. There were probably some of the oldest students who baked potatoes on a fire and talked about the upcoming military service and perhaps about love and sex. There were probably some of the beautiful girls whom he secretly was infatuated by. When Smadar, now thirteen, came to visit her brother, Gili, and was allowed to sleep with them, he looked at her on the sly, and he could feel his heart beating a few extra strokes, but when she looked back, he removed hurriedly his glance and pretended he was busy with something else. The idea of loving Smadar made him sad, but it helped him quell anxiety during the rest of the climb. How, he thought, it would continue day after day, year after year, slowly and tiring, and he would never have the courage to look her in the eye and declare his feelings for her. He began to sing a sad Russian song for himself when he finally approached the top of the tower: "Day after day, year after year, as words without melody . . . long dark nights and the rain that pours endlessly, and all my days disappear as smoke . . ."

A split second roamed the idea to him that if he let go the grip on the ladder now, all pretense would cease, and he would get peace in his sad and wistful heart, but an angry inner voice fought immediately this thought of escapism. "Nonsense with you! You are a born fighter, and you would like to learn the stars to know, for they can get our earthly sorrows to seem insignificant and temporary," and Abraham thought that if he could learn to love the stars as Gili, he would be free of both longing and its heartache.

He reached the final stage and climbed gently up on the concrete floor. When he was at a safe distance of the ladder, he stood and breathed freely and confidently. *I did it!* he thought triumphantly. Shortly after appeared Gili's head up, and Abraham helped him onto the concrete floor. He looked at Gili but could not trace the slightest emotion. While they mounted the telescope on the stand, Abraham was overcome by a sudden urge to be honest, and he took courage and stammered, saying, "I have climbed on the damned ladder at least ten times before, and I'm really looking forward to the day I've got used so much to climb that I stop all the time to think about death."

"It may happen once you begin to concentrate on something other than fear. For example, think how beautiful the sky is or how incomprehensible and magical space is!" said Gili.

"Do you think ever on love?" asked Abraham.

"Not much, if you have girls on your mind!" said Gili.

"No! More on general terms, without any particular girl!" Abraham said.

"I think that science means more to me and that love comes when it will come," said Gili.

"And if it does not come because you are too shy, what do you do?"

"Abraham! What are you talking about? You are the most popular and beloved boy in school, and there are many girls who look at you on the sly. It's coming whether you like it or not," Gili assured him, grinning.

"Do you think so?" Abraham looked at him with pleading eyes.

"Yes, it is just as surely as I know the Milky Way. And I also know that my sister is crazy about you!"

"Is she?"

"Sure!"

"But she is only thirteen!"

"She is already a little woman. She already has a small woman's heart, and she goes after the best." Gili smiled shyly.

"Well," said Abraham, overwhelmed, "we have come up here because of something else. Let's look at sky."

Gili straightened slowly the telescope toward a point on the firmament and locked it tight. "At night, you can clearly see the Milky Way. In the town where I come from, there's already so much streetlight the darkness will be dissolved, so you cannot see the stars so clearly as here."

"So there is still something good with our dark and scary nights," said Abraham and took over the telescope.

"Yes, I can see it clearly. It is beautiful," he said. "The Milky Way is the galaxy that our solar system belongs to, but you probably know that already. In it, there are perhaps 250 billion suns and many of them similar to ours, which means that it might teem with life up there. Do you understand what it might mean for us and our self-understanding and life onward journey?" Gili asked.

"Yes, I understand, but why are you concerned with it?" asked Abraham.

"Because it is exciting, more exciting than anything else! If in our galaxy there is a million developed and organized civilizations, it will be possible one day to get in touch with them, learn from them, transform us, fight diseases that kill us, learn how to avoid wars and infamies . . ."

"Can we visit them and vice versa?" asked Abraham. "There were some scientists who once figured out that an average distance between two developed civilizations in our galaxy may be three hundred light-years. Do you understand this? This means that a spaceship, which moves at a speed of light, an impossibility for us today, will need at least six hundred years traveling both ways. I cannot be sure whether such travel will ever take place, but travel to the planets and star systems that are closer to us will probably be a reality, perhaps already in our time. But in the case of information exchange and communication between developed civilizations, we can already obtain a lot of information via radio waves, and the form of communication is extremely simple and cheap compared to what a giant spaceship demands," added Gili.

"So you think then that if we send them a message in the morning, we must wait six hundred years to get a return message?"

"Yes, but it will, of course, be worthwhile if they can help us with anything, which they are better than us," said Gili.

"There is a Chinese proverb that says, 'When you look at the moon, you yearn to get close to it without being sure whether it can ever succeed, but your longing can give you a focus, which can help you to pull your boots out of the mud!' It was well said!" Abraham chuckled. "It occurred to me on the way up here, so now we can go down unless I get thoughts of death. I would rather think about a possible meeting with other intelligent life that can teach us something about life so that we may one day be able to settle us on other planets, which will be hospitable to such some stunted fools as we!"

WHO WILL SURVIVE?

One Friday afternoon, when Arif had come to fetch Akram home for the weekend, it struck Abraham, who followed him down to the car, that Akram seemed quiet and grim. His father also noticed it and asked, "What is the matter with you, son?"

"Nothing!" said Akram.

"Is something bothering you, Akram?" asked Arif again, now with urgent voice. Akram looked at his father and then at Abraham. "You can say it, even though Abraham is here. He is your twin brother!" ordered Arif.

"Do you know Nasruddin and the cruel Emir?" he asked his father hesitantly.

"The play we saw last week in Tel Aviv!" added Abraham, and Akram nodded affirmatively.

"I've read about it, but why do you care about a play?" asked Arif.

"Is it true that the Arabs are stupid and evil?" asked Akram and looked fearfully at his father. "Are Arabs dumber and more vicious than other peoples?"

"Who said such a thing? There are stupid and evil people among Arabs, among Jews, among people from Denmark, but there are also good and fine people among them."

"Can it be that there are many more among the Arabs?" insisted Akram.

"Allah is great! What's this kind of nonsense you utter, son?" cried Arif.

"Why is it that the Jews are so more modern, better educated, and have a stronger military than all the Arabs together?"

Arif sighed deeply and looked long and intensely at his son. "So this is how you understand it! That just because certain people in a period are stronger than others, they are not stupid or evil? We are talking about wisdom, the wisdom of a long, long time, a wisdom which should bear us to a better future. Not all the mighty are wise, and many of them make terrible havoc in the world and thereby undermine the evolving human course while digging their own graves. I will tell you both a story of wisdom! It's about Nasruddin. It is quite a short story, so it's not going to tire you, and it can help to put a few things in place on the topic of wisdom. So Nasruddin was a ferryman and ferried people from one bank of the river to the other bank. One day came a finely dressed and obese man who had much money and spoke in highly literate language. He wanted to sail to the other shore and began to negotiate the price.

"At one point this obese man interrupted Nasruddin and told him that his language was bad and that those who had not learned to express themselves properly had already lost half of their lives. Nasruddin was silent and began to row. When they got midway, Nasruddin turned toward the man and asked him if he could swim. 'And why should I bother to learn swimming?' said the self-important man with contempt. 'Because If you cannot swim, you are going now to lose your whole life because we sink . . .,' replied Nasrudin.

"What is moral of this story, Abraham? What's the value of one's pretense and power if you cannot swim when you need to swim?"

"It must be something to do in focusing on the essence of life," Abraham said.

"Yes, Abraham sees clearly. We, the Bedouins, and they, our Arab landsmen, have learned to survive under the worst conditions. What do we have? Desert, camels, sheep, and tents and desert winds. Being able to understand and accept the extreme necessity is the foundation of all wisdom: to be able to survive in harsh conditions. Out there, in the big cities, there are many people who philosophize like parrots but can't cope with one day in the desert. In this area of survival, neither Jews nor other smart people can teach us something. Remember it, my boy. And one more thing, son. I would like to see you do well in school so you can join the military, like I did, and excel in the art of war, both with modern tanks and artillery and guerrilla, commandoes, and with marksman skills. I can shoot a man at a distance of one kilometer with my gun. You must be even better. Do you understand?"

Arif gave his son a little push, and Akram nodded without looking at his father. Arif turned to Abraham. "There exists an alliance between us and you. I love you and your father as my son and brother, but between Jews and us, there is a mutual contract, a Hudna, a contract based on common interests, not on love. Love plays no role in this alliance. We say that my enemy's enemy is my friend. This is the situation now, and this will continue to be as long as *Homo sapiens* walk on the earth unless we will evolve away from it. This principle is the foundation of our wisdom. Right now, we have an alliance with the Jews, but who knows what the world will look like in one hundred years? We are in alliance with those who can accept us and respect our survival skills. We have seen many nations come and disappear, go up, and then go down, but we prevailed. As long as they let us live, we will not betray them. It is our wisdom, Akram."

"And if they do not treat us nicely?" Akram asked.

"If they do not, then we have. Allah is great, time and time, and time is on our side. As the saying goes, when the Bedouin revenges after forty years, he mutters, 'I got to hurry!' Do you understand now, what is the source of our wisdom and strength, son?"

"But we are weak in comparison to all the other countries around us," insisted Akram.

"It's true right now but not forever. I will tell you about another strength we have. King of Babylon built a maze of iron and stone, and so he invited the big Bedouin sheik to visit him. He tempted him to go into maze and try to find his way out of it. Throughout the day and night, the great sheik searched for escape without finding it, and in his distress, he called on to God, and God showed him the way out. Before he took leave of the king, he told the sheik that he also had a maze, and the king of Babylon should try one day. He went home and gathered his army and led it to Babylon and the king's castle, surrounded the city wall, and got the king to surrender. He tied the king up and led him by camel out into the Arabian desert and he removed the king's ropes and said to him, 'It is my labyrinth. You get a little water and food, and then you can try to find the way out.' And then he rode away, and ever since, no one has heard or seen anything to the king of Babylon," ended Arif.

"What is this story to do with military power?" asked Akram defiantly.

"Today you can cross the Sahara by car, and any tank can reach our settlements in a few hours . . . In the long run, no one can usurp God's maze. On the contrary, they, the mighty of today, will achieve the opposite by creating desert out of the fertile land if they keep acting arrogant against God and nature. We came from the desert, and it is in us. Kingdoms get up and get dissolved. Empires control many people and collapse. We live frugal and thrifty. We take only what we need. We are not spoiled, and we don't bury us in our waste. It is our strength in the long run, and we will, through focused efforts to become better people, through transformation, survive all these people who think they are superior to us. It will happen because we are of the maze that leads to the Promised Land. Remember this as a metaphor, Abraham!" Arif ended his tale.

"Can we just try to live and be happy without all the things you've told, Dad?" objected Akram gently.

"There are many people who pursue happiness and even believe in the happy life as an end in itself. But happiness and joy is like a blowing wind. You cannot catch them in your hand or harness them. You can feel them in moments, and that can go a long time before they appear. There are people who claim that they live a happy life without unfolding efforts to pursue great mission, but it's pure pretense. The only thing that can give you a feeling of sustained fullness of life is to go for the stars, a Promised Land, and to work focused and targeted for our transformation. Everything else is a smokescreen. Well, hop you two into the car. We drive."

THE YOUNG GUARDIANS

Abraham and his comrades joined the Young guardians movement in the sixth grade through a ceremony where they were wearing blue shirts with red leash on the collar, swore allegiance to both the pioneering spirit and the socialist vision, along with accepting ten commandments, which were the pillars of the movement. After joining the movement, they met with a counselor once a week to acquire and discuss the ideas in the vision and to undergo paramilitary training and character hardening, which included shooting at targets, navigations in the nights, courage and endurance demanding exercises, and talks dealing with introspection and motivation to live up to the ideal of the Guardian.

In their classroom hung a large blackboard, and on it hang the ten commandments:

The Young Guardian:

1) is a truthful man who defends the truth.
2) is an inseparable part of the Jewish people and retains strong ties to the state of Israel, has deep roots in the country's culture, and supports Judaism and Zionism.
3) is engaged in his work and struggles to create a life where work is a productive expression of human creativity and freedom.
4) is politically active and dedicated. He works for freedom, equality, peace and solidarity.
5) is a loyal friend who works with his comrades to achieve progress and to spread the movement's values in the world.

6) develops and maintains free and honest relationship to the members of his group and assumes the responsibility to provide for their welfare.
7) respects and takes good care of nature. He acquires knowledge of it and lives and acts in accordance with the principles of sustainability.
8) is brave, independent, enterprising and critical thinking.
9) builds up a strong character and strives for physical, mental, and spiritual balance.
10) is guided by reason, taking responsibility for his actions, maintains sexual purity, and strives to set an example for the others.

Abraham thought that sexual abstinence was a very big challenge since they slept two boys and two girls in the same room, but even harder was it had to be happy all the time. They sang a particular song almost every time they met to get into this mood of enduring happiness.

> *The young guardians are a happy bunch.*
> *None of them gives up and complains.*
> *Our group is prepared for any task!*

It worried Abraham because he occasionally would sigh and was not happy all the time. He certainly was not sure if he was actually ready for any task granted him, and so he stood there also in the commandments that he also had to be independent and critical, and he was not sure that he was as he followed without doubt the socialistic dogma. During the last year, he had grown up almost sixteen centimeters. His voice had come in transition, and there was growing black hair under his armpits and in the groin, and he cut himself often on the razor blade while trying to remove the sprouting stubble on his chin, and he was plagued by constant and bothersome erections. But there were also uplifting moments. He was a talented, focused and teachable student in school, popular, respected, and well-liked. Nevertheless, he was at times melancholic and felt sad without knowing why, with one exception. He knew for sure he was in love with Smadar, who lived with her father in Rechovot City. He saw her once a fortnight when she and her father came to pick Gili home for weekend in Rehovot. He was often invited but declined always, partly because he had to work in the cowshed on Saturdays but also because he could not relax with her and imagined what a painful scene it would be if she saw his erections. He often thought about what you could talk to a girl about when you went with her hand in hand and how he could get his penis to relax. He could maybe start with something about Leninism, socialism, and some of the ideas the kibbutz was based on. It was important to start relations with a girl with some well-chosen topics, but he could not really get started because he could not talk to anyone about his feelings. They were forbidden. The idea was that, as part of the upbringing of the Guardians, he had to learn to sublimate those feelings and drift and transform them into actions for the benefit of the community and humanity.

When he turned fifteen years old, he and the other group members were ready to be introduced into the tough issues that created the framework for their lives in the kibbutz: Marxism/socialism, Zionism, and Judaism. Because of his good memory and his focus, Abraham learned fairly quickly all the important concepts and embarked on a career as an amateur journalist for the school newspaper, where he wrote enthusiastic articles for the youth. He worked three hours every day after school in the cowshed, where he looked after the cows and milked them and sometimes helped get the pelt of a dead calf. When he finished the day's work at six o'clock, he trained running in the fields, hoping to qualify for the Olympic Games in 1964.

As he was good to gather the youth and keep them engaged and to hold speeches, he was elected as a scout leader for a group of children of ten to twelve years in Ashkelon City. Once a week, he and a girl from the group, Nili, took the bus after school to Ashkelon City ten kilometers away from the kibbutz. In the city, they met young children in the street, and their task was to introduce them to the movement's spirit. Often, they had to deal with fifty to seventy children from the city's poor neighborhoods and organized games, excursions, and cultural events for them. It was the first time in his life that Abraham had received money from the kibbutz because they had to pay for the bus ticket. In the kibbutz, they did not use money. Although they almost spent two hours waiting for the bus and driving back and forth on the bus, which had many stop stations on the way, they spent in additional three hours with the kids; they had no money to buy neither food nor drink. He soon found out that if he could save the bus ticket to the city, he could buy an ice cream for the money and would feel truly spoiled. He only needed to run the ten kilometers along the highway, past some small villages and to the town, and it was no big deal for him.

Inside the city, he met with Nili, and when their activities with the children was over, they went back home on the bus. When they got off the bus, it was pitch-dark, and there were still five kilometers to go back to the kibbutz because there was no bus going to the kibbutz. They went on a road between fields and orchards, and they felt both scared and insecure in the dark, but they were, of course, the brave guardians who learned not to give in for fear. For safety's sake, Abraham found a thick stick, so he was prepared if he should have to defend themselves. He was afraid of wild dogs, which dwelled around the hills and hunted on the fields at night. Some of them suffered from rabies and could find to attack passersby. There were some from the kibbutz who had been bitten and had been through a painful and prolonged treatment. To make the agony with the five kilometers in the dark shortest possible, he suggested, accompanied by Nili, loud protests that they could run back to the kibbutz. It was there on the dark road that he learned that you cannot chase away the darkness with a stick but that you can defend yourself with it, so they were prepared to defend themselves against what could threaten them in the darkness, thereby feeling more protected and less afraid.

On one of his visits to the kibbutz, Arif asked about Abraham's activities in Ashkelon City with the young children, and Abraham replied that they tried to teach them solidarity, love of nature, values of work, generosity, and shared responsibility and to help them become as well tough, courageous, and hardy.

"And what about the other values you seek to liberate people from their limitations, refine them, and to strive to improve the world and for greatness, nobility, and heroism?" Arif asked.

"I do not know for sure whether we aspire for greatness, but we strive to exercise our best. The ideals that you've mentioned, Arif, cannot be communicated directly to the children and not within the framework we have. We see them once a week for three to four hours, and sometimes there are almost seventy of them," Abraham said shyly.

"It is very good to strive for greatness, if one has it in him, and preferably with a degree of humility and if you know where to invest your force and talents," said Arif. "Most people live their lives from day to day and think mostly on their personal and social challenges like earning enough money, fulfilling their needs and to live as enjoyable and convenient as possible, and it is this mind-set and focus which determines what they find challenging and significant in their lives."

"Is there something wrong with this way of life that they and we have?" asked Abraham.

"No. I am not criticizing you. I criticize the lazy and spoiled mentality that is spreading in the world and that results in mental apathy and decadent life view. It is not the ultimate meaning with our lives."

"In the kibbutz, we are proud to be ordinary and work with our hands," Abraham said defiantly. "Sometimes the ordinary people are the salt of the earth!"

"You have not been taught to be ordinary, Abraham. You have been promised a Bustan. You have been promised that if you work hard for it, you will become its gardener," insisted Arif.

Abraham had heard it so many times before and did not want to discuss it more. "Man can work in Bustan and still be ordinary and associate with kids and try to influence them with small means, I would think!"

"An evolving Bustan is something entirely different," Arif said. "Those who have been granted a blessing, a Barakh, and do not try to excel and strive for greatness end up writing their lives on the sand or water. For most people, life consists of living life and cheating themselves with the world's notions of life after life, and that's enough for them, but for a few, life is about transforming life." Arif continued.

"So what on earth is an evolving Bustan for a mission?" Abraham asked irritably.

"I can only have my thoughts on that. I know that it is a task significantly greater than mine that was and is to lead my people into modern times. My pledge is to continue the journey of transforming my wandering people into modern permanent living people and to support you in your journey. Whether you choose to pursue your destiny or ignore it, it is up to you, but stop for heaven's sake your nonsense about being ordinary. Life is what you do in it if you can or neglect to do!" Arif said excitedly.

Abraham couldn't quite follow Arif's thoughts. He was in love with Smadar, and he was going to sublimate his urges, and it was springtime of his life, and he was sometimes sad and frustrated. That was his focus. He often listened to "Summertime" as his heart flooded with grief, pain, and sweetness without knowing why.

Summertime and the living is easy
Fish are jumpin' and the cotton is high
Oh, your daddy's rich and your mommy's good-lookin'
So hush little baby
Don't you cry
One of these mornings, you going to rise up singing
Then you'll spread your wings and you'll take to the sky
But till that morning, there ain't nothin' gonna harm you
With yo daddy an' mammy standin' by

SMADAR

His burning and devouring love for Smadar, his persistent daydreams about her, and the painful erections that he sometimes had to relieve made Abraham doubt his ability to sublimate his urges and turn libido into constructive energy. He was ashamed of the situation but kept it to himself and felt more and more alone with his shame. Once a week, the group met with the scout movement supervisor, who was about twenty years old, to talk about how the group members were doing, and at one point, the debate revolved around all the precious and constructive energy that young people waste on sex and eroticism. The supervisor explained what a great chance it was to be able to help improve the world at a young age instead of wasting time jumping on each other's pants. It sounded convincing to Abraham but not to Akram, who thought it was not "natural."

"Look at the sheep, the donkeys, the camels, the horses, and the people. It works by itself, completely without all the sublimation hysteria!" Akram insisted.

Akram believed that they were on their way into a monk's order and declared that he had no intention of wasting any chances. During one of the meetings, Akram sent him a small note, saying, "If we do not release our libido's drives, we will get a brain which will fry!" Abraham laughed but could not share the secret of his preoccupation in Smadar with Akram. Having spent three meetings discussing every possible aspect of the topic, all members of the group had committed to transforming their libido into cultural, social, work-related, revolutionary, and missionary activities, and each had to identify the areas that they burned most for and would throw themselves over. They had promised that sex and love were indefinitely postponed until the day they had attained sufficient maturity as to be able to understand the depths of love as their supervisor had expressed it.

Afterward, when they met outside, Akram whispered to Abraham, "I now intend to limit myself to pretending. For me, it is all very simple. It's about touch and penetration, and the rest is just some ideological fuck! With us, it is said that a Bedouin has three dreams: succulent spring grass as far as the eye goes, the full moon, and eternal life, and we have three desires: a large grassland, a good Arabian horse, and a benevolent young woman . . . Shall I continue?" Abraham nodded, smiling. "There are three things that are insatiable: the human eye that wants to see more and more, the desert land that can never get enough rain, and the woman's desire for a man. This is how people are in their core regardless all their sublimation. Man is driven by his urges, so I consider this a perversion," ended Akram. Abraham laughed loudly. "Allah the Great!" exclaimed Akram, smiling. "A large miracle has occurred right now. I never thought you could laugh again!"

Abraham smiled, but no matter how much Akram's down-to-earth considerations eased his mind for a while, he thought he ought to follow the collective decision. Akram continued to tease him. He believed that this so-called sublimation miracle cure was, of course, also used to sublimate "crazy people, sinners, dreamers, and not least, the many fanatics who plant crazy ideas in the fiery youth. "When you wake up from your brainwashin' masochistic game, get ready so I can lead you into the Bedouin's sensual way." He laughed and pinched Abraham in his cheek.

THE JOURNEY TO THE MOUNTAINS AND THE BLESSING AT THE SAGA

Being only fifteen years old, Akram was a fully fledged pathfinder, both in the desert and in the other Israeli landscapes. "And you, Abraham, our pathfinder into the future . . . and, Gili, you are our pathfinder among stars." Akram said, laughing. "My father thinks that you will be able to find your way to the stars with difficulty, but you will find them," said Akram to Gili, "but right now, I think we should stick to the ground, where I am at my best, all right?"

One day Akram suggested that they would go hiking in the mountains. He borrowed an Uzi submachine gun in his village, and on Friday afternoon, the three sneaked out of the kibbutz and went on their way through the fields toward Judea's mountains in the east. It was the middle of summer, so they could spend two nights outside the kibbutz without anyone noticing their absence. In the afternoon, they reached the foot of the mountains and had a break. "And now I will make some coffee to keep me awake!" He got up and went to his backpack and pulled out a small cloth bag while Abraham and Gili were staring at him.

"Are you smoking pot?" Abraham asked.

"I have been created to enjoy life, to fight, to smuggle a little here and there, and to be a good friend and warrior! I would like to live a life where I can feel that my heart beats! Mind you two that I will enjoy life a bit? I am two persons: One in the kibbutz and one when I am free of the kibbutz and in my tribe. It is best for me, at least while I'm young, to smoke pot once in a while. We Bedouins are stealing in order to survive. I will be allowed also to be a little thief but with my heart in the right place. With too many injunctions, we lose either our hearts or live pretending to be somebody else, and I don't play this stupid game to my best friends. For me, the man who prevents other people from living a full life is worse than a sinner. There are some of them in the kibbutz, and I'm tired of them!"

"As long as you continue to be a decent young man, it is fine with me," Abraham said. They kept going up the slope as the sun warmed the air.

"There was a time," Akram said, "where I and my siblings were picked up by some riders and tucked away. My father said to us, 'I cannot take you to the hiding place where I'm going because you're only children. By God's grace, neither you nor I have known many ailments, but they exist, and they are countless, and now has an accident hit our house. I leave money to your protectors while I'm gone as long as there is a danger for our lives.' While he spoke, he took three rings out of his pocket and sat them on our fingers. Then he kissed us long and disappeared completely, enveloped in his cape. When he was about thirty steps from us, my mother came out of the tent, and he turned to her. She put her hands to her mouth, and then she lifted her arms in the air and pointed skyward. He bowed deeply, turned, and disappeared into the darkness. 'What was the miracle he was talking about?' I asked my mother. 'It means that you may need to see each other again in heaven, dear Akram,' answered my mother. I saw my father again years later, but ever since, he had become a stranger to me . . . The sadness brought me into a sleep mode, and when I woke up again, it was with a feeling that I no longer belonged to this world and that there had been something terrible. I no longer knew if I saw a nightmare or whether our lives until this moment had been a dream. When I found the pot, it helped this darkness to vanish for some time," Akram said, looking up, avoiding his friends' stares.

A stifling hot westerly winds sent waves of the field scents over them, and butterflies, dragonflies, and wasps annoyed them incessantly. Akram continued his story. "While we, the children, slept, we were led away from the tribal habitat and into Jaffa, where we spent two years with some relatives and constantly surrounded by our bodyguards."

"How was the city then?" asked Abraham.

"It is difficult to describe. I was angry at my father because he did not come to visit us. It was also unusual to see Bedouin children in this town, and we were teased by the Arab children and had no real friends. Not so far from our house, there was a hotel, where there lived waiters, dancers, prostitutes, and their pimps, and it was the closest we came to townspeople. I remember that we saw a superannuated Bedouin who had been an actor in a cabaret and played the wild animal with a dagger between his teeth. He appeared for a Jewish audience and yelled and screamed something resembling war cry, and we were ashamed of us on his behalf. The hardest part was walking around the city streets and watching the many people who lived in poverty and degradation. It seemed to me as if they all had enough in themselves but suffered from this. I was six then, and I felt that I could just disappear without anyone noticing it. We were the pure nothing, and I missed my life in the settlement with my friends. I felt often as if I walked around in a nightmarish city inhabited by devils children, strangers they were for me, although they spoke a language I could understand. I felt their indifference as a blow to the body, and eventually, I began to hate them, or at least most of them, for there were also some who were good enough, and it was often the prostitutes. They could find to buy sodas for us and caress us, perhaps because they understood our deprivation and humiliation. I began to change and not for the better . . ." Akram stopped abruptly. "Let us start to make some food!" he said.

They heated some canned food on a small fireplace. They had only brought five liters of water to each one for two days, so they had to accept a field ration and agreed that this trip part was a good idea. When they had finished, they climbed into their sleeping bags as the evening got cold. Akram agreed to take the first watch and laid the Uzi submachine over his shoulder, after he had given the two others a scanty instruction in how to use it. Gili started talking about the future of space travel while they looked up into the clear sky and stars. Akram teased him and asked how long he had been in love with the stars. Abraham kicked Akram discreetly and said that he would follow Gili's thoughts on the possible existence of intelligent life in space, which in the future could help us develop ourselves further from our primitive state.

"Why are we primitive?" asked Akram, amazed.

"See, people can produce airplanes, cars, boats, medicine, phones, rockets . . . Between us, we are primitive as long as we can slaughter each other such as happened during the Holocaust and as long as we do not try to prevent the evil," Abraham said.

"Our technological advances cannot hide the fact that we both can be extremely short-sighted, cruel, and immensely negative to the atrocities we commit!" said Gili.

They lay on the soft moss on the mountain bed, when Akram fished a new cigarette out of his pocket and lit one for himself while the other two watched him.

"Do you also smoke cigarettes?" asked Gili.

"As you can well see, but only when I do not find myself on holy ground as the case is in the kibbutz!"

"How long time have you been smoking?" asked Abraham softly.

"For about a year!" said Akram.

"Bad habit!" Abraham commented.

Akram shrugged. "I reckon that we can keep some secrets, we three, as long as they do not harm other people."

"Sure we can!" said Abraham. "Men, it's stupid! I can hear my father's cough from a half kilometers away, and he stutters and spits and gets one pneumonia after another, but you know all that, Akram."

"Yes, I know just as well as I know that everything is temporary and that all things pass away. Even the kibbutz socialism and our bloated humanism and human rights will pass away one day, although for most people, it seems unlikely. So yes, I smoke and dance with the girls every now and then and do other things, but I do it without involving all these ego-inflated people who eat like pigs and fart as pigs and behave like pigs. Back then in Jaffa, I lost respect for our family, and my mother and I began to associate with pimps and their girls. When my mother saw my defiance and my growing hatred and the company I came in, she struck me once but gave up fairly quickly to correct me and contacted instead one of my uncles, who at the time took us back to the tribe settlement when the feud between our family and the enemies had died out and soon came to its end with a Sulcha (peace agreement between the feuding parts), which was sealed with a party. But after all these experiences, I let not my mother, neither my father, to decide for me if I don't agree . . ."

Akram paused, and silence descended upon the three friends until Gili asked, "Do you still have contact with the wise man from Jaffa?"

"My father thought I should talk to him because I am uncertain who I really am! All that with being a Bedouin yet live in a kibbutz, thinking to become an officer, Jewish customs, and so on. Sounds easy enough, but for me, it's quite confusing. Well, enough of that!" declared Akram and jumped up.

He served them another round of Arabic coffee.

"It is the real coffee. The smell of real Turkish coffee!" he said and brought the bag in front of their noses.

"I have never tasted real coffee," murmured Abraham.

"Exactly!" said Akram. "Here we do things we have not done before . . . I have a weapon, cigarettes, some fine dope . . . and now coffee. Next time I take something else with me!" He laughed loudly.

They collected some dry branches, and Akram kindled a new fire and put a pot of coffee, water, and sugar. Shortly after, he poured the hot coffee into three small cups and offered around the frothy, aromatic drink, after which he sat crouched and began to drink with soft, slurping sounds.

"And you, Gili!" said Akram. "Why did you leave your family in Denmark, the safe country where they lie down when the enemy comes . . . and why did you come all the way to this strange land? I have heard that in Denmark, they do not know war, hunger, and disease, the chosen course to capitulate to the Germans immediately! What a people!" said Akram.

"You cannot talk about people when you don't know them at all!" protested Gili. "I have only good memories from the years up there. It was the happiest time of my life!"

"Why did you leave this paradise to come here, where you will never surrender to your enemy?" sounded Akram sarcastically.

Gili looked sad. "It was my father's decision! He said that we had to travel. One reason was that my parents were Zionists, and the other was that he learned that more than seven thousand Danes participated voluntarily in the German army on the Eastern Front and perhaps also in concentration camps. They could not bear the thought of meeting this kind of people on the street . . . and felt certain distaste for the Danish people's denial of this shameful chapter in their history. It was this reason he had been named. And so he was offered a job in Weitzman Institute."

"When did your family immigrate to Israel so?" asked Abraham.

"It was in early 1953, when I was seven years. My mother got cancer, and they would both like to travel to Israel, where my father was promised a good position."

"Was it hard for you to come to Israel as a seven-year-old boy?"

"It was probably just as difficult as it was for you, Akram, having to adjust to kibbutz life. I was called Casper in Denmark and had to get used to be called Gili."

"Do you still talk your old native language?" asked Akram.

"Yes, I do. I could well imagine that one day we could travel there together, to Copenhagen, which is a beautiful city, and experience how beautiful and peaceful the country is. We should do that all three of us!"

"I am with!: said Abraham.

"I do not really know! To me, it seems like a boring country, and I do not like people who just surrender and let others fight for them or even support the enemy," muttered Akram.

"They did not have a chance against the Germans!" said Gili.

"It is the same the Jews in Poland and other nations in Europe claimed," said Akram sharply.

Abraham thought that Akram was too harsh on Gili but decided not to intervene. *Perhaps people who change sides may be extra radical*, he thought.

"Between us, we cannot judge the Danes without being in their shoes . . . and they would not risk being subjected to the same treatment as the Jews. In addition, they helped Jews escape to Sweden!" said Gili.

"Yes, in return for their money, we read about it!" added Abraham.

"The vast majority of people at such situation would do the same," interjected Gili. "Now it is up to you, Akram, whether you want to participate in a travel to Denmark or not. I will show you, Abraham, where I was born and grew up, and I have nothing to be ashamed of. You'll like it!"

"Why have you chosen to live in a kibbutz, far away from the exciting life of the city and from your father and sister?" continued Akram relentlessly.

"Well!" stammered Gili. "I grew up in the country as spoiled and soft, and I wished to become a tough boy. I and Smadar knew only the life we had together with my father and mother in Aarhus. But my mother died, and my father could not cope with both of us, and so I suggested that I could live in a kibbutz. I heard and read a lot about life in the wild and about the socialist ideal, and I would like to try it. I would like to try to be tan, wild, and lively, like a Sabra, born a citizen of Israel. I had never tried to run after a butterfly or a green grasshopper, to catch big fat bees, to hear the birds singing everywhere, and to spot an invisible cricket. And I had never seen a bee pull out backward at a flower with pollen on the legs. And especially, I had no idea the joy you feel when the wind blows in a cornfield and embraces one . . ."

"And what about you, Abraham? What's your secret?" asked Akram.

"It is hard for me to explain it . . . I recently read a short story by John Steinbeck called *The Leader of the People*. There, the author describes an old, tired, and worn-out man who lives with his son's family on an American ranch. He is lonely, neglected by his son and his wife, and only his grandson shows love to him and listens to his life story. The old man tells over and over again the same story about how he and other young and brave men crossed the American continent from east to west until they reached the ocean, which set the boundary for their onward journey. This perilous journey was his greatest achievement, and it gave him the greatest moments in his life and gave meaning to his otherwise ordinary life because he had helped to accomplish something special. I came to think that Steinbeck in this short story described something deep in the human soul: the urge to transcend one's own insignificance and the world's known limits and restrictions! Only by doing something extraordinary, something magnificent, people can free themselves from their insignificance and truly understand what their life should be about. They are pioneers and pathfinders seeking new horizons and unknown frontiers . . . I know you will ask why I talk about a short story, but you asked for my secret, and my secret is a feeling that haunts me and will not leave me alone. Is it good enough?" Abraham smiled shyly to his blood friends.

Later on Akram asked Abraham, "But why? What does the future to do with stars or great feats?"

Abraham explained that they express a search for something great that can redeem and transform people. It must have something to do with the future. Akram felt that this response was strange. "Why can't we stay down on earth and live peacefully and enjoy ourselves?" he asked.

"It is because many of us just cannot!" said Abraham. "Between us, we cannot agree on much. In the kibbutz, they talk about better people and a better society, but they are also quite dim-witted and spend lots of time focusing on the trees while they forget the forest."

"What do you mean by that?" asked Akram.

"People talk a lot about focusing on the essentials, but they are best able to do it in words, not so much in actions."

"Are kibbutz' members ordinary people?" asked Gili.

"Yes, the vast majority of them are except quite few."

"Are you ordinary?" asked Gili.

"Time will show what we will become, but I think that we can choose whether we will be one or the other, and it is already very much . . .," Abraham said.

Abraham was on watch the other night from two o'clock to six o'clock in the morning, where he was to wake the others. He lay in his sleeping bag with a firm grip on the machine gun and waited anxiously for the sun to rise. *It will be a splendid sunrise, and I am looking forward to it. Only in those special moments when the morning is still slightly pink and the world slowly wakes while the light spreads one can grasp life's grandeur, mystery, and magic,* he thought. *When the light becomes stronger, it can also have its moments, but the magic belongs to the sunrise.* He was thinking of their conversations and Akram's and Gili's stories and wondered why he could not repay their honesty with his honesty. But he could not tell Gili how crazy in love he was with his sister. There were many things he could not reveal yet.

The darkness was slowly supplanted by a pale pink glow that going up the sky lapsed into gold and would soon envelop the landscape in bright sunlight. He began to see the contours of the landscape around him, the mountains slopes, the fields to the west, and some small fleecy clouds, all of which found their role in the magical game that was created in the awakening world. Abraham took a deep breath and said to himself, "A precious moment of creation. It must be similar creation that dawned on the new created world."

He saw the light embraced and caressed the ripe wheat fields to the west, turning the wheat into golden tapestry. He said to himself that life was worth living for and suffering for with so much beauty, and he knew that this was not a fleeting feeling but a deep realization. At six o'clock, he awakened his friends, and after a quick breakfast, they packed their equipment and got ready to head home. They started the descent from the mountain, and after half an hour's walk, they reached some major wheat fields they would have to go through to get to the dusty way leading to their kibbutz. They moved into the field and felt embraced by a golden green sea of gently dancing, undulating wheat. Abraham sang out loud, while Akram, who walked behind him, kept his eyes intently on the path that his friend stomped in the golden field, while Gili followed silently.

When they came out of the field, Akram became suddenly aware of something and pulled out his Uzi forward. Akram heard and saw better than most people, so he could not understand how the man in the shiny green cloak suddenly stood before them without being noticed by him, Akram.

The man lifted his brown hand as a blessing, and his palm was dissolved in the golden light while his cape shimmered and shone. He asked where they came from and who they were. Abraham had a vague sense of having seen him once before, just as he thought he had heard his strange dialect before, but he was not sure. The man first asked Akram where he came from and who his father was, without commenting on Akram's submachine gun. Then he saluted Abraham in such an exuberant way that he got the feeling to have met him before. Finally, he asked for permission to bless them before they went ahead, but Gili would not accept it because he did not believe in blessings. The man laid hands on Abraham and Akram's curly heads and whispered something for themselves in Arabic.

"What did you say?" Abraham asked.

"Well, that Abraham one day will find out what he looks for and yet does not know, and he will also tell you what it is." He smiled. "And remember, Abraham, a Bustan waiting for you! It will be difficult to create it, but you are a good friend with two pathfinders right now, so you'll be fine!" Now Abraham knew immediately who he was. He was moved and wanted to talk to the man, but the man smiled and muttered, "Time is not mature yet!" And then he disappeared into the light from the morning sun.

"Why would you not let him bless you, Gilli? He might be the Khider I have heard about," asked Akram with a hard gaze.

"You don't even know who the green, shiny man who came out of the blue was, so how could you reject him?" Akram's eyes were filled with tears and looked at Abraham, who had also become very sad without understanding why.

Loneliness and
Everlasting Song

During this period, Abraham isolated himself. He often went to a small hill, where he lay down on the ground. He spoke neither with Akram nor Gili about his difficulties, so the melancholy in his head kept pestering him, but at the same time, he noticed that sadness is not only tiring but also can be nutritious. His thoughts often went in circles about the unfulfilled love for Smadar, grief and longing, and the struggle for freedom, which he vaguely defined as the struggle against oppression, conservatism, and stupidity.

When he had had enough of the sad thoughts, he threw himself into literature, and one day he borrowed a book in the school called *The Legend of Thyl Ulenspiegel and Lamme Goedzak*. He read with great interest this epoch of fighting in Middle Age against the oppressive Inquisition and had the book in his backpack, reading again and again. Abraham identified himself fully with Till, who had a good life appetite. Till was funny, cheerful, and in love with life, although the Inquisition had killed his father and filled his life with grief. He was always hungry and thirsty. He fought ceaselessly against the Inquisition and for his people's freedom. But the most important thing in his life was the love of his childhood, Nele. And Nele, or rather Smadar, went with Abraham through the golden cornfield, smiling as a warm sun and was so pretty that his heart was about to burst. And she sang to him of freedom and love, both immortal, and Abraham listened to her echo that rolled across the field and disappeared into the horizon, and his heart was crying of happiness and longing. He and Nele, Smadar, joined the struggle to free the oppressed people, breaking their shackles of human stupidity, materialism, and shortsighted greed. They fought for a new humanity, which should stand up and move toward a future full of comforting and warming light, progress, and transformation. Abraham and Nele, Smadar, flew up as they were wearing wings and came to hover over the fields and forests, hills and deserts, mountains, and valleys, with a message that a new world has been created for the oppressed masses. Abraham had transformed himself into Till, and he was the bearer of the message of the very last song of liberation, though he did not quite know what it was, but he knew that it existed.

He, Smadar, Akram, and Gili walked around to inflame people to rise against their oppressors. They just lacked Lama Goedzak, the good-natured and loyal dumpling, which was Till's friend, but there was a thick and good-natured boy in his school, so they could take him with them. They walked around and fought all kinds of inquisitors, and although they were many, they could win over them. They stopped once in a while in a tavern; filled their stomach with thick and smoked sausages, ham, and delicious bread; and washed it all down with red wine from their motherland vineyards and supplemented with fried chicken and apples and pears, which they stole from the rich peasants. They were going out to meet the troops who had risen against the Spanish Inquisition, and they fought and defeated the Spanish troops, who fled back to their country. Then Abraham pulled out of the story with his friends and sent Till Ulenspiegel back on stage again to be united with his Nele.

"That is the love I have for Smadar," whispered Abraham to the wheat field. "My love to her cannot die because it also contains a persistent struggle to liberate men from their oppression and limitations. This kind of love can never dry out. Only bourgeois love without a great vision of liberation, and such love dies out because people are concerned only with each other and the small, everyday things and events in life. The bourgeois love is not blessed with stardust as a great Nele–Till love is. It is what I am looking after." Abraham slapped his forehead with his fist: A great cause, a great vision to generate the immortal love. And then he read again the end of the story, which he almost knew by heart.

> *As Nele glanced at herself, she saw that she was naked and rushed to get dressed. She saw that Ulenspiegel also was naked, and she tried to put his clothes on him, but since he did not wake up, she was gripped by fear and began to cry. "If I*

killed him with my magic ointment, I would also die!" Then she heard the sound of bells and saw a group of people with a priest in the lead came towards them and soon came face-to-face with her and looked at Ulenspiegel, who was stretched out in the grass. The priest was drooling with delight and said, "The great idiot Ulenspiegel is dead! Thank God and the law! Hurry to dig a grave so we can get him in the ground, but take his clothes off first!" Nele protested, saying that he was going to freeze underneath without his clothes on, and wild with grief, she bent over to Ulenspiegel's face and kissed him, sobbing bitterly. The priest chanted, "The big motherfucker's dead! Blessed be God!" So they dug a grave, laid Ulenspiegel, into the grave, and covered him with sand. But suddenly, while the pastor read the prayer for the dead, the sand pit began to move, and Ulenspiegel stood up, shook his sandy hair, and grabbed the priest by the throat. "You bloody Inquisitor!" he shouted. "You put me in a grave while I sleep. Where is Nele? Have you buried her?" The priest screamed and fled, and Nele came running toward Ulenspiegel, who said, "Kiss me, my darling!" The rest of the entourage fled too, and only the mayor and an alderman were so shocked, so they lay down in the grass. Ulenspiegel went and shook them and said, "Do you really believe that one can bury Ulenspiegel, Flanders's immortal spirit, and Nele, its heart? Also, she can sleep but never die! Come, Nele!" And he went away with her while he sang his song about the struggle for freedom and love, but no one knows where he went, but the song is with us!"

And Abraham whispered to himself, "The last song for the struggle for freedom and for love cannot die as long as there are people like Ulenspiegel and Nele, but how does it sound this very last song, and how is it different from other songs?" There was something that was invisible for him. He knew that everything on earth was temporary, but this song will live forever, but how!" He closed his eyes and whispered to himself, "Sesame, sesame! Shut up and . . . show me the very last eternal song!"

The hike in the Negev

Akram called Abraham's attention to the bird of prey hovering over the desert with outstretched wings, which flew in circles and then glided downward. Akram could see on the horizon a hazy gray mass under the strong midday sun. "It is either a sheep or a donkey. It's hard to see, but it's either dead or on the verge of dying," said Akram. "How can you see it from this distance? I can only see a small, obscure dot!" said Abraham, amazed.

"I can see. I can see that it moves slightly. It is as if the animal's hind legs are quivering and twitching slightly. I think that it is about to die out!" said Akram.

Three other raptors joined the first, and they circled now as a flock over the place, waiting for the animal to die. "It is a sheep. Now I'm sure," concluded Akram as they marched ahead on the rocky path.

They were a big group of youngsters, around two hundred scouts, and they went into the desert on a march of five days. It was their third day, and they put about thirty kilometers per day with full packs with food, spare clothes, sleeping bags, cookware, and raincoats. The only thing that they should not bear in these five days hike was water that they got supplied every night when they made a camp. It was a demanding trip, although it was early springtime and the temperature were over thirty-five degrees. Akram went next to Abraham, while Gili went a little further back. In front of them was a girl from their class, along with Smadar, who had been allowed to get on this demanding march on the condition that the three boys would take care of her. Smadar and Shlomit had shorts on, and Abraham could not remove his eyes from Smadar's nice ass and beautiful legs.

"If you continue that way, it ends up that you will fall over your own feet and hits your nose!" Akram laughed.

"In what way do you mean?" asked Abraham, blushing.

"You walk like a zombie, totally absorbed by her ass!" whispered Akram so Gili would not hear them.

"Man would think that you had grown up in a Yeshiva (religious school) and had never seen a woman's ass and a couple of naked girls' legs before!"

"Hold your mouth shut!" snarled Abraham.

"I say no more!" Akram said, laughing.

They walked further along the dry riverbed, where the animal was lying, and the birds now sat, poised to pounce on prey. Now Abraham could see that it was indeed a sheep and looked admiringly at Akram. "Gili!" shouted Akram backward. "Can you see the sheep lying down there?" Gili wiped out the sweat from his brow and blew his glasses and looked in the direction that Akram had pointed.

"Shall I help you carry your pack?" asked Abraham.

"No, I can manage it myself," said Gili peevishly.

"Your back is dripping with sweat!" commented Abraham.

"And then what?` retorted Gili

It is springtime, and you sweat as it was tropical summer!" said Akram.

"It is there!" shouted Gili. "The lamb is alive, and they hack into it while it is still alive. We must do something!"

"There's nothing we can do, Gili. It dies now, and it is numb. This is how nature works."

Smadar and Shlomit also caught a glimpse of the massacre taking place, and Shlomit asked if they could do anything to save the sheep. "No, there's nothing we can do. The sheep is done with," said Akram. Smadar looked at Akram with tears in her eyes, and Abraham shrugged and looked away. At one point, they came to a ledge that they had to help one another down from, and then all jumped into a riverbed. While walking there, they heard a sudden rumbling sound behind them, and turning around, they saw large stones that came rolling toward them. Akram turned and listened attentively.

"What is it?" asked Abraham.

"Come out of the riverbed in a hurry!" shouted Akram. "Quickly out! Run up the cliff!"

The others looked confused at him as he yelled and gestured. Abraham pushed Gili in front of him and grabbed Smadar and pulled her up the riverbed while Akram lifted Shlomit. Akram was shouting to the others who went in front of them, oblivious to what was about to happen.

"Overflooding! Run up! There comes a flood!" shouted Akram.

Shortly after, they saw a wave of dark water, rocks, and mud that came rumbling through the riverbed and rolled those who had not reached to save themselves in security, and they could only watch helplessly while ten to twelve of their friends were led away by the stream. When the wave had passed, Abraham shouted to the rest of the group, "We must go out and see if we can help the others! Gili, stay with the girls! Are you coming, Akram?"

A few hundred meters further the riverbed, it struck a turn, and there, in a huge puddle of stone and mud, they found their comrades. They pulled the victims out of the mud and carried them to a dry place, where they began to check whether they were hurt seriously. Most had escaped with bruises and superficial injuries, but two had broken legs, one had a broken back, and two others were unconscious. There were only a few who wept while the others sat with shocked gaze and froze in their wet clothes. There were some who ran out to the highway, which was three kilometers away, to get medical help, while the leaders gathered their groups and told them to check whether somebody was missing. When they had calmed down, the leader of the expedition patted Akram on the shoulder and thanked him for his resourcefulness, which he had shown and which had meant that no life was lost. Akram smiled shyly. Smadar came to Abraham and so long at him.

"Thank you for saving me!" she said and gave him a little hug.

Abraham looked down, shook her hand, and whispered, "It was nothing . . ."

She still looked at him, but he could not look at her and walked over to the injured.

In the evening, they gathered all around a large bonfire to celebrate that the day, after all, ended with a miracle. Each group performed a little sketch, some sang in the choir, and others played the flute and danced while they drank sweet chicory and ate baked potatoes from the fire. At one point, Akram was invited to teach scouts to dance some Bedouin known dances. Gili and Akram whispered together, and so began Gili whistling a tune that Akram had taught him while Akram showed the steps, and little by little, the bonfire come together was turned into dance scene. Smadar tried to pull Abraham into the dancing ring.

"You know that I cannot dance," murmured Abraham.

"You can learn it if you try," she said quietly.

"No. It will not do that!" he replied.

She turned around and mingled with the dancers, while Abraham was angry with himself over his reluctance and uncertainty. He was aware by now that luck is a combination of charm, resolute in action, and creative brain. He knew that resolute in actions played a major role in enhancing luck. Since many people, if not most, guarded their "flanks" too much, being afraid to fail or become objects of sneer/shaming, they reduced their chances of luck, banging on their ports. And now he did it all the same . . .

He saw a young guy with blond hair approaching Smadar and offer her to dance. He held her hand and put his arm around her while Abraham looked into the darkness behind him. When the dancing stopped, Akram and Gili came sweating and sat beside him. "What the hell's the matter with you?" asked Akram. "You are sitting here all by yourself as if you carry the world's grief on your shoulders!"

"I am just not in the mood!" Abraham said, distressed. "I cannot dance."

"So learn it, dammit. You have learned many things by trial and error. You are not a chicken by definition, so why do you do it against yourself? If you do not learn to dance, how will you be able to score a girl, you fool?" lectured Akram.

"You're right! I should learn this . . .," Abraham said resignedly. He looked over to Smadar, who sat with the blond guy, holding her hand, and they seemed to enjoy themselves. She whispered something to him, which made him smile.

Abraham got up abruptly and started walking away into the darkness. Akram jumped and asked, "Where are you going right now?"

Abraham, close to tears, said, "I need to be alone!" Then he added brusquely, "Just keep being seated, Akram. I don't need you as a nanny!" He could see that Smadar sent him a long, searching look. "Why do you make this scene?" her eyes asked.

His heart constricted. It was too much pain, and he could not bring himself to tell her. He was so upset and felt alone in the world. He approached a hill, which he began to climb on. When he came up, he pulled a dagger out of his pocket and was ready, but he could not find out whether he was ready to cry or ready to fight against anything that might emerge from the darkness. Right there, the moon came up behind a cloud and cast its silver light on the hill. He turned and saw a figure standing motionless a few hundred meters away. It must be Akram. *He cannot let go, my annoying twin*, he thought, both defiant and sad as he turned, and continued his speechless hiking up toward the top of the hill and then down again while the night became cooler. He saw the little enticing stars on the horizon and thought that they could be his torches in the darkness that could show him the way, and then he went through a little goat track down another hill that was bathed in moonlight.

Suddenly, he heard a sound that made him stop abruptly and listen, and in the silence, he heard something chuckled and whispered. The gurgling sound came from a rock nearby, and Abraham decided to find out what it was that chuckled. He picked a stone in his left hand and held the dagger ready in his right hand before he crept silently toward the source. When he reached the cliff, he could see a stream that flowed along the rock wall and went into a recess under it, and that rock was surrounded by desert flowers in full bloom and with a heady scent. He threw the stone against the stone recess to scare animals or perhaps a snake that could hide there, but nothing was moving over the water. Then he continued but made sure to pass the large rock where snakes and other vermin could hide. He collected water from the spring up in his hand and drank from it, and suddenly, it was as if a large gate opened up inside him, and he drank and drank while tears welled out of him, and a moment later, he sobbed aloud while he tried to be alert to possible dangers.

"How could you," he said to the little brook, "find me here in my unhappiness? How did you find me all the way from my Bustan? Yes, I drank from you then in my Bustan, I remember, and now you came here when I needed you most . . ." The water chuckled and gurgled and Abraham asked, "Does it perhaps mean that the Bustan as the Green Man promised me is associated with a long and painful walk through the desert?" The water chuckled again, and Abraham felt as if his pain melted away, and he knew he found the right answer as the brook showed him the way. He knew that he, despite all the hardships that surely lay ahead, would again find the thread that was posted for his life, only he had to remember that it was there. He sat by the brook and drank his Bustan water and felt

---

no more pain in his heart, not even the pain of unrequited love, death, or other sorrows. "Where can I find you again?" he asked the water.

"Your wilderness journey will lead you to me and to your evolving Bustan," he seemed to hear.

"And are you my way to the Bustan?" he asked.

"Yes, but you will find me only in the wilderness where the journey toward an evolving Bustan can take place . . ."

The ear-piercing cries from the wild dogs nearby brought him back to reality, but he was not scared or sad any longer. A starry sky of infinite dimensions was unfolding around him, and a small spring in the desert had just told him that he would one day reach his Bustan. He knew he could look forward to a hard and challenging life but that he was prepared to take on, even if the price would be turning his back on love, for an evolving Bustan was the greatest he could achieve.

The feeling was scary but also magnificent. Suddenly, he realized that only people who manage to sacrifice much of their comfort and habits and were willing to wander through deserts were able to rise above a life that is shackled by commonplaces, illusions, and emptiness. He knew that somehow that night, an invisible force had handed him a helping hand to find the secret of creating an evolving Bustan in the desert. Suddenly, he heard a cry that faded away in echoes through the hillside. He hurried to get up as he swore to himself that he would not reveal the location of the brook for his friends now, perhaps first many years from now. He left the rocky, dry, and fragrant desert behind and went in the direction of the cries, which had called him back to the present moment, and when he was halfway down the hill, he saw a figure came up to meet him.

"It is me, Abraham!" Akram cried out in the darkness.

"What the hell are you doing here, Akram?"

"What the are you doing here?" cried Akram angrily. "I've been looking for you for a few hours, man!"

"Few hours?" repeated Abraham, uncomprehending.

"You can thank me for not telling the leader on your disappearance. He would send everyone out looking for you. It would not have been fun for you!"

"Pardon, Akram! I am sorry for making this trouble. I must have lost track of time!"

Akram gave him a hard hug and then looked into his eyes. "This trick you will never do again to me!" he said sternly. "I would not be able to forgive you again, and my father would not forgive me for not being there for you!" he snorted while saying it. Abraham gave him a hug and muttered that it had nothing to do with him or others. "So what you have been looking for? Gili said that it can only be heartbreak or revelation! Is he right?" Akram laughed through tears.

"I think it were both at once!" Abraham said quietly. "But now my heartache's evaporated and . . . regarding the revelation . . . Yeah, I cannot talk about it yet because I cannot distinguish between what I have seen and what was pure fantasy . . ."

They started to go back to the camp with Akram in front. "What did you see up there?" he asked casually. "I do not ask for the revelation!"

"I met something that I cannot describe now. Maybe it's something your father knows . . . Well, now I can see that both Gili and Smadar are awaiting for us down there. Why don't they sleep?" asked Abraham, wondering.

"Ask them! I could not persuade them not to be troubled by your behavior."

They hugged him both, and he was about to cry and mumbled an incoherent excuse since Smadar looked at him with tears in her eyes. "What have you seen up there?" asked Gili.

"I cannot talk about it now!" Abraham whispered hoarsely. "Maybe another day!"

"Abraham had a revelation," said Akram

, "and then I have gone through all those years and thought that my friend was an atheist!"

The next morning, they continued the journey, and Smadar came to Abraham and asked shyly whether it was her fault that he had gone from the party. He looked at her, cleared his throat, and said in a hoarse voice, "I cannot talk about it now, but I hope that one day I can show you what I've seen. It was great, and I'm not sad anymore!"

"I will be glad to see it," she said and gave him a hug.

SMADAR

It was summer 1964. The Combines drove on the kibbutz wheat fields that stretched as far as the eye could see. They drove day and night, harvested the wheat, and spat straw in bundled straw bales. Abraham and some of the other young people took turns to drive a big tractor with a pickup truck as they loaded the bales up. Smadar also joined the fieldwork, but since lifting bales on the cart was too demanding, she stood on the platform, along with two other girls, and stacked the bales. The sun was going down behind the dusty cypresses, and Abraham was sweaty but happy, and the day's work was soon over. He thought that soon, all who had taken part in harvesting would surrender to a well-deserved rest after the day's work, but as soon as the evening breeze surged in from the sea and summer evening violet silk screen unfolded, he could feel that all his fatigue disappeared. There were some people who laughed and whistled in the gathering darkness, and he heard Smadar call his name in the darkening evening. "I am coming!" he cried as he went in the direction of her voice. It was an enchanted evening, and he was excited to tend a fire and cook the food that they had brought with them, and he looked forward to the cool, black, and sweet malt beer. Maybe he would also take courage and put his arm around Smadar's shoulder and look her in the eyes and finally tell her what he had felt for her in the last four years. She was just the most beautiful and loveliest girl he had ever seen, with her golden hair, her cute face with the most beautiful blue eyes, and her slim body and beautiful skin. She was intelligent, attentive, knowledgeable, and lively. He was supposed to be soon enlisted into the army for two and a half years, so if he was to tell her, it had to be now, he thought. He knew he had to control himself and be open about his feelings. Akram suggested that he should be both open and eager but also cautious.

Somebody had lit the bonfire, and she had to be there with the other girls. The fire blazed up, and the people who stood around the fire looked like shadows that danced in black and red movements. There were more and more people coming from the fields, and some of them began to sing, accompanied by a mouth harmonica. Now he could catch a glimpse of her. She turned and looked at him in the velvety darkness, and he went straight up to her and put his arms around her as if it was the most natural thing in the world to do, and she pressed her warm body against him. They kissed, and she pulled him into the circle of the young people who passed the time until the food was hot with three-voiced song. Abraham sang without taking his eyes off her, completely intoxicated by her scent, the smell of new harvested grain and the cool, salty breeze from the sea. He thought that he had never sniffed somebody as pretty and that he wanted to prolong this moment into eternity, and here ended his restless quest.

So began another girl to sing with crisp voice, and the mouth harmonica followed, and some of the people stood and started dancing. Smadar pulled him up and began to dance around the fire. I dance! I dance and sing for life! Smadar danced like a dream, and he was enchanted by her beautiful oval face, her elegant neck, and her supple body and beautiful legs. She had a short white dress, a white cotton shirt, and light sandals. She moved gracefully, aware of how beautiful she was, and every movement pulled him further into a magical universe of love and total surrender. So the food was ready, and they sat on the ground and ate hungrily, holding hands.

When they had finished, she jumped and pulled him gently but insistently in the shirt. He stood, and she took his hand and led him into the warm darkness with a dedication he had never seen in her before. "Come!" she whispered to him.

"Where to?" he asked, taken aback.

"You will find out soon." She smiled with a cocky kid voice.

He turned to her and hugged her, and she put her arms around him and kissed him, and then she freed herself and pulled him away from the noise of the company and to a dark spot in the field, where she again kissed him, lay down, and pulled him down on. All of a sudden, he knew what to do as she turned suddenly into a woman with a glowing sensuality. She moved under him in strong spurts. As he penetrated her, he felt on his back and the shoulder her sharp nails. He was seized by her desire, and they disappeared into a vortex that threw them toward the sky, tinkled and in a gentle motion and brought them slowly back to the present in total exhaustion.

They lay side by side on the ground; he caressed her breasts, and she looked up at the moon, which rose against the sky, and whispered in his ear, "Now you're mine!"

"Yes, I am yours!" he whispered back.

"And you will never leave me?"

"No, never!" he replied firmly.

"So it cannot be better!" she whispered. "I just have to believe in it!"

"What do you mean by that?" He lifted himself on his elbows.

"It has nothing to do with you, Avri. It's me . . . There is a voice inside me that I need to calm down and get it to be quiet. Don't you have more than one voice in your head?" she asked, and then she looked into his eyes. Abraham thought about it.

"No," he replied. "I have only one voice, but it can become capricious and also melancholic. It's my voice, but it changes and surprises me all the time, and I do not know always how it will grow up to become more stable."

"It was a fine answer, Avri. Shall we sleep here tonight?"

"It is too dangerous because of the wild dogs and tractors, which come when it gets light, but we can go back to the kibbutz and sleep there if you wish."

"So you take no chances?" She laughed.

"Not when I'm with you and not without my submachine gun, but we can do it another time with submachine gun and mosquito net." He laughed.

She kissed him, and then they hugged each other and did some more things as only young new lovers can do on the way through the fields.

Was there a Green Man?

"Akram has told me about your covenant, and I asked why you three have made it mixing your blood, and he said because his fate was closely related to you and Gili and that the decision was taken many years ago, when he was very young. So was there really a Green Man?" asked Smadar.

"I do not know. I really don't," Abraham said.

"I think there was a Green Man... Akram and even my brother believe that you were blessed as a child!" insisted Smadar. "Can you remember what he told you when you were a child?"

"He told me that I should cultivate a Bustan, not a real one, an evolving one . . . He told me to water it, give it fertilizer, provide appropriate spacing between the trees and fell the weak and diseased trees, plant new and strong trees instead, and so on . . . So he said it was not an ordinary Bustan but gave instructions as it was one, which had confused me ever since . . ."

"What did he say more?"

"There was no more. Oops, yes, now I remember one more thing. He said that I would have to cut down the trees that were no longer useful in the Bustan, but I did not understand it then."

"Akram told me that his grandfather was there and knew that he would soon die and that the torch of the vision regarding the Bustan had to be given to a man who could bear it, and you were chosen. It was all something his grandfather knew because he could see beyond the veil of time and place that humans cannot penetrate due to the burden of their daily life and prejudices. And then he lifted you up and blessed you, turning you against the four corners of the world . . . and told you never to forget this day. Do you remember it now, Avri?"

"Yes, but it scares me to think about it!" he whispered and looked away.

Military time

Abraham and Akram started their military service a rainy day in October 1964, while Gili, who was a little younger first, was enlisted four months later. They all had wanted to perform their military service in an elite unit in the infantry, but it was not possible as Gili, via connections, was already appointed to a post in the intelligence service. The first weeks passed quickly. They were new recruits who had to get used to the sergeants, humiliation and crude behavior, noise and stress, lack of sleep, marching exercise, and poor food and dirty beds and barracks. They were given uniforms and were tonsured and then followed something that looked like a recruitment campaign in which representatives of the various military branches competed to get the best recruits to their respective units.

Eventually, and after conducting a march of thirty kilometers in high pace, they were enrolled into elite unit. The winter was harsh and rainy, and the first four months of training were harsh and demanding. They started at five in the morning, and most of the training took place outdoors. They slept in a tent, and when it rained, their sleeping bags and clothes were often under water; they waded through the mud, was soaked, and had neither clean or dry clothes to change. They were subjected to all sorts of punishments for the most trivial conduct and completed a hard day with being on guard two hours in the night. Fortunately, they slept in the same small tent, and through some connections, they put their hands on a piece of plastic so they could isolate the tent against the worst rain while they dug trenches around the tent, so the rain was led away. It helped, but they were cold and dirty and felt very far away from the comforts of civilization.

Their friendship became even stronger, and they developed a common jargon, spirit, and humor, and their fellow soldiers called them the Supermen twins and with good reason. They excelled both in terms of perseverance, camaraderie, shooting practice, navigation, and leadership and excelled particularly in difficult situations where colleagues were about to give up because of fatigue and exhaustion. Akram excelled especially as a sharpshooter and was given extra training, while Abraham was a born leader and a beloved mate, and gradually, they accustomed themselves to life in the wild, training, humiliation, dirt and stench, too little sleep, and night shifts. They often took the shifts from others as to earn some extra money.

There was a young guy from the town who teased Akram with his Bedouin background, and when he, despite repeated warnings, did not stop the harassment, the other recruits decided to take matters into their own hands and beat him in place. It happened one night when they threw a blanket over his head while he slept and beat him through the covers, and afterward, he was gentle as a lamb.

The first and only leave in the recruiting period fell in January 1965, and at that time Abraham had, through extra shifts, saved enough money to buy a new jacket. It was the first time he could buy cloth for himself, so he asked his mother for some advice. She encouraged him to buy a more expensive and better coat than he had thought of. "You must learn to spend money, my Puritan. The hard time is over, even in our kibbutz. People would like to have nice clothes instead of the schmatta (old clothes) we used to go in!" she said.

"Are you against the idea of something cheap?" he asked her.

"You remind me of a woman who went into a store to buy a variety and chose the cheapest. The clerk made her aware that a cheap product is often of poor quality, but when she insisted that a variety is a variety and that it should just be used for waving, he sold her the cheapest. It was a hot day, so she began to wave with it on the way out of the store, and a little later, it broke down. She fumed and went back to the store, where she scolded the clerk and accused him of cheating customers."

"How did you fan?" he asked coldly.

"How did I do it? I waved it to and fro in front of me on. What else?" she shouted excitedly. "Very strange! You bought one which is not designed for waving. It is intended to keep it still while a person is waving his head instead, replied the clerk. So think about it again, and I want to help you!" said his mother.

114

"I do not dangle my head," Abraham said angrily.

"I am not so sure," replied his mother.

"I hope you do not get the headache of too much sarcasm and worries," he replied dryly.

The time flew by until March 1965, when they finished their recruitment period. They finished both with honors. During the closing ceremony, their commandant held a little speech in which he said he deliberately had abused their body and souls and challenged their moral principles. He knew it had been a difficult time for many of them and that many hated him and the other officers and sergeants of a good heart but that there was method in the madness and continued that the goal was to train them into competent combat troops of the best kind, what in English is call: break - make and shake! "We have crushed you as civilians but built you up as combat soldiers, and now we shake your hands as equals combat soldiers!" He finished the speech.

"Akram and Abraham had distinguished themselves in this course! Tread force!" the officer of their unit ordered. "You two Siamese twins from the kibbutz had shown a good example, and what a good friendship is worth. I had not spared you of hardships. You had supported those who had it even harder and did the hard training and the night shifts without complaints and had shown leadership!" So he gave them his hand and wished them a good progress on corporal school, where they were to continue their military career. Abraham was proud of their achievements but still angry about the humiliations that this particular officer had exposed them to.

Before they were transferred to corporal school in Shivta in the Negev, they held a farewell party, to which were also invited girls from the nearby kibbutzim. He remembered the party clearly because it was the first time where they suddenly could fully relax and enjoy a party after the shake-break-make bloody months. At last, the roads and paths in the military base were not "electrified," any longer so they did not need to run all the time as recruits. At last, sergeants stopped cursing them and calling them idiots.

Now he sat together with Akram in the decorated military dining hall while colleagues came by and patted them on the shoulder and shared their delight of being chosen as excellent recruits. They looked at the girls and listened to the music, but they did not get up and offered the girls up, Abraham because he had Smadar and "could not dance with another woman" and Akram because he would not let him sit alone. Akram ended nonetheless on the dancing floor when he was invited by a girl, and Abraham thought with a pang of envy that it was these dances Akram had taken care to learn while he was with Abu Sina in Jaffa. Abraham was also welcomed by the girls, but he refused again and again and explained that he could not dance. He was aware that he had learned a lot about this and that from kibbutz life, but he felt sad about his inability to cut loose and plunge into youthful erotic infatuation, and the thought about Smadar, whom he had not seen for two months, made him even more sad. He looked at Akram, who, as easily and elegantly, swung a pretty girl around, while he, with great aplomb and agility, pulled her close to him. *It is this I will never be able to do,* he thought sadly. *I must concentrate on my tongue's eloquence and my brain's endowment, but it is perhaps not what the young women look for.*

Somebody started singing, "She loves you, ya, ya, ya," while the dances became wilder, and then they continued with another song that overwhelmed him: "If I fell in love with you, would you promise to be true . . .," and the others continued to dance, and Akram kissed the girl on the mouth. Akram came up to him, dripping with sweat, and took him by the hand while he bawled, "Do you always need to be such a sad and dried-boned saint? It is a celebration for us, and when do you think it will happen again? Come on, Abraham, I'm tired of your solitude."

"You in your chair, filled with despair. Nobody can be so sad with gloom. Everywhere you sit and you stare."

Then he waved a girl to him and said, "Dinale! Here sits my best friend who graduated with honors yesterday, and now the corporal school is awaiting both of us . . . He is good as gold and even very clever, and he is popular and sporty, but he cannot dance! He can dance a little chain dance and circle dance, but the slow dance that is danced here he does not know. I would be grateful if you would teach him that!" he said and kissed her hand.

She smiled at Abraham, and he smiled at her. "My naughty friend is right, although I find it hard to admit it," he said hoarsely.

"You are so cute!" she said, taking his hand.

She danced very close, and he tried to follow along and suddenly realized that he danced and also was about to get an erection. She crept even closer to him under George Adamos's "Tombe La Neige," and soon, he found himself in a dreamlike embrace with a warm and sensual body and arms that closed around him. And then it dawned on him that Dina, who, five minutes ago, had been a stranger, had broken through his armor, had awakened his libido, and had made him free in a new way. You did not always cultivate the solemn love that also led to anxiety and idealization. But he was doubtful whether it was this freedom he wished to attain.

Shortly before they should leave to their new training camp in Shivta, Gili appeared up with the new team recruits. He had succeeded to persuade his father that he could team up with his two friends, and they were all happy as it meant that with a little luck, they could go together through the whole military service.

SMADAR AND ABRAHAM

The fig tree was big and old, and Abraham got hold of a branch that was overflowing with ripe fruits. It had been almost two months since he had last seen Smadar, but now he had a leave from the army for five days before he was to start on an infantry officer course. "Can you pick some while I hold the branch down?" he asked.

When she had picked a ten to twelve pieces, Abraham let the branch jump again and took a juicy dark fig from her outstretched hand. So he asked her to close her eyes and open her mouth while he stripped the fruit open with his fingers and popped it into her mouth. She was sucking the juicy and sweet fruit in it and squinted. "Paradise! Now it's my turn!"

They repeated the ritual, kissed each other passionately, and laughed aloud. The light was softer and would soon dusk buckle them into a mosaic of bright colors. Smadar saw impassively at him. "What are you thinking of?" he asked.

"Of you!" she replied shyly.

"How do you think of me?"

"Only of you!" she replied.

"How?"

"It is difficult to explain . . . Last winter, I heard a radio program about a young boy who was born blind. His greatest wish was to be able to fly like Icarus but more shrewdly that his wings would not be burned by the sun. He said he had already seen the invisible life on earth but that he needed to see it out from above, free of the usual context. He imagined that what would open itself to his mind's eye would be so beautiful and at the same time so horrifying and sad because it was all temporary and transitory, and it might well be that the beautiful, the ugly, and the evil exist without definitive answers or redemption. I came to think of you after I saw the program." She looked at him, and Abraham was suddenly both embarrassed and upset. He cleared his throat and stroked her tenderly on the cheek.

"Yes, it reminds me of a dream I had when I was about fifteen years. I ran toward a springboard for long spring and, nearing the plank, assured that I was going to set a new personal record in the long jump while my companions and some of kibbutz members stood around and watched me. I put in a perfect spring and continued to soar through the air. I exceeded my own record then the national Israel's record, and eventually, also the world record was behind me, but I still had momentum and continued to rise higher and higher up to the sky to everyone's silent amazement. At last, after having hovered around and up and down bathed in sunlight, I landed quietly on the ground. I turned my back on the people, who looked shocked and astounded at me, and rushed to the dining room, where I drank a cup of tea and took something to eat. Then I resumed my usual life as if nothing miraculous had taken place shortly before. I have since wondered over this dream because I saw something up there that the others could not see, but what was it I saw and why I went on with my life as if nothing had happened, I don't know."

"My brother says you are special," whispered Smadar. "Are you not special? Are Gili and Akram not being special? Many people have a special quality or potential in them, but whether they end up developing it or not for the common good depends on many things. I have not done anything special yet, ergo, I'm not special . . . only in my love to you I try my best. In this regard, I am extra special!" He laughed as he embraced her. "Abraham, I'm sometimes oversensitive, and I can tell if someone is special!"

"I know it, Smadar. But I'm not ready to carry other burdens in my life now than my military service. I would like to have it over with as quickly as possible so I can focus more on you and what I want with my life," he said and kissed her tenderly. "There is something I want to show you, Smadar! Every time I think of it, I get tears in my eyes . . . and you're a part of it. There is a very special water source, a hidden brook, in the desert. I found it then when I disappeared from you. I found it because I was so in love with you but did not know how I was going to show it. It seemed as though I found the source of this reason. Unfulfilled love leads to a fulfilled one . . . You probably remember this night!"

119

"Yes, I can remember that. I could feel your sadness, but I could not interpret it."

"It was because of you that I found it, and it helped me finding courage to show you my love. Now I'm sure of it!"

"Will you show me the source?" she asked with an expectant smile.

"Yes! I will show you the brook because it led me to you. The water tasted like the water from my old Bustan, and I wonder if the water traveled the long way in order to tell me in my desperation something that's greater than my petty life . . ."

"I certainly believe that it is true," she whispered, and he laid arms around her and kissed her tenderly and passionately, with tears streaming down his cheeks. The world was shrouded in semidarkness when they came to themselves again in the soft grass under the tree. He heard something hiss nearby and jumped.

"What is it?" Smadar sounded frightened.

"Lay quiet!" he whispered. "We have an intruder, a poisonous snake. Let me deal with it!"

"No, Abraham!" she whispered.

"Smadar, shut up!" he said firmly.

He picked a thick branch from the ground and was moving between Smadar, lying naked on the ground, and the snake, which raised its head, threatening him. With a lightning stroke, he hit the snake in the middle of the body, so it rolled along the ground. It tried to straighten up again, but Abraham was immediately over it and struck it on the head and body. The snake gathered its last strength and tried to throw itself at him, but he remained at a distance, kept hitting it with the branch, and when it finally was heavily wounded and incapacitated on the ground, he crushed its head.

"Why did you do that? We could have run away," cried Smadar.

"We would run away naked as Adam and Eve?" he shouted excitedly. "I once run away from such a beast. Never again! I cannot talk about it now . . . but I will not run away!" he said grimly. She continued to sob while they got dressed. "Why are you crying?" he asked as he held her and stroked her hair.

"When I saw you and the snake and the way you killed it, I could not recognize you. I was just stunned inside me."

"It was me. I had it in me for a long time. It is my inner warrior. Otherwise, I cannot cope with this harsh and strange world. There is enough room, also for the sweet, but the warrior is also a friend!" He smiled to her.

"All of a sudden, I was afraid of losing you." She sniffed. "I do not think that I can hold on to happiness for more than a short time and then only with my fingertip . . ."

"Why? I am here with you . . ."

"You saw it yourself! The happiest day in my life with you, and then comes a snake up, which is both toxic and a bad omen! I was so afraid for you both . . ."

Abraham kissed her tenderly. "You should not be afraid of me. I can promise you. But I have a score to settle with these poisonous snakes, how crazy that may sound. I'll tell you why one day." She looked at him with tears in her eyes.

"So you won't leave me?"

Abraham held her close to him. "Why would I? You know . . ."

"Most people leave each other, Abraham," she said, sounding like a lost child.

"It is not everyone doing it, and I will definitely not leave you!"

"Can I be sure of it?"

"You can be sure of it. Never!" he assured her.

WAR

In early May 1967, Abraham completed his military service as a lieutenant in the infantry. After he flatly rejected an offer to sign up a professional officer contract, he returned to his kibbutz. He and Smadar, who were exempt from military service because of her asthma, planned to go on a long trip to Europe, which should start in Denmark, where they could stay with the old friends of her family. Akram had signed a professional contract for three years in the army and continued as officer in the same unit. He continued to visit the kibbutz in the weekends to meet with Abraham and a Danish girl named Lena, who was a volunteer in the kibbutz at the time. Gili, now a sergeant, was still missing four months before he could finish his military service and start at the university in Haifa.

In a way, Abraham was relieved to be free of the strict framework of military service, and he was happy to see Smadar more often, but at the same time, he felt a kind of melancholy. He had created in the military service many close ties, and the distance and a new life routine made it hard to entertain them. The years where they had been challenged to their utmost and shaken together formed some very strong and close friendships, which only soldiers under difficult conditions can shape, but he also knew that these friendships were bound to die out when life pulled them apart. And then there was the matter of taking responsibility in the kibbutz working and administrative life. The thought scared him in itself, but he had no doubt whether he should stay in the kibbutz. He was also a little afraid of becoming a hardened combatant and wrote as a reminder to himself, "Miserable is the man who has lost his child heart" as Lao-tzu had written.

And what about education, he was asked by the kibbutz secretary? They wanted to make him into a teacher in high school of the local school. He wanted to study at university and knew that he could manage it. Yet he was afraid that his life would become banal and routine prone without other challenges than those the kibbutz could offer him. He knew he was too restless to settle down in a kibbutz or a bourgeois life for the rest of his life with marriage and family as the Bustan was playing all the time on the back of his mind and where and how could he find out where it was supposed to be created and in which form.

He began working in the kibbutz chicken house with some sixty thousands chicken for meat hens laying eggs, and after one year, he was granted the responsibility for the whole chicken business. He was to run this business until he could start in the teacher seminar, which the kibbutz had planned for him. In the kibbutz, a person could not say no to a job offer or even choose his career, but he was not ready to commit, and a journey to Europe could buy him time to find out what it was he would like to invest his energy in. He told the kibbutz's secretary and his friends that he was planning a Europe trip with Smadar. "I will never be able to calm down if I do not get out and away from the kibbutz to see how the rest of the world looks like," he said. He planned to seek leave from the kibbutz for four months from March 1968.

"And what if they refuse to grant you the leave?" asked Smadar.

"For me, there are two options if they do not accept my request: either a short postponement of the date of our journey so we can negotiate a new agreement or if they refuse altogether to let us travel in the next two years, I leave the kibbutz. I never thought of this possibility before, but I can't see another possibility," Abraham said with tears in his eyes.

"I would not like you to do it for my sake. You've spent your whole life here," said Smadar.

"It is also the last resort, but I cannot, at the age of twenty-two years, accept being tied down to a life that I have not yet chosen. For me, it's casus belli (reason for war), and it cannot be different." They had already begun to plan the trip and had figured out that they could survive for four months for their joint savings.

In May 1967, Egypt closed the Suez Canal to Israeli ships and then quickly escalated the situation, and the war drums began to rumble. When Nasser refused to back off and sent troops to the Egyptian–Israeli border,

Israel launched a total mobilization, and Abraham was called up as a reservist.

Like thousands of other soldiers, he, Akram, and Gili were forced to wait fourteen days in uncertainty whether it was going to be a war or a diplomatic solution that could resolve the conflict. They spent the waiting time with different pastimes; there was a club for coffee lovers and another group where they drank whiskey and exchanged views on the different brand taste and quality. When they had been sufficiently drunk, there were always some horny soldiers who climbed into one of the armored personnel carriers and enjoyed themselves by drawing particular women body parts as they put it force. They were, however, easily distracted, and one day their attention was caught by two small black beetles copulating. The event lasted about twenty minutes, and there were no limits to the attention of the whiskey-drinking soldiers. They built up embankments around the beetles to see if they could pull one another up, and they could, an endeavor that got the young soldiers to be even more ecstatic.

Abraham and the other officers let them enjoy themselves because who knew if they would get through the war? Akram, Abraham, and Gili often sat together and read letters from Smadar, Akram's Danish girlfriend Lene, and a girl named Tova, whom Gili was starting to date with a month earlier.

"Hello, three holy men from the kibbutz!" shouted a tipsy sergeant. "Come and see the most wonderful intercourse that is drawn down here. I've never seen anything like it. Come in here and get a taste of our nectar. Tomorrow we are at war, but while we are alive, there applies only one slogan: drink, eat, and fuck all what you can because tomorrow your soul will fly away! Are you coming?"

Abraham laughed and made them aware that they were already fully occupied in the wagon but that they would not mind a quick unauthorized exhibition in the open. A tipsy corporal climbed out to show the officers and Gili their fantastic production of the vaginas, which they had drawn in all sorts of shapes, colors, and expressions. "Akram will judge!" Abraham grinned and sent the bundle of drawings on to him. Akram looked through the drawings and chose four, which he believed were the most expressive and the most stimulating, and that was how they passed the waiting time.

The girls wrote almost daily about how much they missed them, and the three sat ready with their weapons, kept little track of their soldiers' catching flies and drawing vulvas, and waited and waited. Some of the soldiers, who had never been concerned with religion, started going to the improvised synagogue services as rabbis of every conceivable observances held and where they promised the participants that God would protect them and lead them to victory.

The three looked at their comfort-seeking soldiers and said nothing but thought theirs. "That's life under these circumstances." The three agreed. "In such situation," Abraham concluded, "it is normal that young people are attracted to black holes, God holes, and other holes in females to keep the fear and uncertainty out."

"And what does Tova say that her peace-loving Dane is going to war?" Akram teased Gili.

"Win decisively or otherwise surrender immediately, if I remember correctly!" He laughed. "I wrote to her that I have two bodyguards, you and Abraham, and that you two take good care of me. Especially you, Akram, your horny warrior," said Gili.

"I will do my best, Dane, for we have undertaken a blood oath as you probably remember . . .," returned Akram. They smiled to one another and then kept quiet for a while.

"I do not know why I'm so damn sensitive and sentimental in these days," said Gili and looked at them with tears in his eyes.

"You must bear over with me!" Akram gave him a hug, and Abraham cleared his throat and looked at Gili intensely.

"I have the feeling that we are going to win it, and the war will not last long, so let's talk about what to do after the war, Gili," Abraham said.

"I had actually decided first to tell you the good news after the war . . . certainly not to tempt fate, but now, when you ask, I may as well say it straight away. My father bought tickets to the US for both of us in October, where we will visit Carl Sagan at Stanford. Do you remember that I told you about him!"

"Yes, we remember," said Abraham.

"Okay! He can get me a scholarship to read astrophysics! So my dream comes really true," cried Gili.

"Great, really great, but why are you weeping?" asked Abraham, shaken.

"It is because . . . so we're going to be separated, and I cannot bear the thought . . ."

"Between us, will we continue to keep in touch as we have promised each other a long time ago. And I will also soon travel abroad with Smadar, and who knows, maybe we can meet somewhere in the big world?" Abraham smiled.

"Assholes! You are traveling away from your baby brother. I can first travel three years from now when my contract expires, so what about me?" exclaimed Akram angrily.

"None of us is leaving or forgetting the other two. Do not look like this, Akram. We stick together. I know," said Gili.

"Fine, Gili," muttered Akram. "I believe in you the next five seconds." He smiled mischievously.

GILI'S DREAM

The evening before the war broke out, Gili came to speak to Abraham, and they went for a walk in a nearby pine forest. "Is something wrong?" Abraham asked gently.

"If something happens to me . . .," said Gili with a dark look on his face.

"I will not listen to the kind, Gili," said Abraham, upset.

"I do not think that something will happen to me, but if something happens, will you help Smadar in the beginning? She is sensitive and vulnerable. She's like our mother . . ." Abraham stood still for a moment, and then he nodded. "Good," Gili said, sighing. "I just wish that she becomes a part of our blood covenant . . ."

"She is a part of the covenant," sounded Abraham with a sad voice.

"Well, I believe you. But I also want to tell you about a dream I had for three nights ago. Do you know about how to understand dreams?"

"I have read a bit about it, but I am an amateur in this area."

"Never mind," Gili cut off him vehemently. "If you understand any of it, then it's good enough. Let me tell you about my dream. Is it okay?" Abraham nodded again. "I dreamed that we three were in the kibbutz. It was night, and we lay in our beds. Suddenly, I decided to stand up in the middle of the night. I got dressed and put on my sandals and left the kibbutz without anyone noticing it. I felt relieved and yet sorrowful because I ran away from our pact. After a long march, I got sore legs and had to sit on a rock beside a dusty, wide, and long road that continued into the horizon. There were a lot of people passing by, completely oblivious of my presence as I was invisible, but then came a seller with a large basket, which

127

offered me to buy some oranges. I said that I was returning to my father in the town and that I had no money on me because we did not use money in the kibbutz. 'If you come from the kibbutz, you get them for free, and if you proceed down this road right up to the horizon, you come to a place where you will be completely free. You will be able to do everything you want, you will not have to do the honors for the people in military clothing, and you will be able to eat all of the oranges, you feel like . . .'

"Then I told him that I have two friends in the kibbutz and that we have entered into a covenant, and I asked if I could take them also with me, for they also like oranges. I know it sounds stupid, Abraham, but let me finish this dream . . . 'Well, you cannot take them now with you, but they'll come another time, later on. You need not worry about them,' he said. 'I ran from home,' I told him, 'but if they cannot come along me, I will now turn around and go back to my friends . . .' 'Don't turn back, for there will soon come a guide that will show you the way, and he will tell you very good news . . .,' and suddenly, he was turning to another man on the road, and this one told me that the war was over. 'Who has won?' I asked the newcomer. 'You have won!' 'Have they signed a peace agreement?' 'Not yet,' he replied, "but perhaps they will sign it another day . . .' And then he began to throw many beautiful oranges in the air as he deftly caught up again with hands and feet. 'I love oranges!' he shouted. 'Because they are big, juicy, and sweet! You can drill a hole in them and suck the juice out as if they were rich women breasts!' he shouted as if he was a sergeant: 'Forward march, Corporal!' and he began to march, and I came with him, away from you . . ."

"It was a dream, Gili . . . a dream and not an omen. You've even said once that if you sink into the world of shadows, you risk turning into your own horror and shadow," Abraham said.

"You're right. I know. I just had to hear you say it again. I feel already much better now." Abraham patted him on the shoulder, and they gave each other a long hug. "I feel good now," Gili said, smiling, "but remember what you have promised me regarding Smadar."

"I heard you, and I keep my promise. Let's change the subject!" Abraham smiled, but he could feel a small stab in his heart.

"Thanks, Abraham!" said Gili softly.

THE WAR BREAKS OUT

And then the war broke out. The night before the war broke out, Abraham was removed to an artillery unit, where he was given command of a battery of four guns. He protested strongly and was promised that as soon as possible, he would be moved back to its original unit. And then hell broke loose. While he was training with his new unit, he was told to move quickly to Jerusalem. Roads were blocked by military vehicles, tanks, and armored personnel carriers headed for the same place. Night fell, and he and his force had to stay overnight in a small valley twenty kilometers outside Jerusalem. The next day at dawn, they proceeded toward the city and stopped at the city's central bus station to await new orders. Shortly after, they drove in a long column of military vehicles up the mountains encircling the city and crossed the border with Jordan and down to the first Arab city, Ramallah, where they had their first firefight, and his crew driver was injured. The rest of the war was a bad dream in which he for the first time in his life saw the bloated corpses of Jordanian soldiers on roadside, wounded soldiers on their stretchers, and plunder that both his own soldiers and soldiers from other units participated in. He wanted to stop it, but his sergeant advised against it, saying that they would not listen to them. He realized very quickly that all agreed rules for war conduct were suspended and replaced by others and harsher.

In Jericho, he tried to take five Jordanian soldiers to as prisoner, but they were mowed down by his soldiers before he could force them to surrender. He saw all this and had to accept the grim reality of death, destruction, brutality, and mad euphoria, which bewitched some of his soldiers. He saw the rapidly growing war economy and the robbers that drove their trucks stuffed with looted goodies back to Israel proper. He saw how a distant family member, along with other reservists, break into the city bank and steal millions of dinars. Others got hold of the truck and began to move all sorts of goods, automobiles, and machineries back to Israel. It was something he had never been able to imagine, but now he saw it with his own eyes.

His unit continued on to the Syrian Golan Heights, he was fed up with what he saw, but many of his soldiers were in the clutches of euphoria of the triumph. In Syria, he saw something that he also had difficulty accepting. A Syrian soldier without a gun had strayed into their ranks and had been taken prisoner, and Abraham and another soldier took him to the high commander of the column. When the officer saw the prisoner, he ordered Abraham to shoot him on the spot. Abraham refused, but his soldier was willing to carry out the order and gave the prisoner a moment to make one last prayer, and then he shot him in the neck. Abraham was furious but could not raise objections as they were at war, and he could not defy a higher-ranking officer. He went furiously back to his unit, along with the soldier, but made clear to him that in the future, he would not have anything to do with him.

Abraham met his distant relative after one battle, when his relative and his soldiers crossed his column with trucks with stolen property. Menachem stopped his convoy and came smiling up to him and his crew, along with some of his men. "Bravo," they cried. "Well done, boys. We need some warriors like you." Abraham's soldiers, who were tired and dirty, looked questioningly at him, and he had to explain that Menachem was a relative. Menachem asked on the battles Abraham's unit had been involved in and pulled him aside and asked him whether there was anything he would send to Israel, where he had an errand, and Abraham asked him to call Smadar and tell her that everything was in order. "Was that all?" asked Menachem and patted him on the shoulder.

"What have you got on the trucks?" asked Abraham.

"The less you know, the better!" said Menachem offhand.

"I know!" said Abraham.

"So close your mouth! The guys that you see here can be dangerous. Do you need some more trouble than this war?"

Abraham had just heard one of the guys from the column boasting that he had raped a woman in her home and told laughingly that she had been like a rutting goat. "Is it a threat?"

"No, a fact. They are not the best company to mingle around with!"

Menachem said. Then he pulled a pile of crumpled banknotes out of his pocket as he tried to put them into Abraham's hands, but Abraham refused. "Yes, I'm speculator, war profiteer, and I need these guys. We do not live in a fantasy kibbutz. Here, we grab what we can get our hands on . . .," he admitted, gloating about Abraham's moral. He pushed back the crumpled banknotes into Abraham's hands and said, "Stop acting like a saint. Saints do not belong in this world. Take what you can get, enjoy it, and enjoy your life," so he gave him a pat on the shoulder and went back to his column.

This meeting with his unscrupulous family member and his gang disgusted him deeply, and he was furious, but his task now was to look after himself and his soldiers, and the other issues had to wait for another time.

What the kind of world I've got into, he thought. *I thought that we had to defend our country, not to behave callous and disgusting. The ideals of the socialist revolution are too far away here, too lofty here. In peacetime, they in the kibbutz allowed ourselves to be dreamers and fantasize about a better world and better people, but the meeting with the war hit him like a shell shock. At the same time, he had a sense of helplessness. This he had to learn to deal with after the war, but how does one come to terms with the boundless greed and evil, which apparently are hiding just under the surface of civility in these people while they harbored deep and close camaraderie with one another? This mixing of the vile with very close relation may be one of life's paradoxes.* He shook his head. Abraham handed the crumpled banknotes out to his soldiers while he still felt sullied by Menachem's farewell salute: "And remember! One day, when you get tired of kibbutz monastery, I can help you with any business. I need an honest man like you. When this dirty war is finished, we will go out and eat at the best restaurant in Tel Aviv. Remember it now, Abraham!"

Abraham looked at his soldiers and felt disgusted both by them and the war, which was quite different from what he had imagined. He climbed on his car and gave the order to proceed to the next battlefield.

GILI'S DEATH

Gili was hit by a mortar shell early in the morning. He got a drop, and they carried him gently behind a sand dune, while Akram and Abraham were summoned and stood now beside him and smiled to conceal their dismay. "What has happened to me?" whispered Gili.

"There is nothing special!" Abraham said aloud. "A mortar struck down next to you, and you were slightly injured. Does it hurt?"

"No!" he replied.

"It is not serious. I will take your shirt off! Let me know if it does hurt," said Akram.

"What happened? I cannot feel my legs . . .," he whispered.

"Quiet, quiet, Gili," whispered Abraham. "Between us, we are going to fix it all. We remove the shirt."

"Let it be there!" Gili became suddenly angry.

"You were wounded in the stomach. That's why we remove your shirt, and soon, we will drive you to the hospital."

Gili closed his eyes and fell silent. So began his upper lip to quiver, and he got tears in his eyes. "Will you contact my father, Smadar, and Tova and tell them what has happened to me?" He looked beseechingly at Abraham. Abraham nodded. "Why am I so thirsty? It is as if it is burning inside me and around . . ."

Abraham looked questioningly at Akram. "Soon, you will get something to drink," said Akram. "But we should just first give you the drop. Abraham, can you wash his face a little?"

Abraham washed gently Gili's face and hair. The shootings around them ceased, and a military vehicle stopped alongside them, and Gili was lifted gently into the vehicle on a stretcher. He began to sigh and asked Akram to take off his shoes, and Akram replied that he would do it right away and leaned down over the broken leg and had to bite his lip not to cry.

"How does it feel now without boots?" asked Abraham. "You are lucky! Now you will be taken to the hospital and will be rigged, and that's the end of your war . . ."

"Take care of my boots. They are made especially for me! You know how quick I get wobbles," he whispered.

Akram and Abraham jumped into the carriage and sat beside him, and the command car began to drive. "Abraham, where does all the light come from? It's like everything lights up here . . . and I thought it was already night!" Gili whispered.

"You know the light in the desert is very strong. The sand reflects the light, and so it seems like it's all a big light party," murmured Abraham.

"I am not tired at all, although I have not slept many nights," said Gili.

"It is good," Abraham said.

"If it does not bother you, I will just close my eyes." Gili sighed.

The car reached the way, and Gili opened his eyes. "Where am I, Dad?" he asked with vibrating voice.

Abraham stroked his cheek and whispered to him, "We go home, Gili . . ."

Gili looked at him with glassy eyes and whispered, "I recognized her immediately when she came to me with the flowers. She spoke to me, and I recognized her voice. I'm fine, Mom, I said. I feel much better now. They do it well here. You can see that father is sitting there and telling me stories. I am just a little tired. You can put the telescope here and sing a song to me . . . or do you want me to play something for you?" Abraham bit his lips, and Akram looked at him with tears flowing down his cheeks. Gili's face darkened, but suddenly, he opened his eyes again. "Abraham," he asked, "is Akram here also?"

"Yes, Gili. I am here, and I am holding your hand. Do you need something?" said Akram hoarsely.

Gili breathed shallow and quick while pink bubbles began to flow out of his mouth. "Why are you looking at me that way?" he asked suddenly. Abraham looked at him. His eyes were closed. "Why don't you let mom sit next to me? She is my mom . . ."

"Now I have given her my seat. She sits next to you . . .," Abraham said.

"It is fine. Mother, Abraham and Akram are my best friends . . . and you've heard of them. Isn't that right?"

"Right!" murmured Abraham.

"Now I feel better," he whispered.

Shortly afterward, his death qualm started. There were several pink bubbles coming out of his mouth, and his breathing was short and troubled, and after a final effort, his chest sank down, and he lay still. The light over the mountains trembled and danced, and Abraham and Akram embraced each other, and Akram patted his friend on the back and said, "It is all over now!"

THE END OF THE WAR

They were many soldiers in the bus. They drove northward toward Israel proper. They were dirty and exhausted and lay wherever there was some room. Abraham and Akram were dozing in the back seat. They had planned to do a short stay at the military base, which was also the bus last station, so they could wash and change clothes, and then they would drive to the kibbutz in Akram's jeep and lay down to sleep in a clean bed. It was the only thing they wanted to do right now. Abraham's father had visited Gili's father in the hospital together with Smadar and had told Abraham that his condition had deteriorated and that he was admitted to the psychiatric department for further investigation while it went downhill with his physical state and that he had lost much weight. Abraham planned to visit him along together with Smadar when he had slept and had recovered slightly.

The bus growled, and he looked around him and saw his comrades sleeping in all impossible positions. He closed his eyes and thought about how they could go on after Gili's death and how they could have confidence in life again and how he could sum up this chapter of his life. "All right, we won a great victory . . . but we lost our best friend, and he died in front of my eyes. Maybe we were not good enough at safeguarding him . . . and maybe I'll never get to feel my heart again because right now, it's like, it's completely dead!" Abraham could not reconcile himself with the loss of his friend, the galaxy's explorer who aimed for the stars and who was their hope and Orpheus. "Yes, he was my Orpheus," thought Abraham while tears trickled from the corner of his eye. "And now we've lost him, and he is no longer on our journey through life, and I have no longer a melody to follow . . . I should not think of it right now when I am damn exhausted.

The thought of his death exhausts me furthermore, and I need to sleep away from life for a long time."

Suddenly, he heard the tune from the bus radio that they had called Gili's melody shortly before their world was shattered. He touched Akram beside him and whispered, "Listen, Akram. They play Gili's song!" And through the engine humming, the snoring soldiers, the song spread beyond their tired and dirty bodies, floated through their wounded minds, and embraced the two tired young men who now had seen and experienced life's brutal arbitrariness. It felt like a caress on their sweaty foreheads and, for just a magic moment, wiped out all the dead corpses, the dying screams, and the horror that they had experienced. In a magic moment was darkness displaced while Abraham and Akram listened with open eyes.

"Like a bridge over troubled water, I will lay me down . . .," sang Simon & Garfunkel with their silky voices as a cool breeze in the summer heat, caressing, consoling, and redeeming, and Gili was there again with them.

Abraham whispered to Akram, "It may well be that I am crazy, but I feel that our Orpheus sent us a greeting from up there. What do you think?" Akram nodded, and life seemed to be a little easier to bear.

The Accident

Abraham felt for the first time since the war happy and excited and looking forward to Smadar's visit. They had agreed that she should come so they could discuss the final details about the trip to Denmark. He had been given four months' leave from the kibbutz and was looking forward to "the free life" as he had presented it for Smadar. It was Saturday morning, and they had agreed to meet at ten o'clock by the water tower, where she could park the car. It was nine, and he lay in his bed and sang the song for himself as he had done times before to keep his memories at bay. "The morning will dawn and will burst forth, and I will keep being awake all night and wait for you. I will follow you on the road and wait for your smile in the hazy summer morning. You will show up in your purple dress, and your eyes will shine with subdued glow. You will smile to passersby, and a red rose will bloom in your hair. You will sing a song with words you'd forgotten, and you will laugh without knowing why when we will get together. We will run and drink of life's cheerfulness along the sandy beach. We will swallow the whole city. We will sing the crazy songs in the buses, and then we will sit at the entrance to your house and talk, maybe for one hundred hours, and this will go on and on, when we will be together . . ."

He had just got up from his bed when somebody knocked hard on his door, and his father and mother and a nurse came in and asked him to sit down, which he rejected. So his father said something he did not really understand but perceived as a bad dream. It was about a car that had been crushed under a truck at the entrance to the kibbutz and someone who had died on the spot. *What has this mess to do with me?* he thought irritably. He also heard someone mention Smadar's name, and he heard someone scream and saw himself from above. *Who is screaming so violently?* he thought.

137

There were lots of people coming into his small room and held him in his arms and tried to calm him down. His parents tried to talk to him, but he saw them from a long foggy distance and could not understand why they came and what they were doing in his room, all these bloody people.

He saw that the nurse took a syringe out and walked toward him. He jumped and grabbed his dagger, his shoes, and a thick stick and stormed out of the room, beside himself and so violently that he came to overthrow the few people who tried to stop him. He ran toward the hills and hid in the orchard. He took off his shirt and his shoes, put the dagger in his belt, and started walking. How long he walked, he did not know. He lost the sense of the passing time, but when he woke up, it was half dark, and he had strayed into the neighborhood of a bunch of wild dogs, growling. They started to pursue him. He looked around for a tree where he could seek refuge but did not get to safety before the dogs reached him, so he had to defend himself with his stick. He lashed out at them and hit a couple of them on the back and body and stuck the dagger in a third, who had bitten him in the leg. The rest of the pack disappeared, and he bandaged his leg with his one sock and stopped the bleeding with the other, before he went on through the hills and crossed the main road leading to the beach at Ashkelon City. He was sure that Smadar was waiting for him there.

Around midnight, he suddenly saw Akram twenty meters behind him, but he decided to ignore him because he constantly followed Smadar, who was running in front of him in the grove shadows as she looked back at him and encouraged him to follow. He looked at his dirty and tattered clothes, his injured leg, and the stick he still kept in his hand and the dagger in his belt that was completely plastered by the dog's blood. "Hello, Hello!" Smadar shouted from inside the orange trees. He tried to follow her, though he could barely control his legs and staggered through the trees and bushes as she disappeared again away into some foggy landscape, and he could still hear Akram behind him. He did not understand why he ran after Smadar in the middle of the night, far away from the kibbutz, and with Akram on his heels.

"What is he doing here? What is she doing here? What am I doing here?" he asked himself while his thoughts raged in his head, but he could not hold them out; he was still following after Smadar's voice that rang in front of him like silver bells. "Smadar, please stop!" he shouted. "I cannot run more. I cannot find you!" But she did not answer. Now and then, he caught her when she danced among the trees, but then she suddenly disappeared again when he reached the place where he had seen her. He went round and round and lost track of time and felt a heavy weariness in his mind, but he would not stop in the middle of the grove. "What are you doing here?" he shouted to Akram, who came closer. "Fuck off, Akram. I do not need you here."

Akram, who had his machine gun over his shoulder, looked long at him and said, "I have as much right to walk in the grove as you, and besides, it's best that we will go down to the beach. All people are ending finally down at the beach . . ."

For some reason, Akram's words sounded like a revelation. It was obvious. Of course, she was down by the beach. Smadar liked the sea and waited for him down there to take a swim with him when the sun rose. He might as well meet her there, but he could not find the way out of the grove. "You will not follow me!" he warned his friend. "I have already killed three wild dogs . . . There's nothing that can stop me now!"

Akram looked earnestly at him and said, "I'm not here to stop you, only to take care of you so you do not get to harm yourself."

"I do not need your help!" he screamed. "I can find her by myself!" And then he fell into a deep ditch with water in the bottom. He climbed with great difficulty again and stood at the edge, trembling with cold.

"I did not come here by myself to help you. Just a little company up to the shore," said Akram and came a few steps closer. "Arif had asked me to come and show you the way to the shore. He is my father, and he is a high-ranking officer as you know. He gave me an order!"

"Arif gave you order to keep an eye on me?" asked Abraham, wondering.

"Yes! I got an order!" said Akram. "Do you want my jacket? You are soaked up with water, and you are freezing!"

"No. I will be fine. I have to find Smadar on the beach. I need to talk to her. Why does she run all the time away from me? You can walk behind me when Arif had said so. But when I find her, you may well take back home. Is it a deal?"

Akram sighed and whispered, "Yes, it's a deal . . . but before I go, can we eat breakfast on the beach. Is it okay, Abraham?"

Abraham nodded but could feel the tears pressed in his eyes, and he squatted down and wept quietly while Akram stood still beside him. "Don't touch me!" he snarled through tears.

"I do nothing. I stand completely motionless," said Akram in soft voice.

Abraham got up and looked at his stick and his dagger. He looked around and then asked suddenly, "What am I doing here in the middle of the night?"

"You are looking for Smadar!" said Akram.

"Yes, it's true. I'm looking for her, and she is down at the beach. She comes when the sun rises. Shall we go down?" He looked at his hands and shrugged. "I cannot find my way in this forest. Where did the wood come from? Can you find your way, Akram?"

"Yes, I can find the way to the beach!" said Akram in subdued voice. "I will follow you down so you can get some sleep before it is morning, and then we will see . . ."

Abraham nodded. "I do not know what is happening around me. It's as if I do not understand what is happening . . . I did not mean it when I threatened you, just so you know, it's not meant harshly. I don't understand myself. I guess I am confused . . ." He was looking pleadingly at his friend.

"I know it, Abraham," said Akram. "May I now help you out of the woods? May I hold your hand and show you the way?"

"Yes," whispered Abraham. "I cannot even find my way here. I do not even know what it is for a grove we ended up in and why she appears and disappears again and again." He wept silently, and Akram grabbed his arm and led him gently back to the road. He followed, fumbling and stumbling. "Thanks. I do not think that I have been so tired before, and my head is driving around and around like a carrousel."

Akram covered him with his jacket and hoped that Abraham's senses would return when he had slept. He just had to be patient and wait until Abraham could see the brutal reality.

"What kind of a lake is it to the right?" asked Abraham with weak voice. "What kind of country is it we are in?"

"It's just the moonlight that causes the field to look like water, but it is a field, not a lake," said Akram.

Abraham drew anyway Akram to right as he was afraid of falling into the water, but Akram reassured him that he knew the way to the beach and that he would avoid falling into the water. "It is good," Abraham said. "It is here like an enchanted forest. I was not aware that there are such forest landscapes so close to the kibbutz. Do you think Smadar can figure it out?" he asked, looking uneasily at his friend.

"Yes!" said Akram, "I'm sure!"

"I've read so much about that people can disappear in the vast forests, and it has nearly happened to me. Without you, I would not have found my way."

"This is something which happens again and again with forests. People lose their way," said Akram. "Man must have a compass, and I have mine."

"You are always prepared for everything!" noted Abraham. "Why would your father want you to keep an eye on me?"

"He was afraid that you would end up in a forest like this. You know he has big plans for you, so he will not risk that you disappear."

Abraham thought about it for a while, and they continued toward the beach. "What are his plans?" he asked.

"He says you must be the gardener in the evolving orchard, Bustan, and therefore, he wanted me to look out after you so that when the time comes, you can deal with your task."

It's something I have heard before," murmured Abraham, "but I have never quite understood it!"

"My father says you will understand it when the time is ripe. You will also be able to understand this night better when you have slept a bit."

They walked some way in silence but then Abraham asked, "Why do you go with this machine gun? The war is over!"

"In order to protect you and me in the forest! You were bitten by the wild dogs, and who knows what kind of beasts may try to attack us here!"

"I could defend myself with the stick and dagger. I did it with three of them before the rest fled."

"It was well done, but tomorrow we will have to go to the hospital or on the kibbutz clinic so you can get a vaccination against rabies."

"We will go to the hospital!" Abraham said, determined.

"It is fine with me!" said Akram.

They approached the harbor, which was bordering on the beach, as Akram stopped by a large old tree. "What are we doing here?" Abraham asked, and he felt that his voice sounded as if it came out through a conch.

"Please lie down here under the tree. I keep watch and will wake you up when the sun is up."

"But what about Smadar?"

"I keep an eye on whether she comes over. You know my senses are very sharp . . ."

Abraham nodded and lay down, and Akram put his jacket over him and sat beside him and lit a cigarette. Abraham looked at the moon, and the moon looked at Abraham. The moon sent his silvery beams at him and stroked his face, and the stars in the distance began to move up in the nearing space. He thought they were moving like the enchanted forest. They invited him to dance, and he was lifted higher and higher, and he saw Smadar's shadow dancing between them, and he whispered to her, "Well, that's where you hide! I have been looking after you. Do you not float down to me?"

"I cannot any longer," she whispered. "I cannot come down more, Abraham."

"Why can't you?" he asked.

"You know it, Abraham. When the sun rises, you will understand it all . . ."

Abraham could feel the tears welling up in his eyes, and his heart was bursting with pain, and he began to sob, for now he knew it . . .

In the morning, he was awakened by Akram and saw a jeep with a young soldier who was parked a little farther up the road. "Good morning!" Akram said and helped Abraham to stand. "Let us eat something! My driver took a breakfast with him."

Abraham looked out over the sea, saying, "I know that I was out of my fucking mind, and you do not have to tell me that. I know she is dead. Is it right?"

"It's true," said Akram quietly.

"And you kept an eye on me because I got nuts?" Akram nodded. "It was nice of you!" murmured Abraham. Akram looked down at the sand. "And what do we do when we have eaten breakfast?" Abraham asked.

"Afterward, we will drive to the hospital, and you must have an injection against rabies."

"And what afterward?"

"She will be buried today in the afternoon. Will you come, or will you spend the day together with my father?"

"Will you be there for the funeral on my behalf? I cannot do it now!"

"Fine! I drive you to my father. There, you can stay as long as you need and wish."

"Thanks!" Abraham said and put his hand on his friend's shoulder. Akram turned and embraced him, and they stood for a long time with tears streaming down their cheeks.

LAST TALK WITH ARIF

Arif came to the kibbutz in the afternoon and as so often without notice. He kissed Abraham on the forehead and suggested they went for a little walk. "What is happening with you, Avri?" he asked as they walked on the dusty road, past the green iron gate toward the cemetery.

"Nothing new! What about you?"

"I go on a pension from next year," said Arif gloomily.

"Is it of your own free will? Have you not been there since 1948, when the war started?"

"If we take into account my contribution to Israel before the war, so I've been in service more than thirty years, and I am nearing sixty years old, and I am one of the oldest officers. I've been waiting for my last promotion for almost ten years, and now I have got it, and I look forward to also tell your father the good news."

"Great! Congratulations, Arif!"

"They dragged me around for too long, but now I've got it!"

"When we are back at my parents' house, we must celebrate it!"

"No! There is nothing to celebrate. They discriminated against me for too long because of my origin, but now they could no longer get around it. It is the only thing there is to celebrate. But I came today to talk with you about you, Avri, not about me."

"About me? What should we talk about? Have we not talked enough about me?"

"I have a good story to tell. You have nothing against a good story, right?"

"I've got used to your stories and know that they always lead to self-examination, but just come up with it!" Abraham smiled, strained.

"It is a good story about the creation of the world, which I have heard from an old Persian Jew," said Arif.

"And it has a moral?" Abraham laughed.

"There is a moral, if you bother to look for it!"

"The question is, whether it makes sense to search for moral in this world!" murmured Abraham bitterly.

"If you are looking for a moral, you may find it!" Arif said. Abraham nodded affirmatively. "When God created the world, he created three types of people. He created one type, who worked hard, earned his bread in his face's sweat, and followed all the rules. He always went on the same track and was disciplined enough to never come out of its fixed route. This kind of people followed instructions as camels in a caravan, and therefore, man called them *camel people*. The second type which the almighty created were those who could rise above everyday banalities and hover over life pettiness and generate therefore higher perspectives of life. They see the world from a bird's view, and therefore, they are called *bird people*. The third type was strong, enduring, and quickly running people with small wings, who could not lift themselves up because they were too heavy. When they feel danger or face a challenge, they run away as fast as they can or stick their heads in the sand. Those God called *ostrich people*," ended Arif and looked at Abraham.

"Very fine story!" retorted Abraham, clicking with his tongue. "And what then?"

"What type are you? You must soon decide!" noted Arif dryly.

Abraham was silent for a moment and then said with a timid voice, "I do not know who I am now. I do not know myself anymore. I only know that my life is fucked up, and how long it will keep being like this, I do not know. Basta!"

"But if you could choose to be one type, which one would you choose?" insisted Arif.

"In old days, I would prefer to be alternately a bird and a camel, or both, with both their strengths so that I could adapt myself and switch strategy, as you taught me, in line with changing contexts. Now I have come far away from these considerations."

Arif looked at him with an expressionless face and said, "So you have chosen, Avri!"

"I have not the strength to all that. Leave me in peace!"

"Your strength and your courage will come back! I'm sure, and you are already on your way . . ."

"What kind of way I am on? What is this nonsense? I'm half crazy. I'm looking at the clouds, and they speak to me and make a sign from her and him. I try not to talk to them, but sometimes I forget about it and wave to them . . .," sobbed Abraham.

Arif gave him a hug and whispered, "I know that you have not lost your senses. It's a temporary pain, and it will subside."

"How can you say this?" Abraham said and slapped on his chest.

"In this chest, there is only pain and emptiness. Nothing else!"

"You feel self-pity. But the dead do not come back, and you'll have to say goodbye to them and move on. You must slowly move them away as the stone I hold here, further and further away from your focus so you get your vision back! They're going to approve of it because you allow yourself to rediscover the meaning of your life, and you will not forget them either. Neither Gili nor Smadar want to hold you back from pursuing your destiny. Do you understand that?" Abraham nodded, his face buried in his hands. "It is enough now with your self-pity, Avri. It is not your destiny to cry over something that we have no influence over," said Arif, comforting.

"How do you stop the pain? It decides over me," he wept.

"Well, you decide where to place your pain, slowly remove it away from your heart, and then it will start to subside. When you start to believe that you can find love again, which will replace your love to them, and you will use it as a foundation to pursue your destiny . . . then you will be cured of your sorrow."

"And if it's never going to happen?"

"It is going to happen, Avri. I can see it coming, but if you are in doubt, let us conclude a bet." Arif smiled.

"It is nice of you to encourage me, but you say it not because you believe that I can make it . . .," Abraham said.

"No, no, and no! It's going to happen! I'll give you just a little push!" said Arif.

"Thanks. I'll try to believe in it!"

"You will slowly, almost without realizing it, find a small path which will lead you to a path that will lead you to a big road. I can see it for myself. The road will come to you . . ."

"A road that comes to one?" Abraham said doubtfully.

"Yes, if you help it actively . . . so your road will come to you!" stated Arif.

"How do you know all this?" asked Abraham, looking with warmth on his old mentor.

"In Persia, there lived a time a man named Rumi, who said, 'I was first created as a stone, and it took some time before I turned myself into a plant and then went there again immensely long time before I turned myself into an animal, and then millions of years passed by before I turned myself into the person I am today. What can prevent me from turning myself one day into an angel?' Rumi knew that our ultimate destination is to transform, further evolve, and improve ourselves incessantly. It is your destiny to pursue this option, creating an evolving Bustan. It is your secret, and it is also the essence of the Barakh that you was granted as a child. Do you understand that now?"

TOMORROW

The night sky was dressed in glittering stars, and a majestic moon threw its lemon yellow light on the sleeping kibbutz and the fields, and even a dog's stubborn barking in the otherwise quiet night could not break the magic. *It's a good night for a good farewell,* thought Abraham. He did not sleep all night as he wished to follow it all the way until it was challenged by the fledgling morning that would continue into an explosion of sunlight that would chase the night and its demons on the run, a symbol of an emerging new era that would hopefully dominate his life from now on. He had already packed his few things in an old suitcase, which he had borrowed from his parents, and now he brewed a cup of strong Arabic coffee. He sat in his chair and looked out the window onto the world he had grown up in and which was now shrouded in the night's magic as both were so familiar yet already strange as if he saw it through kaleidoscopic glasses. He took a deep breath and could feel that he was able to put his life sorrows behind him, even those who were still sighing inside him. He could turn his back on all of them.

The radio broadcast sounded as he came all the way from distant worlds that he looked forward to exploring. It sounded like the sounds of a conch shell, where time flows forever. When he closed his eyes, he heard a chorus of voices that wished him bon voyage. It startled him when he saw a beautiful woman with big blue eyes came floating out of the conch shell. She had a red dress on and looked attentively at him, and then she said something he could not quite hear because it sounded as the voice came rolling from somewhere far away, but he understood what she tried to say to him. "Yes, Smadar!" he said. "I now take on the journey that you and I had planned, and I hope that you approve of it." She looked at him with a sad expression, and he looked back at her and felt that he could accommodate her and their sorrow. "I have learned how to accommodate sorrow," he said. "I have stopped to escape from it, I sing it a lullaby when it is unbearable, and it falls asleep like a baby." She sang something that sounded as if it flowed through the conch shell and slowly began to dissolve and disappeared altogether. He took a sip of coffee and thought, *I now walk on the new way.*

He switched off the radio, opened the window, and looked intently at the skyline until he spotted among millions of tiny glittering stars a little one to the right of Carl's wagon, and this was Gili. Gili winked and smiled at Abraham, who returned the smile and raised his hand in greeting, and then Gili glided slowly down toward the horizon and singing until they faced each other, united in the same song, for this was the way stars-people and people who loved them meet.

"So the day has come!" the star said.

"Yes, I never thought it would come . . ."

"Are you still afraid?" asked Gili.

"A little bit, but when I know you're up there, I can cope with the fear . . . I believe so anyway." Abraham smiled. The star laughed, and it sounded like thousand small silver bells that ring harmoniously.

"I hope that I am not the only support you get along the way . . .," it said.

"No, you're not the only one, but you are always beside me! Tell me, Gili, how is it to be up there?"

"It is all right. One gets used to being a star. What about you and your sorrow?"

"I was silent for a long time. I could not find words . . . You watched me all the way, didn't you?" asked Abraham softly.

"Yes, I saw it all . . ."

"Also with Smadar and your father?"

"Up here, close to eternity, we look different on mortal life." The star grinned.

"And what about my evolving Bustan? Can you see it, or is it just a mirage and castles in the air?"

"I can see it clearly!" said the star.

"Are we to say goodbye now forever, Gili? Can I talk to you living in other countries?"

"Do you remember our blood ties? I will always be with you whenever you will need me . . .," sounded Gili's voice, echoing through the twinkling firmament.

"In that case, I feel much better now," Abraham said, waving goodbye. The star began to sing while it rose as it was the way the stars-people say goodbye to their beloved people.

Darkness was beginning to retreat, and the morning mist appeared. Abraham went out of the house and through the kibbutz, where he had grown up and where all the people he had known always lay now in their beds and slept. He had to leave them, and he did not know whether it would be for a short period or forever, but he felt clear-minded. He turned off the light in his room, locked the door, and went with his suitcase toward the shattered water tower, where the car stood, and put his suitcase into the car. The darkness was disappearing, and the mountains to the east spread an orange stain out into a sea of light that pierced the shadows. It embraced him like a soft, warm waterfall and sent a beam of light over the car. He stood bathed in light, half blinded, and then it happened suddenly.

Suddenly, the sun opened his childhood tunnel for him, and he was in it, and its light swept all the evil and sorrow and pain away. Abraham stood in the light and noticed how a smile grew inside him, like a flower that folds its petals out. *I smile, I smile inside me*, he thought, laughing. *I smile again, I smile again inside me* . . . "Light, light!" he called the vibrating, redeeming light. "Here I am!" said the light. "Is this the way to the evolving Bustan, or do I dream jus now?"

"The way is inside me . . . with some pain and sorrow, which you will be able to bear," answered the light, "and you are heading toward the Bustan." And Abraham could feel how he was filled with gratitude.

"So who has chosen that I should follow this path?" he asked.

"This choice came from within you, and you will breathe life into it, if that's what you want and if you are faithful to it. The choice can die if you forget it, and then it disappears into nothingness! Are you still ready to pursue your choice?" asked the light.

"Yes! Yes!" resonated Abraham's voice inside his head.

He drove to his parents' house, where the light was turned on. His parents and his little brother were sitting around the dining table and drank tea but stood when he came in. He looked at his parents, and suddenly, it dawned on him how shriveled and helpless they looked. He hugged his mother long. She cried a little, and he patted her on the back. Then he gave his father a long hug. His father kept him close to him and pressed his stubble on his cheeks. "Drive carefully, Abraham!" whispered his father. His father turned to his brother. "Keep an eye on him!" he said.

The two brothers walked toward the car, and before getting into it, Abraham turned around for one last time. His parents stood at the entrance to their apartment, and he thought that they looked very lonely and sad, but a voice in him whispered, "Remember Lot's wife. Do not turn around. Today you start pursuing your destiny."

"I drive!" Abraham said to his younger brother.

"It is fine . . . But beware that you will not be blinded. The light is already very strong and blinding," said his brother.

"Between us, we will run into it!" Abraham grinned.

When he started the car, he saw him suddenly as if he grew out of the overwhelming sea of light, which they found themselves within. Abraham stopped breathing and stared at the Green Man in the shiny green robe whom he had known since childhood, but he never quite had believed in his existence. The man raised his hand in a farewell gesture and smiled kindly to him. He stood there for a moment like a motionless sculpture engulfed in a strong dancing green light.

"What is it? Who is he?" asked his brother, overwhelmed.

"You don't know him!" replied Abraham and began to drive.

And a new morning was born when the light broke out and engulfed the Green Man, leaving only a faint green glow on the morning sky.

PART III

Maturity and Old Age – the days of blowing life into the evolving Bustan

Free thinking + available information + experience-based knowledge + mental capacity and emotional balance = wisdom + far sight.

—BK

CHAPTER 1

It is winter 2045, and the hot, dry wind is blowing outside, darkening the daylight with its multitude of small grains of sand from the Arabian Desert. The heat outside is unbearable, so I sit inside, in this chilly room conditioned by our local fusion energy reactor, watching my hands, these wrinkled hands that have served me for 100 years. I cannot believe it, but then again, there are so many other events in my life that I cannot really believe either. Like the way my life's story began. Would you believe it if you did not know who I am and what I have done? Would you believe that your own stories are streams and brooks coming out of my story, which started in an Arabic Bustan (orchard) in old Palestine for almost 100 years ago? I know it sounds absurd, but there it truly all began. I was chosen to choose when I was sitting in a berry tree one summer day in an Arabic Bustan at the age of four.

The Green Man passed by, addressed me, and asked me to sing a song and utter a wish. I said, "I wish to tend a Bustan like this." He explained to me thoroughly what it meant to be a gardener of such a Bustan. He explained to me that in a blooming Bustan, there were many different trees, and one had to water them in a hot climate like ours. He asked me whether the trees needed anything else. I shouted proudly that they needed chicken manure since I had seen my father spreading chicken manure in a ditch under our trees around the house. He asked me whether there was more one could do. I shrugged because I did not know. "Well," he said, "there must be a reasonable distance between the trees. Otherwise, they will not get enough nourishment and sunlight and will wither. If you plant them very close, only the strongest will survive, and their fruits will be tasteless. Can you imagine anything else?"

I did not know what to answer. He told me that in a Bustan, the gardener has to uproot the weeds all the time. Otherwise, they would strangle the trees. "A good gardener will do this weeding all the time if he wants a healthy and prosperous Bustan."

And lastly, he said something that almost made me weep: that trees get old and sick like us humans. A gardener has to care for them and heal them if possible. But when there is no hope, he has to uproot them and plant new ones instead.

"Do they have to be uprooted?" I pleaded.

"Yes," he said.

He explained to me that this is important to keep a Bustan healthy and ever-evolving. And I agreed to the conditions presented to me by the Green Man for becoming a Bustan gardener. I was only close to four, but he took my words as a pact between him and me. And so I was blessed. I got his blessing to go ahead and create such a Bustan. Later on, he found some other, more or less plausible, reasons for choosing me, but for me, it did not matter any longer. I was chosen, coerced, and seduced, but I decided to follow the mission, and I did just that.

Sometimes groups of students on a "back to the core" course come and stop by the ranch and come to see me, the fossilized, unlikely hero of their civilization. I wonder how they look at me, the man who set out to change human civilization but almost always reluctantly, always doubtful. Do they view me as a pathetic old man, a strange piece of antiquity rather than one of their own? Or do they see me as the great founder of their civilization and of the new brave world? I really do not know. At times, a child in my class asks me why I seem so full of sorrow. I could tell them. Yet I always stall. And I stutter. I don't want to get into my personal loss. My old man's voice starts quivering even more than usual. I never could hide the fact that I am made of the same flesh and blood and virtues and frailties, which have made the *Homo sapiens* into what he is. For many years, I too was subjected to unbending lusts like sexual desire, but I fought all these excesses throughout my grown-up life and sublimated their energies for the sake of a great cause. There were only few ones who almost succeeded in toppling my capacity for sublimation and derailing my quest to transcend *Homo sapiens.*

One day in my office, a dramatic battle had been going on in my mind and had reached its peak. It was a day I was plagued with a strong feeling of unease in my mind—a bright March day 2008. For the first time in my life, I felt the pain of giving up on my species, *Homo sapiens*. I remember this premonition infiltrating my mind as if I had crossed an unseen boundary as if "the dice had been thrown!" I felt nauseated and terrified on this spring day, realizing that I was crossing a line that might end up in despair from now on. It became apparent to me that my own species might not be wise enough to solve its intractable, self-created problems. I felt as though I were Judah, although the comparison was utterly absurd at the time as I had betrayed that which is most sacred for humans: the faith that we can prevail in the face of mortal dangers. I came to betray the ones I loved, not believing in them any longer. Not because I wished to be Judah but because I knew that they did not know what they were doing.

All of a sudden, a young woman appeared in the clinic in the afternoon and asked to talk to me. Without making an appointment, she just walked in and wished to see me. She was seated in the waiting room, this dazzling beauty, as I followed another client out. She stood and greeted me on my way as I turned and intended to go into my office. I turned toward her and greeted her in return, and she asked for my name and presented herself. She was a beautiful young woman, and I admit that in our first session, I had lost some of my cognitive sharpness. But I regained it slowly. So what did I find out about her? My first impression of her was of a young, attractive woman of Jewish or Spanish origin with a vivid personality: charming and unaffected, with lots of warmth, and an eager appetite for pleasure. She enjoyed the quotidian details of her life and described them with relish: the motley household in which she lived, the psychology lessons she took, the walks she took through the shopping heaven of the city. On one level then, she was a dazzling, beautiful young woman of her time: emancipated, educated, and urbane, with professional ambitions and a penchant for a bohemian lifestyle. She had a variety of lovers, she admitted, as well as some intimates and a circle of interesting friends. She was a percipient observer, aware of the issues and movements of her time: postmodernism, self-realization, feminism, ecology, etc. Her passing remarks about such things showed penetrating and distilled insight.

But capable though she was of extroversion and engagement, her most intense interest was focused on understanding the complexities, blessings, and curses of human folly. Her essential existence, she reminded me before exposing her true nature, took place in reflecting upon this most denied virtue. She had a rather strange name, Moria, which she claimed was rather common there, where she had grown up. She revealed herself in her diary, which she wanted me to glimpse at, she was impassioned, erotically volatile, restless, and often tormented. In the early entries, she repeatedly recorded swings from elation to brooding melancholy, from embracing excitement to depressed withdrawal, and from expansive flights of fantasy to besetting self-doubt. She could easily be seen as one of the scores of oversensitive, slightly neurotic young women. Moria herself thought in psychological terms. But they were also insufficient, for Moria had the kind of genius for introspection that converted symptoms into significance and joined self-examination to philosophical investigation. Her self-exploration in the sessions was a continuous, animated dialogue with herself, a constant drive toward her own truth. She knew how to follow subtle movements of her feelings and how to question and criticize herself. Even in states of extreme distress, she retained an unerring sense of emotional proportion, a kind of perfect inner pitch. She recognized her own tendencies to false exaltation and self-denigration, her attraction to grandiose ideas, and her possessive greed; she upbraided herself for them and countered them with insistence on moderation.

"My protracted headaches, so much masochism; my abundant compassion, so much self-gratification," she wrote in her diary.

Moria knew she had to master her own excesses and conflicts and to "give some form to the chaos" inside her. She chose me as her guide and treated me, in the beginning, as if I were a guru. She knew very well that I read Erasmus from Rotterdam's classical book *In Praise of Folly*. She knew, too, that I knew what the name Moria meant, so she said, "You understand, please don't ask dumb questions regarding my name, especially when I told you how common it is!"

She was obviously flirting with me and quite openly tried to seduce me. By today's standards, we were not supposed to engage in such a manner with our clients, but I was closer to "crossing this river" than ever before. From the very beginning, I could sense something unusual about Moria. But what was it? Was it the queer name? Why would parents give a child such a name referring to foolishness? I sensed that she hid more behind the feminine, assertive, talkative, beautiful, neurotic young woman. This feeling of unspecified alarm was increased by one of her first remarks. She said that one thing that had attracted her attention to me was my paraphrase in my blog of the expression of Saadi: "Poor greedy one!

Whenever he runs, he is after food, and death is after him. I wrote, "Poor greedy ones. Whenever they run after their whims, folly kicks them from behind into the clutches of oblivion." Moria said that upon reading it, she felt an intimacy with me, and I shuddered because this reminded me of one special client a long time before.

It happened at the beginning of my professional career, when I had some consultations with a very peculiar man. He just popped into my clinic one day and asked for me. He was an Israeli of Arabic origin, in the middle of his forties, well educated, charming, and wise but somehow elusive. He had heard of me and explained that he had chosen me because of the similarity in our backgrounds. He gave me his name but no address or phone number. He would call me if he needed contact with me in addition to the fixed appointments, he said.

In those days, when going to a psychologist was not yet popular, some people behaved with much secrecy. So I accepted this condition. He suffered from diffuse anxiety, which hampered him in some spiritual activities, he explained. I remembered him because he had said very special things that kept popping up in my mind. Talking about his anxiety, he had said to me, "Horibilis mors pertrubat!"

"What did you say?" I said. "I do not understand Latin." He said that it meant "terrible death preoccupies him." "Are you sick?" I asked.

"Not so far as I know!"

"So who are you afraid for?" I inquired. He ignored my question.

"Do you agree with what I say now?" he just went on. "If not the perfection of the human soul, then greed until death becomes man's ultimate goal." I was astounded. He really took me by surprise. He looked at me imploringly and repeated, "Do you agree?"

After some frantic thoughts, I said cautiously, "If not the perfection of the human mind and soul, then folly to death will become our goal . . ."

Then he muttered, "The oven is hot—bake the bread!"

He was a bit crazy in his own way, and I will probably never know whether he told me a true story or an allegory that he was traveling and had stopped in this particular country to study how people thrive when they have the best welfare system in the world. What moved my heart listening to this story was the memory of my own Bustan and his candid manner and great humbleness. We talked some more, but now he had changed track. "Have you got a mission in the world?" I asked him.

"Have you got a mission, or are you just a passerby?" he asked me, smiling.

This way of turning my questions on me irritated me, but I decided to pursue this course for a short time. "I help people," I replied.

"You mend people, right," he commented, "but opportunity is precious, and time is a sword, yet you do not have a mission."

He cancelled the next appointment and did not call again. He just disappeared as he had appeared in the clinic, without leaving a trace. I do not know what he gained from our talks, but his question has followed me ever since. "Have you got a mission in life?" There must be some quivering "yes" somewhere inside me, for why else would I be invaded by this terrifying premonition on the fate of man? My occasional experiences of these unusual encounters with some extraordinary people make my mind whirl, but they are also moments of awe and grace.

CHAPTER 2

It was December 22, 2008. Just a few days before Christmas, Moria came to talk with me once more because, as she explained, it would be almost another fourteen days before we talked again due to the holidays. She was lovely, dressed up, and came with a little present for me, which she wanted me to open under the Christmas tree. I said to her that it was not customary to give or receive presents from my clients, and she nodded and said that she understood, but too much rigidity could end up in stupidity, so she pleaded with me to accept hers. "One of Moria's 'small piercing needles,'" I muttered. "What was this for? You know the rules!" She sat and looked at me for some time, saying nothing. "What do you want to talk about?" I asked after a while.

"About a deal!"

"A new deal? We have already made one concerning your dissertation. Is it not enough?"

"I wish to expand this deal!"

"What do you mean? And may I say from the start that I am not interested in more deals with you?"

"You may. Maybe I have a proposition which you cannot refuse."

I shuddered. "So what is your proposition?" I said, a bit tense, a bit amused.

"Well! You can write an updated version of *In Praise of Folly*, and I can help you with it—"

"Stop! I am not interested. There is no reason to continue." I became irritated by her overt attempt to mobilize me to her projects.

159

"I did not finish my proposition, Abraham. You are being paid to listen!"

"Fine! Go ahead."

"I can help you in updating it, and I know that you look for something. I can help you to detect it."

"Do I look for something? What is this something which I do not know of?"

"You know it but are afraid of it. You had for quite some time a notion of some calling, but you could not define its substance and meaning! I can help you."

"How can you help me? You know very little about me."

"I know much about you, Abraham, maybe more than you know."

It was an incredulous assertion. "This discussion, Moria, is too bizarre for me. I stop here."

"Listen to me! There is too much at stake for both you and me to stop this now. Listen to what I have just said and give yourself time to think it over. All right? We have taken the highway to extinction, and our present leaders lead us, blindfolded, in this direction."

"What are you talking about now?" I was startled by her abrupt change of focus.

"I am talking about our common future or the end of such a future. Earth doesn't really care whether we live or become extinct. It just gets grumpy and simply wipes out species that threaten its survival, including humans, as we get too threatening. And we are causing the sixth mass extinction in a flash of geologic time. And you can see in this critical time human folly in its splendor as nobody else, and it must be recorded and pointed out."

"What for?" I sighed.

"What for! Do you not wish to ring the bells to warn the dummies! I assumed that this was the kernel of your calling!" She looked at me indignantly and continued. "Respected scientists warn of imminent energy shortages as geologic fuel supplies run out. Wall Street executives dismiss their predictions as myths and call for more drilling. Environmentalists describe the destruction to the earth from burning coal, oil, and natural gas. Economists ignore them and describe the danger to the earth of failing to burn coal, oil, and natural gas. Geology researchers report fresh findings about what the earth was like millions of years ago. So their warnings just cancel out one another, and you know where it all leads to this time, don't you? Yes, it leads to the finite story of their folly! Maybe our last chance to prevent the endgame of our species is to write this book on folly and supplement it with huge ringing bells," she said, looking pleadingly at me.

CHAPTER 3

As we proceeded with our sessions, my heart longed for her, regardless of what she told me about her life. It was a terrible thing to be dominated by such a seductive young woman. It was almost torture and yet infinite delight. Her look, her smile, her hair fluttering in the wind coming through the window, the little lines of her face, the slightest movements of her features all delighted me, upset me, and entranced me. She had captured me by her gestures, her mannerisms, and even by her clothes, which seemed to take on a peculiar charm as soon as she wore them. Her dress seemed to me inimitable. I became bewitched, and I wished to regain my self-control, and there was only one way, after she had achieved full recovery.

"Why should we terminate the sessions or change our rhythm?" she asked me in a harsh voice. "Do you view this as an elegant way of getting rid of me because you are in love with me, and it irritates you?" I said nothing, just watched her. "You know, Abraham, I am dead tired of this game. Let me put it this way: there is not going to be any termination of the contact unless you accept the deal."

"In this case, I am forced to tell you that I finish this contact whether you wish it or not," I said angrily.

She looked at me with cold eyes. I thought that in a moment or two, she would get out of her chair, curse me, and leave the room, never to come again. I was prepared for it. The past had taught me to deal with these uncomfortable situations. "Are you screwed up, man?" she asked me angrily. "Do you wish me to force you the make the deal?"

"Can you force me?" I said coldly.

"So you want me to do it, stubborn creature?" she hissed.

"All right! I will do this, although I had planned to wait for the confession."

"What confession, Moria? Did you keep something essential about your life out of our talks?"

"Sure I did!" She smiled. "To say it shortly, I am not what you think I am. I am not the Moria who you thought you talked to, sir. I deceived you all the way through."

What was going on? My mind was fleeing. Through the clinic windows, I could see the street crowded with people. They could feel the gentle breeze that wafted over the city on a warm springtime evening. It made me feel like going out somewhere, I did not care where, under the trees, and made me dream of moonlit lakes. I heaved a deep sigh and said, "Ah! I am growing old. It's sad. Formerly, on evenings like this, I felt full of life. Now I only feel that I am getting behind the pace of things. I feel bad about it."

With a glow in her eyes, she answered, "Well, my boy, this is how humans grow old, more often than not without noticing it in the least."

"I have always been merry, healthy, vigorous, and all the rest. I do not bother about age, but I understand you, all right. As one sees oneself in the mirror every day, one does not realize the work of age because it modifies the countenance so gently that the changes are unnoticeable. It is for this reason alone that people do not die of sorrow. This is under my command as well." With this sentence, she brought me back to my unfolding nightmare. She had gone completely nuts. "What is under your command, Moria?" I gasped.

"I control the merciful denial process of growing age, of course. What else? Now, Abraham, pull yourself together and listen to what may be the shock of your life." She watched me for some time and then continued. "It is time to tell you that I am not any neurotic par excellence Moria. I put on a show for you. I am not a simple Moria. I am another being." And then looking at me, giggling, she added, "You were deceived all the way through, old buddy."

It took me some time to regain my composure. She was telling me the truth. There was something in her appearance that was congruent in the most authentic way, and it scared me. "So who are you?" I gasped.

"I am the real Moria!" she emphasized, looking at me as I sat dumbstruck.

"Moria. Yes, Moria!" I was dumbfounded by her confession.

"Moria is my name. It is not used in the world for children." She cracked up laughing. "I am the only one who bears it, as far as I know."

"Say, why did your parents choose for you such a difficult name to bear?"

"They did not. Stop playing a fool, Abraham. You know exactly who I am!"

"Stop playing insane yourself!" I shouted. "Do you wish me to believe that you are some kind of apparition? You went too deep into your fantasy, and you cannot discern reality from fantasy. I am not . . ."

"Stop panicking, Abraham! I am Moria, and I can materialize whenever I wish to. I am the most cherished goddess of mankind and the best-wired goddess in their silly brains. I am the grand maestro of human cacophony, of the 'quacking frogs in the pond,' who are deceived to believe that they can avoid their oblivion . . . I form and maintain their frame of mind, their self-interest, the short-term gain, the long-term pain, the short-term resurrection, the long-term self-destruction, the confounding of wisdom by illusions and delusions, and the replacing of the aspiration for megalopsychia with megalomania and monomania. You name it. Do you get it now?"

"Stop this!" I said to her angrily. "I am not going to listen."

"Erasmus, who wrote my first biography, was a very gifted and knowledgeable fool," she said, looking at me with green catlike eyes. "He really tried to make fun of me by praising me. But he turned out to be both the fool and my obsessed admirer in this game. He was almost forgotten, and I have become more glorious, grandiose, and grand than ever before. I am more popular than ever, especially in your new era. But this is not the matter which preoccupies me mostly. It is just these old memories which overwhelm me once in a while," she whispered while tears welled up in her green eyes.

I shuddered. She was raving mad. "I do not get your point, Moria. Can you talk so I can follow you?"

"I try, but these memories well up . . ." She sighed.

For some ten minutes, I was in a state best described as mixture of rejection, confusion, and disbelief, but then she proved it to me, in front of my eyes, by what I would consider to be semi-miracle or impossible demonstrations. What had really happened, or what I conceived had happened, was impossible to discern. I remember retreating toward the window that became, all of a sudden, moon-flooded. I watched as Moria made the light of the desk lamp go out. A wave of icy feeling washed over me as she hissed. She pushed her head that now shone with yellow cat eyes toward me, stretching out her arm as far as she could, and she began to pluck at my shirt with her fingernails. Her arm started to stretch as if it were made of rubber. Finally, her fingers caught my throat and turned me around as if it were the easiest thing to do. I pressed myself to the wall and tried to remove her hands from my throat but could not. My last hour, I felt, had come. The window swung wide open, and the freshness of the night and the scent of lime blossoms flooded the room. At that moment, the bells of some church rang out behind our building. Where did the ringing come from in this peculiar hour? I thought in frenzy while Moria stopped pressuring my throat with her rubber steel fingers. Wild fury distorted her face as she swore hoarsely, and I collapsed to the floor. The clocks rang again, Moria gnashed her teeth, and her hair stood on end. When the bell ringing ceased for a moment, I regained my strength and senses and stumbled to my feet. I went toward the moonlighted window, heaving for air.

"Would you now accept the deal?" Moria asked me with her sweet voice, her eyes changing colors all the time and her face changing expressions as if it were made of rubber. I bent my head down, and a kind of a snort came out of my throat.

"I give in. I bend to your will."

She rose out of her chair, caressed my shoulder and back, gave me a kiss on my forehead, and said, "I knew you would concede!"

Just as the heart-stopping sound of bells was heard again from the street and from all over the city, I turned around to confide in Moria on this bizarre experience, but she was traceless gone from the office.

CHAPTER 4

Moria decided to tell me parts of my life story as she put it so I could reflect over it. Without almost noticing it, our roles had been reversed. It seemed that I was trying to find some red thread in my life, but why?

"And now I will tell the touching story of three adolescents. Ready?" Moria proceeded.

"Just shoot!" I said.

"There was this covenant you and your friends had committed yourselves to when you were children," she started saying.

"Yes, I remember."

"Akram was your friend," said Moria contemplatively. "He was a boy from a nomad clan in the Negev desert. You grew up together on the kibbutz because his father, Arif, the renowned pathfinder in the Arabian and Negev deserts, wanted him to absorb the spirit of what he called the Jewish Age of Efficiency. Arif wanted his son to help his fellow nomads to manage their transition to modernity. He wanted Akram to unite the force of the desert, which bears the winds of eternity, with the cleverness of the Jews and the Barakh he felt you had been endowed with. Gili was your second friend. He was a city boy—"

"Just wait a moment. What kind of Barakh had old Arif talked about?" I interrupted Moria.

"So we have to go back to the Bustan story," said Moria impatiently. "Arif, the son of Naim, believed his old father when he told him that the Khider, some celestial prophet from the Sufi tradition, had blessed you on a certain day . . . but neither you nor your father believed it."

"Fine, but what about Gili?" I asked.

"If Akram was your pathfinder, Gili was your star pathfinder, an astronomer. He knew a great deal about the stars, galaxies, future space travels, black holes, and galactic springs."

"His father was a remarkable scientist in Israel."

"Akram was a pathfinder on the ground. Gili was the pathfinder in the skies. And you? What was your contribution?"

"Well, I considered myself to be the glue who made the three of us stick together. We were very different."

"And what was this role like?"

"Well, they joked about my being their chief ideologue, the one who had written down what you called the covenant, the one who could see into the mists of the future. They had to come up with something because there was nothing special about me."

"And what did you do then?"

"Like children, we made the oath by pricking our fingers with a knife and mixing our blood together. This was basically a covenant like the 'All for one, one for all!'"

"Did you all observe this rule?" she asked.

"Why do you torment me with these memories? Why do you wish to drag it out of my mouth?"

"You seem to be very emotional about it forty years later."

"When we grow older, we realize how much they meant and how much we have lost." She watched me closely. "One day Akram suggested a journey to the desert."

"That's right! He took a gun from somebody in his village, and we went on this tour up the mountains of Judea."

"And you three spent two nights camping up in the mountains, heating up your conserves on a little fire in a hidden cave, and rationing your drinking water in a military fashion."

"We shamelessly spread the word that we would spend the weekend in Akram's village."

"In your sleeping bags at night—Akram with his loaded gun—Gili told you stories about future space travels. Akram teased him, asking him who he had been in love with before he fell in love with the stars. And you kicked Akram gently, knowing that Gili, who had lost his mother to cancer at the age of seven, started to be preoccupied by the stars at about the same time."

"Yes, I remember." The memories began welling up.

"On the way down from the mountains, Akram asked you, 'But why? What had his mother to do with the stars?' You explained that longings are longings, and what you missed you might get back by being preoccupied or obsessed by something different in form or essence. Not a stupid reply for a young boy like you, Abraham."

"I do not remember this reply!"

"But Akram did remember." I became thoughtful and silent, and Moria again watched me closely. Then she continued. "Waking up in the early morning, you started descending from the mountains. Passing through an endless wheat field, Gili was anxious. You and Akram thought it was a great thing to do, to move in this golden green sea of gently dancing wheat. You sang out loud while Gili watched the path you made in the wheat field in silence. When you came out of the field, something happened. Do you remember?"

I nodded. "Even Akram was taken by surprise. Although he could see and hear better than all of us, he could not understand from where a strange-looking bearded man in a shining green cloak appeared just in front of us. He raised his hand in blessing, and his palm disappeared in the golden glow of the sunlight as it was the source of light, and his cloak shimmered and gleamed."

"He asked you where you had come from and who you were, leaning on his fine curved stick made of ivory."

"Yes. I had the vague feeling of having seen him once before, but I was not certain. He talked in a different dialect. He asked Akram where he came from and who his father was without commenting about Akram's possessing a gun. And then he greeted me in such a gracious manner that again I felt as if he knew me. He tried to talk with Gili, but Gili answered him shortly. He wanted to bless us, but Gili would not be blessed since he did not believe in such things. So the man put his hands on Akram's head and my head at the same time, whispering the blessings to himself. 'What did you say?' Akram asked him. 'Oh, you will find out one day.' He smiled. 'Ask your father, and he will tell you, Akram! And as for you, Abraham, you will have to find it by yourself!' And then he departed, disappearing in the long, glowing rays of the morning sun. I thought to myself again where had I seen him before. I could not remember . . . I thought about this quite a lot after the war."

"You mean, after Gili got killed."

I was taken aback. "Yes! I have thought about whether Gili would have been among us today if he had been blessed on that day. How come Akram and I have survived to this ripe old age? I became a bit odd after losing two dear friends of mine, Gili and a girl whom I loved."

"Yes, Smadar, who was killed by a car."

"I wish some parts of my life could have been obscured from you, Moria."

"Am I not supposed to tell you your unauthorized life story?"

"Yes! This was the deal! But can you be a bit more considerate?"

"It is not my priority, Abraham."

"Sure. Why did I not figure it out before?"

Thinking about Gili and his death and the Green Man with his blessings and the period after Smadar's death, I realized that this had been the hardest trial of my life. I was on the verge of giving up. After this, something happened to my heart. It could not ache any more in the same way.

"I would not bet with anybody regarding whether it was the hardest trial of your life," Moria whispered. I shuddered but said nothing.

CHAPTER 5

"He was there again at the time when you were lost in deep grief after Smadar's tragic death," Moria said. "You could not see him, but he was there, watching you all the way from the fields of your kibbutz to the seashore. Even when you fought the wild coyotes in the night, he was there with you as he was there when the stars started comforting you."

"I did not see him. I felt insane this night but safe. I saw Akram, who came from his army service, and walked next to me through the orchards all the way to the sea."

"He was there all the time," Moria intoned. "He sent me to ease your mind, Abraham. I was reluctant, but he pleaded with me to go. 'Just one day,' he said to me. So I made you crazy for one day." She smiled. "'One day you will thank me for doing just that,' he said to me. I am still waiting impatiently," she said in a tired voice.

All of a sudden, I could see something through the cracks of this complex, foolish, self-content, adoring, and radiant being. Maybe she was also tired of her double game. Maybe she was also at a turning point of her existence, or whatever it could be, where she needed some drastic changes of the rules. She was in need of some new excitements and challenges. I could imagine that human beings must have been—in the long run—both terribly foreseeable and boring for such a being as Moria, who was hooked on novelties.

"I made you delirious so you could reach the sea and experience the night vision, where the stars came closer to you, dancing and chanting in the clear summer night. Do you remember the dancing green star which swayed above your tree? Do you remember what it said to you?"

"I remember," I said.

"There he was, your Green Man, your obsession."

"Was that him? I thought it was Gilli…"

"Can you recall what he told you, this swaying green star, while you were insane?"

"Yes, he told me not to give up, that there was a mission awaiting me. He told me that I had to bear the torch further. 'What kind of torch?' I shouted.'

"And he told you what kind of torch it was. He said you would find out in due time, right?"

I nodded. "Why did you all have to be there? I would have managed my pain." I sighed.

Moria clasped her hands. "I do not know why he chose you. Personally, I think he was mistaken and delusional about you, but I am not supposed to interfere with his decision-making. He is an alchemist of a kind," she murmured to herself.

"What kind of alchemist?" I insisted. "I do not understand him. He named some facts, but they do not make sense to me. There is this grand scheme in his head about a better chance for a new race. He has not confided in me, but he surely tries to rewrite the history of intelligent life, claiming it would grant greater benefits for us all. What were the facts he named, Moria? Can you come to the point?"

"Do not harass me," she hissed. "All right, the great alchemist master said that the fire of idealism and vision, which you had possessed from early age due partly to your kibbutz and Israeli background, combined with the fluid master plan on an evolving Bustan, which you kept in your heart even though you did not understand it fully, and with the perspectives the apocalyptic tragedy of your people opened in your mind, resembled a meaningful pattern he had once recognized. If you put into this pot of magic potion a good knowledge of the desert and its winds, which blow eternally . . . yes, that's what he said . . . they blow eternally. If you add to it your active participation in wars, the inclusive tradition of Jews which produced the fruits of great ideas and minds, he thought, then we could all change the rules of the game. Does it make sense? Not for me, anyway, but he is supposed to be the most knowing and the wisest among us!"

"Did he tell you more?"

"He said that you have come close to finding the properties of the fluid, mutable permanence. Do not ask me what he meant by this. He said that you might devise a way out of the trap of sapiens fixated lifespan, which could make intelligent life partly free at last of self-deception, mortality and . . . of me!" she cried all of a sudden.

"I am sorry, Moria. Sometimes I forget that you also have other feelings." I gave her a hug, and she held on to me for some time, trying to hide her face so I could not see the tears in her eyes. But now I understood that also in their world, there were divisions, like between these two; Moria was the incarnated hedonism, while the Green Man was the search for perfection. But why was I courted by both of them at the same time?

CHAPTER 6

The week after, I tried to appease her mind. I was aware that I was losing control over myself, but I could not resist her intoxicating presence and her occasional flirtatious hugs. So I started by offering to tell her the story about Akram and me, hoping to save us from an unpleasant confrontation.

"Go ahead," she said, touching my leg accidentally with her thigh, sending a warm feeling through my whole being.

"As children, we had walked the narrow path behind the hills. I still recall the sensations I felt on this walk. It was springtime with its fragrance: scents of mint and many more strange flavors of bushes and the spring flowers. Many years later, Akram and I walked again on the same narrow, dusty trail, and the wildflowers were gone. The horizon around us was framed by the almond trees in bloom on the small hills, and the vague smell of pesticide was everywhere. The powerful scents and fragrance of yesterday were gone. From a distance, I could see some of the cypress trees around the cemetery, where many people whom I knew, including my parents, had been buried a long time ago. I just wanted to revive the magic, to retrieve the tracks to my hidden Bustan, to feel again alive by the moving spirit of a grand mission . . .

"Akram looked around him, squinted at the bright light, and said, 'Where is it, pathfinder?' I pleaded with him to be patient. To the east, the bluish mountains were erected toward the dark blue sky as a crystal wall protecting a magical world behind them. The mountains, with their stern crags and inaccessible cliffs, brought back the magic of childhood, when they had been conceived by an imaginative child's fantasy as precious blue

---

crystals, which he could have gotten half a kingdom's worth for rescuing the beautiful princess. Far away to the west, I could sense the salty scent of the sea with its caressing blue waves, those waves who bore my little tanned bronze body. The seashore was my good friend, with its fine white sand on which huge crabs ran to and fro, hiding in their holes. This was the seashore where we collected amazing shells in our childhood, shells which had been able to whisper the tale of the deep sea and its treasures and how life was to evolve. Now they were all gone. 'I know the way, trust me!' I told him, sensing that he was a bit tense. It was springtime, and we were sweating and panting heavily.

"We two had gotten a bit old in our bodies, yet in my mind, I became for a moment the little child from the old times coming back to my green, green grass of home. And down the path, we went, and there, right there, my childhood Bustan, which once had bloomed there and formed my life, lay buried under the almond trees. I knew for sure that this was the right location since some of the old fence of thorny bushes was left there, those thorny bushes that each summer had given us their sweet, thorny fruits. 'This is the place,' I assured him. 'Here it all started for me, Akram. Here, on this very spot, the most beautiful garden had been flourishing. A sustainable creation in the midst of the dry, arid landscape, and it had graced the landscape around it, twinkling to the flickering stars, and from here, it vanished years ago, but it can rise again, awakening sleeping souls. Here it hides, waiting to be revived by somebody!' 'Nice story,' he sighed again, 'but then what?' 'There must be more to our lives than just slow decay. Once we believed in a mission!' I said, turning my face away from him.

"Akram muttered, 'Don't bother me with fairy tales from our background as if we can help people or humanity! Life, for me, is the same as it always was, unruffled by events like this or others, indifferent to the joys and sorrows of man, mute and incomprehensible as the sphinx. But the stage on which this everlasting tragedy we call life is enacted changes constantly and avoids monotony. This seems to be the real plot, but I do not see a designer for it.' I sighed. 'I have heard this before, Akram. I just came from the cemetery, where I put some flowers on my parents' graves. There, I met all the people whom I had known so well. Many of them, like my parents, used their best years to accomplish things that were far beyond their personal interests and of the utmost necessity in a much broader context. They had immigrated to Israel in their youth. They had created a new form of society that served as the foundation of the young country. They were far from happy at times, yet they made a difference in their own time and for the future. We do struggle for grand meaning with our lives, in utter defiance of life's ultimate silence, and this is how we form it. There is no other way!' I sighed.

"'You sigh! How far did you come with this pursuit, or is it just pep talk?' he commented. 'You know why I sigh. I did not come far!' The sun was going down, coloring the sky with crimson red, orange, and violet, while we started on our way back home. While walking on the hills, light and shadows were mingling on the field with the graceful wheat. 'So you got a calling many years ago, but what came out of it?' Akram was mocking me again. 'No, I did not!' 'So what is it you're trying to tell me?' 'I do not know. I am confused!' I retorted. 'I'd hoped you could help me sort up my thoughts as your father did once.' 'Working for a Bustan!' he stated. 'No! For an evolving Bustan,' I said, but I just do not know how it should be!'

"Darkness came tiptoeing on the hills, and the first stars were flickering and blazing up in the sky, inviting and enchanting. Soon, Orion, the Great Hunter, would dominate the sky overhead. Could he sense, looking at the night sky, that we were a part of something incredibly awesome and wonderful, a quest more marvelous than most of us could imagine? 'Look up at them!' I pointed up toward the glimmering stars. 'What about them?' 'They are also a part of it,' I said. 'I sense it! To the stars, through difficulty, might be the essence of the evolving Bustan. That was the voice of Gilli to this pursuit' He gazed at me. 'I am talking about evolving life! Do you get me. I am talking about Gili!' 'Not really. What it has with Gili to do?' he muttered. 'Never mind. I know it has to do with us three!' I said.

What did Akram do? He just walked beside me there, like most of us who wanted to make a difference but remained what we least of all wished to be: ordinary, temporary guests in this world" . . .

"Maybe, Moria, it was meant to be so that this question would keep haunting all the people in this world with its unsolvable suspension. Maybe that is what life is all about: living in the ceaseless suspension of impotence. Or maybe we just keep hiding from ourselves. I wish I knew how to resolve this Gordian knot."

"In any case, you work now hard, Abraham, and he will be delighted to hear this." Moria patted me on my shoulder.

CHAPTER 7

"Now, Abraham, lean back, and I will tell you the most revealing story of your life—your Exodus."

"My Exodus? I have never been a part of any Exodus unless you refer to the Bible and my forefathers."

"It was a Friday evening, and you went to the seashore as you had done so many times before. Summer was about to lose its force, and you were soon to depart from your old life. You were leaving, perhaps for a long time, and you knew that. You sensed the turmoil in your mind, realizing how definite it would be. They were all there, friends and acquaintances whom you loved and who had followed you since childhood. Now they were lying on the sand. Some of them jumped into the water and swam beyond the bursting, foaming waves. Two were playing beach tennis. It seemed to you that you dozed a little bit or fell asleep. You were young and still sorrowful due to Gili's death in the war and Smadar's death shortly afterward, and you wondered if you could ever escape from this pain. Maybe a new love that had no connection with what had already happened? Was that enough to remove the pain? And where was one now supposed to look for the last ultimate hymn? Did it exist at all in this misery-stricken world?

"With half-closed eyes, you saw a figure approaching. It moved like a wildcat in the soft sand. You opened your eyes and saw your friend's dark brown body and uncertain smile. Akram stood by, with drops of water running down his body. He approached you with two easy steps, and now the water drops fell down onto your warm body. 'Thanks, now I'm awake,' you said. He bent down and looked at you with his black eyes. 'Won't you miss this beach, this high blue sky, and the crabs running across the sand?'

'You know the answer!' you said dryly. 'So why on earth do you do it? I have already asked this question once before.' 'And I've answered it, Akram. A string has broken in me, and I have lost my melody, and it is a good enough answer for the time being, right?' 'Probably, and anyway, it was my father who predicted it. Remember?' 'Yes! Arif had come to see me long before I made the decision. Tell him that I will always keep both of you in my mind and will look for new paths as long as I live. He will understand.' 'There is something else . . .' Akram sat down on the wet sand. 'What is it?' 'Are you still cross with me?' 'No. You disappointed me then as I disappointed myself. Gili and Smadar died, and I folded into myself and forgot the living. Can you forgive me for that?' you whispered with eyes closed. 'And you? Well, have you forgiven?' Akram whispered. You opened your eyes. Akram's eyes were full of tears. 'Sure. What did you think?' you said softly to him. 'Am I perhaps a pure angel?' 'You have never done something like the thing I had committed,' he said. 'I'm no angel. I was wrong! I knew afterward I had made a big mistake. I felt sorry for myself and did not think of what you had gone through . . . maybe I can write to you from there. This will make it easier.' 'It sounds strange that you were wrong.' 'I remember your father telling me that if one corrects one's own mistakes, life becomes bearable. There is great wisdom behind these words. We are all flesh and blood . . .' 'You adore him, right?' 'I greatly appreciate him, but for me, he is also only a human being.' 'You are right. To me, he was a father who always kept a certain distance,' whispered Akram. 'That was something I noticed!' you said and smiled. 'But just remember that he formed you into what you are today. Not a bad deal at all!' Akram looked at the horizon, watching how the sun was slowly gliding as a magnificent red ball into the sea.

"'He once told me that a child who fears his father is the one who may be granted the greatest love from his father,' you told Akram. 'Did he say so?' 'Yes. He is proud of you.' Akram smiled shyly and cleared his throat. 'Who can I talk to when you are gone?' 'You can talk with other people whom you will come to appreciate. It can be him or her down there. Find some other interesting people. If you have communicated once well with a good man, so it is no longer something miraculous to find others you can talk with. If you have won one man's confidence, so also can you win others.' 'You have promised to write me, Avri.' 'And I will! I'm not going to search forever! So there is no reason to look at this departure as a definite tragedy. We will meet again, I am certain. Cheer up, man!'

"You two looked out over the water. A few sailboats were sailing toward the north, perhaps to Jaffa or farther away. I couldn't stay silent any longer..."

"Moria! Why do you tell me all this? I remember it as it happened yesterday . . ."

"You do not remember what you need to remember he, the Khidr said, so let me finish!"

"Again, you use this 'he' to make me shut up!" I shouted.

"May I finish what I am supposed to tell you about the golden cord?" I nodded, resigned. Moria began again. "'When I was a little boy,' you said to Akram, 'just before you and your father came to hide in our kibbutz, afraid of the blood revenge, my parents had taken me to the seashore, where I saw the lightshow of the sunset. It was the same sea, twilight with the smell of salt, of people and voices, but I could hear nothing because of the sound of the sea waves splashing on the shore. I thought about a song that I had once heard on the radio. It told a story about a boat with a golden sail moving on the quiet sea. And all its sailors, the grownups and the children, were trying to bring a whale up on the boat. I imagined that golden boat in the water, the children my age all dressed in blue and white as sailors, who drew with a rope a laughing whale up against the boat. Then my father came, dripping, and demanded that I should go into the sea with him. But I was afraid of the waves. My father said, "Huh? Afraid? Why? A wave is nothing to be afraid of!" He took me in his arms and threw me into the water.' Then you turned toward Akram and asked, 'Why are you looking at me in this way?' 'I just listen, Abraham,' he said. 'Continue, please.'

"You looked up at the darkening sky and said, 'Here the story ends. You know my father.' You both looked at your friends on the beach. 'When I think of this, I am glad that we found each other,' you said. 'Yes . . . Do you want me to do anything, Abraham?' 'Well, I suppose my dog might return, and if it happens, nobody will look after it . . . You know dogs almost always return . . .' 'I will be there for it.' 'Thanks! My heart is at ease. This is the right solution!' 'You do not have to come, if it is too . . . I can handle it myself,' said Akram. 'I want to . . . I'd better say goodbye to her because afterward, I will not allow myself to feel such pain anymore. I have decided that it should not be allowed to eat me up. I have wasted too much time on this self-pity, and I am done with it . . . I think so anyway.' And you smiled. 'Go and see Lena. She is waiting for you, Akram.'

"You glanced at Akram, who walked away toward his girlfriend and the others.

That last night, you all stayed on the beach. You wanted to cherish it and stayed awake, watching the others sleeping. After all, it was a special night for you. Morning dawned. The small flashes of light created a fantastic, colorful display in the sky. You watched the others waking up and fixing breakfast, and in the late morning hours, you all drove back to the kibbutz. The dog came to greet you as dogs always do. Akram, next to you, turned and asked, 'When will you be ready?' 'About two hours, at the east entrance,' you said. Then Akram nodded.

"There, by the water tower, bearing the deep bullet marks of the last war, you tried to make her come to you, calling, whispering her name, but she just stood there as if knowing what future you had planned for her. Standing there at a safe distance, she was glancing at you as what she knew you were soon going to become: Judas, the traitor. Bad conscience was creeping into you. After all, you had neglected her after Smadar's death. You had handed her to the nearby police station as a watchdog, but all three times, she had run the ten-kilometer distance straight back to you, escaping both iron chains and good food. Those blaming eyes became more and more unbearable each time. You knelt on your knees and rubbed your face against her nose. You scratched her ears and body. Afterward, you put a leash around her neck and walked with her toward the dining room. In the kitchen, you found a large bone with a little meat on it. The dog went with you to your room, and there, she got the bone. You took two sleeping pills, which you had received from your mother, crushed them, and mixed them well with water. You pushed the water bowl over to her, and she drank everything that was in it.

"From there, you went with her in the warm midday along the hard path to the kibbutz's east entrance. There, in a remote corner where the cows were slaughtered, you stopped. There was a small ditch which was used to bury the dead chickens from the chicken coop. You tied one end of the wire to an iron bar which supported the frame at which the cows were bound for slaughter. This place had not been used for a long time, and the weeds and nettles grew wild. You sat down beside the dog, caressing her forehead, and waited. After a short time, she began to yawn. First, she sat down and thereafter began to doze off when Akram came. 'Can you do it right away?' you asked. Akram nodded. 'You do not need to watch it. You can go and come back in a minute,' he said to you. 'No, I want to stay.'

'As you wish,' said Akram, almost whispering. He lifted the rifle up to his shoulder and aimed at her head. It was as though she could feel something. She tried to stand up but failed and fell down. She growled angrily at him. Akram waited a moment until she was calm.

"You heard two quick shots. She was hit at the forehead and fell to the ground. There she lay. 'Thanks,' you whispered. 'I could not do it! She did not suffer. I saw it.' 'Do you want me to help you with the rest?' Akram asked. 'No! You have already done much. I'll finish it.' 'Then I will go now. Will you come to us at four for coffee?' 'I may come a little later, if it's okay.' 'Come whenever you can,' said Akram and started walking. 'Akram,' you whispered, 'you should know that I said thanks, but I owe you much more. She died without noticing it. I saw it. I'm glad that she did not suffer at all.'

Akram looked, for the first time, very sad. 'Abraham, will you come to us when you are ready? I'll make the strongest cup of Turkish coffee for you. You need it. You have not slept all night.' 'Okay, we will meet soon.' 'It's a little sad! You loved her.' 'There was nothing else to do.' 'Would you . . . ?' 'I'll come when I can.' And your voice broke . . . Akram went up to you, gave you a squeeze on your shoulder, and walked toward the tower. You waited until he disappeared behind the cowshed. You went back to the dog, which lay on the ground. You loosened the leash the dog had on her neck and pulled her gently down into the ditch. You avoided looking at her smashed face. You took a pitchfork that stood beside the ditch and began to throw soil on the warm body. After covering her with a thick layer of soil, you threw the pitchfork and went away toward the fields. You found yourself in the middle of the field, far away from the kibbutz. The grain was high and golden, ready for harvest. You lay down on the earth and thought that the kibbutz had changed in recent years. And now you parted from it, and the pain did not leave you.

"How could you leave it behind you? You knew that you had already tried different things in life, and one thing was the worst of all. You would not have pitied yourself. You grabbed your fingers and started counting. 'So I lost some friends years ago . . . I lost, in the war, my best friend from the pact, Gili, a soul friend. Then I lost the girl I loved very much, Smadar. It is all the same now. I saw people die in war, disease, and traffic accidents. And now the fifth finger, I have lost a dog with an angel's eyes, and I am Judas. She was faithful to me until the last moment, and she had confidence in me.' This last finger was apparently the worst for you right there. And you felt sorry for yourself, repeating to yourself, surrounded by the corn:

'I can't bear it anymore . . . I can't bear it any longer . . .' You cried a little, and then it was easier to think clearly again. 'Of course, I can,' you said to yourself. 'I do not need self-pity.'

"You sat down in the field amidst the golden whispering corn. Suddenly, a gust of wind rustling through the corn passed by, and it seemed to you that there was a gentle voice coming out of the golden straw. It was like a hymn you had heard once long before. You listened attentively to this both known and unknown hymn that flowed toward you from some secret location. You did not know where it came from, but it felt like balm for your soul. When you got up and started walking toward the kibbutz, you knew that your life's great pain would remain there and that you had left it behind you," said Moria, and she folded her hands.

"Is that all? And where is my exodus in this . . . event?"

"I was also told that when you had left the kibbutz, a week later in the morning, you saw a man in a green gown standing by on the sideway and greeting you with his hand. Your brother saw it too, right?"

"Yes, and he asked me who the man was, and I replied, 'No one you know.'"

"I would not put too much stress on this episode, but he wished me to tell you that there, your Exodus had started. I do not understand a thing of it, but I had to tell you according to our contract. I get so tired telling such a sad story." Moria sighed.

CHAPTER 8

On December 17, 2009, heavy snow fell on Shopping Heaven. It shone in the morning with such beauty, a pure white carpet. In the Climate Conference, the parties were deadlocked in endless skirmishes on procedures and in power games. The dirty game of politics, when it tried to hide its inaptitude, was clearly displayed. Once again, the short sight of the builders of Babylon's tower, using their incompatible languages, was dominating the arena, but this time there was no good God to spread people around the world as if to start from the beginning. This time God was absent, and there was no place to go.

I invited all my family members, on this very fine and sunny day, to have a look at my new office. After more than twenty-four years, I had left my workplace, which I had started together with few other people back in the 1980s, and I was now ready to start a freelance existence. Upon hearing this news, Moria congratulated me, sighed deeply, and said, "At last!"

"I do not get it!" I looked at her sternly. "What at last?"

"At last you move yourself from this cozy, secure confinement. I was sure you would be stuck down in your workplace to your last day."

"Why do you care?"

"I want you to deliver the best observation on humans' folly, and one cannot do it well if one is such a fool who dares not risk anything new."

"Interesting observation," I commented coldly. "I thought that my record showed something different, but you probably think that I have grown soft, bored, and frightened . . ."

"You are sometimes boring, even though you do not like to hear it."

"Well," I said coldly, "and so were you with all your immense charm and seductive power."

She looked at me, smiled broadly, gave me a big hug, and kissed me on my lips a bit too long and a bit too deep, and then she turned around and left my office as on a catwalk.

CHAPTER 9

It was December 30, 2009. In the afternoon, Moria called me on the phone. "It is me!" she intoned, a bit distanced.

"What a surprise!" I exclaimed. "So we can wish each other happy New Year, Moria!"

"This was my intention." She chuckled.

"I wish you a good year," I said.

"I wish you too. I wish also to say goodbye. I am leaving the city tomorrow."

I fell silent for a while. Then I came to my senses and stammered, "But we did not complete the conditions of the contract. You said it yourself . . ."

"You have done pretty well updating me so far, and I am certain that you will do a good job on my book. And besides, I wish to cherish a good memory of you, Abraham. I really feel for you, and I cannot take our conflicts any longer. If you could love banalities as much as you yearn after the edges of knowledge . . . but this is just wishful thinking on my part. You could have been such a great lover, and we could have been such a great match." She sighed.

I was on the verge of tears. I had never loved a woman—or whatever Moria was—so foolishly intense and with such devastating contradictions. But I had to control myself. "Why did you choose to make the deal with me and then fight me all the way through? It seems that you choose sometimes without being fully aware of your choice," I said.

"Because you had to fight with me as Jacob did, who fought the angel in Jarbook." She sighed.

"And what was the meaning of this, Moria?"

184

"Do not ask me now. The answer will become obvious if you pass your trials."

"Give me a sign!" I insisted.

"The Green Man, the last ultimate hymn, the evolving Bustan, and the fluid, mutable permanence—if you do not believe in their being real, how can you ever gestalt a miracle which creates new reality?"

"New reality?"

"This is the only chance you have to win the bet . . ."

"So this bet again!" I chuckled. "Are you leaving me now?"

"Yes, I am done with you for the time being, my sweet vagabond!"

"Will we meet again?" I was in an emotional turmoil but tried to control the tremors in my voice.

"It all depends on how well you pass your trials and . . . on what you come to choose."

"What am I supposed to choose, Moria?"

"This answer will blow in the wind for some time, my love. Farewell!"

And there was a sound of kiss and some abrupt sobbing as the phone clicked off, and she was gone. Losing Moria all of a sudden was a blow to me and brought up in me very old and painful feelings. In this process, I became aware of how many voices inhabited my mind. To this very day, the impact she had upon me, and not the least of her departure, was so profound that it was hard for me for a long time to recognize my old person. In the beginning, I thought that she had bewitched me in some way, but this was not the case. At the time she left me, the COP15 Climate Conference ended in a disastrous failure, and I had a strong premonition on its future global consequences. I saw Moria time and again on the TV, broadcasting in Bella Centre during the days the conference took place, playing some central mediating role. It made me feel like a lost child, watching her. She seemed to stand just a bit behind all the peacocks of politicians and diplomats who were interviewed by the channels, brightly smiling and immensely glowing and popular. I was trying to figure out what she was doing there and called some connections. I was told that Maria Buchman—this was now her name—was renowned for her good contacts, skills abroad, and interest in climate questions. She was therefore hired by the Climate Ministry of Denmark to accommodate diplomats and politicians and to facilitate workable compromises.

After the total failure of the conference, Maria was interviewed on

CNN and BBC. She was asked to point out whether the state minister of Denmark was responsible for the conference's catastrophic outcome. "No," she said empathetically. "It failed for another reason. You see, the workers of the world cannot unite. The religious people of the world cannot unite either, and this is also the case for the capitalists of the world. All of them cannot unite, but in this conference, in Denmark, where people were measured to be the happiest in the world, all the fools of the world have united!" and she smiled all over her face, making a V sign. Everybody around her was dumbfounded, but she just smiled her enchanting smile, waved with her hand, and went away. Her statement spawned jokes and demands for immediate apology, but nobody could find her, and the flat where she had been living in the middle of Shopping Heaven was found vacant and empty. I could have screamed, witnessing these macabre scenes, but nobody would believe a word I said. Now she was gone, leaving no trace at all. As the New Year commenced, I felt I was the greatest fool of them all.

CHAPTER 10

It happened on a springtime day of 2015, when my wife and I were seated on a bench after a walk around the lake. The warm breeze caressed us, and we were watching the swans and ducks swimming around while the seagulls above were diving over the mirror-blank water, tearing the idyll apart with their shrieks. Then a tall man dressed in a green gown came walking toward us. There was something rather unusual about him. He had a withdrawn look. An idea shot through my mind: he must be feeling the reality of being a passenger in an alien ship, not in command, not deciding the course, the communications going unheard. The stranger, as he moved closer, eyed me broodingly with the sun on his chestnut beard and hair and on the green gown he was wearing, which gleamed in the sun. He was about seven feet tall, somewhere around forty-five years old, well-built, and walking with impressive elegance. His face reminded me of an Assyrian king whom I had seen once in my childhood, depicted in an ancient painting. This was my last coherent observation before things started rolling as if I were in a dream.

The man walked a few meters past us and then turned around and sat on the other side of the bench and was watching the houses in front of us intensely. My wife and I were engaged in some metaphysical subject when he turned toward us all of a sudden and joined the conversation. "Excuse me for interfering so impudently, but this is a matter of great urgency for me . . . If I'm not mistaken, you were saying to your wife that since God is in the minds of people, there can't be a paradigm which surpasses this attachment or motivates people to believe in their own mission," he asked, turning his piercing coal-black eyes on me.

Coming closer to the age of seventy, I kept repeating compulsively this matter with God, trying to rearrange this insight as to find a crack where new light would come out and illuminate me, but it felt more and more like a recurring nightmare, and my wife was visibly tired of my repetitions. "You were listening, all right." I was taken by surprise. "I was talking to my wife about it when you were about twenty meters away. Could you catch my words from that distance?"

"Well, I did!" He squinted in a strange manner.

"How interesting!" I exclaimed nervously, thinking that I had probably begun to talk loudly, like an old man losing his hearing.

"And do you agree with your man?´ he inquired, looking at my wife.

"Well," she hesitated, looking at me, unsure about this whole situation. "Yes, this is how our reality looks," she said.

"Reality is something which can be formed, I assume," he commented politely.

"Not as much as we wish to," I intercepted. "There is no total free will for us, and there is the unbridgeable gap between what we wish to do and are capable of doing, as you probably know!"

The foreigner leaned against the backrest of the bench and asked, "Are you atheists?"

"Yes," I replied.

"Are you too?" he asked my perplexed wife.

"Sort of." She was clearly annoyed by this intrusive, impolite stranger.

"How delightful!" he exclaimed. "So you do not believe that certain reality is in the making, although we cannot perceive it clearly?" he asked her again.

Now confused by this approach, she said, "May I ask you to present yourself? Who am I talking to?"

"Well, I can see the pattern of the future. Not as deterministic but as the unfolding of intelligent will power," he just continued as if he had not heard her. "I will let your man tell you who I am once I have talked to him. May I beg you to leave us for a short while? I know your man, and I wish to talk to him about something of utmost importance?"

This scene began to remind me of something, but I just could not recall more than déjà vu. Was it something I had experienced before, heard of, read of, or dreamt of? My mind stood still. I nodded to my wife, and she stood, being acquainted with my habit of talking to strange and queer people. She said, with a faint smile, "Well, I will walk around the lake and come back again." The stranger bowed with respect. And away she went.

"Do you live here?" I asked the man.

"You can say so! Right now I live here."

"So you should know that in our country, there's nothing surprising about atheism," I said with politeness. "Some of us have long ago given up believing in all those stories about God and revelations."

"But might I enquire," the man begun after some reflection, "how you manage without belief in God or something greater than your own navel?"

"Say, is it necessary to choose between God and my navel? Can you imagine that between these two poles may exist some transcending meaning, which is much more in touch with both the human potential megalopsychia and its mutable reality?"

"Bravo!" exclaimed the stranger. "Bravo. You have exactly repeated the views of a mortal I once talked to."

As I spoke, I thought, *But who on earth is this fellow? And how does he speak our language so well although he looks like an Arabic immigrant?*

"You know me," he said as if he could read my mind. "We have met before. When I saw you before, you had a strong inner voice, but now . . . like the drippings of an old man . . . No, please, do not stop me or leave."

"Who are you? Where do you know me from?"

"We met a few times before."

And all of a sudden, in front of my eyes, the shiny green light enveloped him. "Now I know!" I cried. "I thought you would never come again."

"Well, here I am!" He smiled broadly.

It took me some time to regain my composure. "Here you come again and start insulting me," I said with a quivering voice. "What on earth do you want from me? Where have you been in all these years, when I was waiting for some sign? I am an old man now!"

"I came to deliver a massage, but first, I should be certain of something. This Homo stupidligence of yours, what is it all about?" Knowing that it was just a rhetorical question because he probably knew all about me, I explained shortly about the shortsighted and greed-prone behavior of Homo stupidligence and the gap between his thought and action. I concluded that self-destructive behavior was rooted in this malfunction.

"So this is how it ends up for you? Being a grumpy, old, pessimist sitting on a bank?" he scolded me.

"Have you got nothing better to say?" he continued.

"It does not matter what I mean or say. Human beings have their own logic, and they will not listen as long as they can dance around the golden calf and nurture their illusions. So you are right, my voice is impotent."

"What about trying the old voice from the Bible: 'Who is for the Lord, summon around me'?"

"I do not believe in any Lord, as you know . . ."

"It was meant allegorically. Who is for a sustainable, an evolving Bustan, summon around me?"

"Here we go again, like with your fairy tale about the Bustan, which I believed in all those years, but it was absurd from the very start . . . a Bustan cannot evolve, sir."

"Oh, do you really think so? But it was not a fairy tale. It was a detailed instruction, Abraham. Not complete instruction, though, and this is why I am here again. Now listen, Abraham!"

He remembered my name. "You remembered my name all these years!" Tears welled up in my eyes.

"Sure!" he said matter-of-factly. "Sometimes it can be mystifying to be a man like you, a man who decided to live a pleasant, resigned life suited for an old person without special virtues . . . and you have planned to do it to the very end and here all of a sudden." He stared right into my eyes. "A trivial matter takes place, you may think, but it is not . . . because for no good reason, you suddenly wake up from a long, deep slumber, and you are so involved in something greater than your own navel that you leave all your family and friends behind you."

"Do not start . . . I am not going to listen to this incredulous talk from you too. Do not talk to me as if I were a puppet on the strings. I am not going anywhere. You are too late!" I said bitterly. "I waited for some message too long time, from 1980 to 2012, and I was getting crazy waiting. In the meantime, I have forgotten all the magic and fantasies and have accepted my destiny."

"You're not going to resign before you know better! But wouldn't it be nearer the truth to say that something quite different was directing your life and fate?" The man gave an eerie sound of laughter.

"Like leaving my family, three children and six grandchildren, for something foggy, which I have become too old and too feeble for?" I had been dwelling on his unpleasant remark about my leaving my wife and three children because I had heard it before and was on the verge of walking away. But I knew the man, and he did not waste his time in petty conversation.

"Please be patient with me, Abraham. I am not here to force you but to plead with you . . . Once you understand the contours of the scheme, it will be up to you to decide, with the remains of your self-determination, what is right for you to do."

And there I sat on a springtime day, entering into the shadowy last part of my life. I did not wish to listen anymore. I was an old man by now, and I wished just to be left alone. "Oh, the force in the things," I prayed quietly, my eyes closed. "You have spared me from the void of existence and brought me some light in this suffering world. I do not wish to lead thy erring daughters and brothers out of the darkness. I do not wish to be a stern and merciful father to them in thy false name. I am tired of the repetition of thy righteous wrath that we, as an instrument for your calling, have to bear."

"Do not be profane, Abraham." His voice intruded my prayers. "Do not become a blasphemer just because you lack resolve right now."

"Stand back!" I said to him angrily, gesturing to him to keep away from me. "I am taking command of my own ship in the name of my sanity . . . so do not push me around."

"Very well," he paused. "This is what I had imagined. First, the inevitable melodrama before any sensible thought can dawn in your stubborn mind. I give you the time to absorb the idea that the deliverance of the evolving Bustan is awaiting you, Abraham. I will come to this very place at a time of your choosing!"

And he stood on his feet and disappeared among the green trees and bushes as he had done in the Bustan of my childhood a long time before, moving through the branches as if they were just green sunrays.

CHAPTER 11

On the morning of October 17, 2015, when I became seventy, two things happened. When I opened my eyes, the sun shone in the most beautiful blue sky I had seen for a long time. In our backyard, the most beautiful sunflower stood erect, smiling at me. I could not believe my own eyes as sunflowers in our region blossom in July and, at the latest, in August. I went down to see it, and it was real. It stood there and greeted me in the still fresh autumn day while the sun caressed my cheeks. *It must be a present from Moria,* I thought. I patted my flower and felt alleviated but also restless. I told my wife I had to get this restlessness out of my body and my mind by walking vigorously around the lake. It was the finest autumn day, with sunshine and just a few white clouds floating in the blue sky. In old times, I would have interpreted such a fine birthday as a sign to "go for it" in life, but now I was mentally resigned yet with a disturbing feeling of both excitement and premonition.

I cycled to the lake and walked around it three times. Now I was both tense and weary, so I sat on a bench, where the way made a curve, and closed my eyes, trying to bring some order to my tormented mind. I could feel him coming. Some green glow penetrated through my eyelids and hit my closed eyes. It was impossible, but that was what happened to me. I removed my hands from my eyes and opened them, and he was coming, right across from me, in his glowing green cloak. He was a bit changed this time: long and lanky with a scanty little beard and gray hair on his temples. His eyes were the redeeming, rejuvenating feature. They were starry like those of a young girl in love. The black irises seemed to thaw away and stream upon the large protruding whites of his eyes. I was sitting on a

---

bench, basking in the sun, in some frenzied pain, when this man appeared at my side. He stopped beside my bench and looked at me.

"Happy birthday, Abraham," he intoned in this voice, which was so familiar. "Did you like Moria's present to you?"

"Why did you come when I have reconciled myself to my age?" I asked.

"You have not given up, old man!" He smiled brightly.

"Oh, I have resigned, and this is my Bustan. This is how far I came with my daydreams and your promises."

"A promise had been made. But one has to become worthy of acquiring an evolving Bustan."

"Yes, that was what you said long time ago, but you did not tell me how one makes himself deserve such one . . . and besides, how does this crazy thing that you want me to do relates to an evolving Bustan? A Bustan, as I understand it, is a tranquil heaven one creates, but you wish me to do something entirely different with confrontations, schisms, pain, and departure."

"What do you think the reason for my return might be? Is it in order to mock you? I came in order to add the missing information for your particular Bustan."

"Why do you come now when it is obviously too late?"

"It is not too late. I could not give you this information when you were a little child or an adolescent or middle-aged. It would not have made sense at all."

"What kind of information do you think I am more ready to receive now than before?"

"That if your Bustan is to prevail, it must evolve."

"What? Here we are again!"

"Evolve! It is not a tranquil one. There are three items of instruction which I have hidden from you all these years."

"What are they, Nudnik?" I cursed.

"I will let you know now, but keep your mouth shut for at least five minutes after I have finished." I nodded. "If your Bustan is to evolve, the first thing to do is to introduce into it new and better fruit trees. As the science of genetics expands, entirely new trees will be available, and the gardener will inhabit his Bustan with them. Soon, you will be introduced to new genetic engineering revolutionary technologies, which will make it possible to upgrade sapiens. These will be your new trees for the future:

---

wiser and more farsighted beings than sapiens to inhabit and take over this evolving earth-Bustan!

"The second thing is to the stars with difficulties. You will use the insight of genetics, space travel, and hibernation to supply the trees, or what can become a tree, nutrients, and moisture that can sustain them without soil, bring them in suspended hibernation wherever you wish to plant them, even on a spaceships on their way to new worlds, where they will germinate.

"The third and last thing is something you will first comprehend at the end of your life: a Bustan becomes ever-evolving when the gardeners become the trees, and the trees become the gardeners. It is imperative that all the trees in it evolve to become gardeners in order to generate the fluid, mutable, permanent state of creators."

I was dumbfounded and could not utter a word. Then I stammered, "Can you repeat it slowly, please?" He did it, and it occurred to me that all these years, he had not trusted my feeble mind. He was right about it, but my mind was still feeble. He stood and walked to and fro for a while, and then he sat and contemplated for a long time. Then he looked over the lake, toward the artificial island, where the seagulls and ducks were walking or resting.

"You have time enough, Abraham. If you only wish, you have got the time!"

"May I walk alone around the lake to think about this fluid, mutable permanence and the gardener who becomes the tree and vice versa? It will take half an hour." He nodded, and I started walking. I became really furious on my walk. I had to admit that he had spoken remarkably well, with a childish directness and as though he himself had lived through the whole adventure of human history. I understood the new instructions, but I was too old. Back at where he waited, I started to argue, of course. He asked for something to eat, and I took him to a nearby café, where our argument became still more heated. He sat on a bench beside me, watching me, leaning against the table, now and then laughing with the inoffensive laughter of an innocent child, or was it innocent?

"So what do we need in order to get started, Abraham?"

"Some daredevil and a portion of craziness, both of which I do not possess."

"I remember well that as a young boy, you were pretty much obsessed by Trotsky oratory magic. You ran in the fields while training your voice and eloquence in order to become such a Trotsky, who could inflame the Red Army and the Soviet proletariat against its enemy."

"I was once a boy who believed in revolution."

"All right, you deserted the revolutionary idea but not the idea of reforming people. Am I right?" I nodded, remembering how unacceptable it was for me to accept Moria's notion of life: to live your life to get the best pleasure out of it. "What about the superimposition of the will power of the exceptional people, not the proletariat?"

"Like what?"

"Like the idea of Ayn Rand, for example. She stirred a lot of feelings by granting people the idea of becoming exceptional by working for the dollar. She talked about the exceptional hero who earned much money because of his virtues, who was free to unfold his desires, and who despised mediocrity and bureaucracy, and this idea was cherished by lots of people."

"You mean Ayn Rand's view of the hero? To create a society of exceptional heroes who don't care about social institutions or bureaucracy and who detest the mediocre? How are they to survive or thrive on their own?"

"Why should it be a problem? Don't you believe ingenuity of great men to be the best guide for humanity toward something great? She promoted what you seem to like: the concept of man as a heroic being with his own happiness as the moral purpose of his life, with productive achievement as his noblest activity, and reason as his only absolute."

"See, I like her rejection of faith in overdose as antithetical to reason. But Rand opposed any form of mysticism or supernaturalism, including organized religion. Instead, she embraced rational egoism, rational self-interest, as the only proper guiding moral principle. I do not approve of it either as a viable moral guideline or as a practical long-term strategy. This was the philosophy of American business men on Wall Street, and when the economy collapsed due to their vanity, greed, and speculations, who had to bail them out? They were the citizens whom they had despised."

"Why this?" he inquired.

"She advocated a sort of ruthless elitism. She said something to the extent that the masses were but mud to walk on, fuel to use for those who deserve it. But if this is the medicine which is needed, what is wrong with it then?" he went on.

"Do you wish to provoke me, or do you really mean what you say?" I asked him angrily. "Why do you talk about all these disturbed people, like Trotsky and Ayn Rand?"

"Why? Who do you wish me to talk about as a model?"

"A model to whom? To me?"

"Yes, so you can kick yourself out of your passivity. Moses?"

"Moses. Good heavens . . . I wish to make my point straight. It repulses me to think of this kind of elitism which Ayn Rand and Trotsky proposed. It is neither practical nor humane to function only on the level of untested idealism or of pure rationality . . . so I do not see your point, sir."

"You will, hopefully, one day! So what do you say about Moses?"

"Right now, it irritates me as you attempt to instruct me by mentioning names like Trotsky, who blindly believed in the wisdom and right to power of the proletarian, and Rand, who became so anticommunist as to end up in the extreme opposite."

"Did Moses?"

"Who talks about Moses? What he has got to do with this subject?"

"I do! I just try to guide you to find your own preferences."

"There are no preferences for me. There is just this mental quagmire, which for most of us indicates the nearing of the end. I am an old man. If I believe in anything, it is the temporariness of everything."

"Pardon me, but I do not listen to this nonsense. I say that among the Jewish ideational inheritance, there must be one with whom you can identify and whose mission and calling you can modify to suit our time . . . After all, this folk has existed for more than four thousand years, so some of their ideas were vital and time resistant ideas as to make them survive . . ."

"Like Moses's guidelines or exodus?"

"For example, there is a crack in everything where the light comes in . . .," he mused. "I see no crack, and I see no light, not in Trotsky or in Ayn Rand!"

"So leave them alone, man. They were just an example of the vitality of the mind and its pitfalls when it goes on overdrive."

"So who are we left with? Moses?"

"Now you are starting to sound more sensible, Abraham."

"A crack in everything . . . Moses is outdated as you may know."

"Do you mean his whole message?" My mind drifted away to a French saying: "Nothing lasts longer than temporary." This is deterministic! All masterpieces and human achievements have had limited validity and duration. However, many of us have difficulty in accepting this deterministic condition, that we and our deeds cannot be eternal. Like eager and self-centered children at the beach, many of us work with the wet sand, building extravagant sandcastles. Many will endeavor to construct protective ramparts and embankments around the sandcastles in an attempt to obstruct the tide. Even worse, while they are constructing their embattlements, they are at the same time destroying the castle from the inside through assuming a sectarian, esoteric, elitist attitude, paralyzed with inner rivalry. In their futile attempt to form permanency in this ever-changing reality, they often forget the original characteristics of their creations; they can exist only for a limited period of time.

"Moses is outdated!" I stated. "The fundamental questions we ask ourselves have persisted, but the answers and their solutions will keep changing as long as there is intelligent life."

"That is exactly my point," the Green Man triumphed. "There must be new replies to the same questions. Look at Moses and the exodus!"

"But I do not see them as something you can renew and make fresh. History is not a matter of rewriting it."

"You will see it in due time." He clasped me on my shoulder. We sat until twilight fell over the lake. I said I had to depart, and he stood, so tall that he almost reached the ceiling of the café, muttering as he glanced out of the window and pointed at me. "Help them! You must help them!" he murmured this sternly as though issuing a command, as though conscious of his power over someone. This little performance was not to my taste, but I said nothing. He looked at me and then said, "By the way, I am the evolver!"

"What does this name mean?" I asked.

"I promote the paradigm of megalopsychia in high intelligent life. I promote sustainability, evolvement, and becoming creators. My motto is, 'Wisdom appears when illusions/delusions/blindness disappear.'"

"What have you just said?"

"You will understand it in due time." And he left me in his usual manner.

CHAPTER 12

It was March 2016 when he appeared for the third time. "Well, have you come to your senses?" he greeted me with a great smile. And he was right. Something very strange seemed to have grown up inside me. There was this surge of new energy as I was reborn anew. There was this itch for action after a long lull and apathy. Everybody around me asked time and again, "What has happened to you? You seem more vital than we have seen you in the last ten years." The only thing I could say in response was "I just do not know. It feels as if something is sprouting up in me."

"That sounds promising," the green Man said.

"What were these things which made you choose me?"

"They are all unconnected symbols for you at the moment. Well, there was the spirit of vision, kindled by your kibbutz background, and the foundation of your nation at approximately the same time. The spirit of creating something anew was strong in your childhood and granted you the knowledge of what real Megalopsychia is all about. You learned to see this rare aspiration and force temporarily surfacing in the hearts of ordinary people, and you absorbed it and learned how to rekindle it in your own heart . . . and then there was the Holocaust . . ."

"What has the Holocaust to do with me and you?"

"Do not interrupt me, please! You asked me for the constellation, and you will get it, but the connections you will have to find out by yourself as you have figured out your way so far. The Holocaust was the biggest tragedy of modern time, showing how humanity could go astray and making it urgent to find some outlet, a lasting meaning for it in order to prevent its beast from rising up again. Have you thought about it?" I nodded, realizing that he knew much more about my inner thoughts than anybody. "Then there was the Bustan, where I met you for the first time. Your kibbutz was placed on the boundary of the desert, where the winds blow into eternity. There, every exodus of great missions had passed by on their way to a Promised Land. For one reason or another, you were coached by the spiritual teacher Arif, the pathfinder, and his son, Akram, was your closet friend and guardian. You had experienced sorrow, wars, and trials and the collapse of your visions due to human short sight. You had experienced all these events without losing your heart.

"The last test was the most demanding of them all. When you settled down in Denmark, you were for years exposed to the eroding forces of mental numbness, security, welfare, and everyday pettiness, which were considered essential here, but you revolted against this masked but sneaking numbness of the great soul. You kept fighting and searching for a mission and calling grander than this safety in the frog dam. This rare constellation of experiences made you into a possible candidate. Do you understand it better now?"

I looked at him. "I assumed for years that it all started with your appearance in the Bustan. The rest does not make much sense to me!"

"Does it make sense to you, great psychologist, that stuffed, buffed, indulgent, leisurely, and comfort-seeking people would not be able to kindle such fire, to nurture such a torch? You know them! Does it make sense to you that you had to be groomed for the mission through much experience?"

"But why am I alone?"

"You are far from being alone. All around the world, people like you are awakening, and all of them will join the ranks once they hear the trumpet, once humanity's sufferings will become unbearable. You are just the whistleblower, the trumpet!"

"I am the trumpet . . . and nothing more?"

"Once you start trumpeting and the process gets started, they will do fine without you. You are but a catalyst in this historic turn."

"So I will be able to leave if I wish?"

"Yes! They will let you go once they can manage on their own."

"That sounds less frightening, although I still do not know how I am to go about this business . . ."

"Now, Abraham, we can make a very clear-cut deal."

"How can I figure out something when I just do not know the rules of the game?"

"The rules of the game are simple. You will have to start an exodus and settle down in new settlements for your chosen branch of human beings. You will start a poker game on the survival chances of intelligent life. That is all there is to it!"

"Who are we playing against? Who are my contenders?"

"You have greeted them before. These human beings guided by folly. Folly is their malign virus. Now you are also a player in it, for otherwise, why should we bother with you, dummy? Got it now?" I shook my head in disbelief. Was I to challenge human folly and to give intelligent life a new chance? It could not be done. He shouted now. "You wrote about it yourself how some fundamental rules of nature are reversed or annulled sometimes . . . You wrote it all, but you just do not take it into account!"

"What did I write?" I asked meekly.

"You wrote, 'Just remember that once in a while, the fundamental laws of the universe seem momentarily suspended and not only does everything go right, but nothing seems to be able to keep it from going right. In the same spirit of semi-miracles, we can make ourselves fuse what we are with what we wish to be and into what we must become. I am not sure why it must be so, but it is. It helps to know though.'"

I put my hands on my cheeks and whispered, "I did not mean it that way."

"But you had activated the force that way!'" he roared. "Show me what you have written so far," he said in an icy voice.

"Not that much."

"Show it to me!" he roared.

"Here it is!" I gave him a rolled piece of paper. He started reading it aloud.

CHAPTER 13

The new paradigm will promote the following:

Firstly: Enduring global sustainability in all major areas like economy, ecology, demography, and social values in accordance with the principles of prudence, solidarity, modesty in consumption, and cooperation.

Secondly: A strategic struggle against the worst ill effects of human stupidity expressed in self-destructive and destructive behavior, in apathy and paralyzing self-deceptive systems, and in the worship of mammon.

Thirdly is the acceptance that intelligent life is influenced by randomness, coincidence, and luck, but we can reduce its ill effects by learning to decipher its irregular regularity. God has no control or power over randomness or human stupidity.

Fourth: Intelligent life's utmost meaning lays in pursuing further evolvement and greater mastery of life, including challenging its confines and striving to transcend itself.

The fifth: A detailed yet personalized program will be devised for creators to pursue megalopsychia (the greatness of the spirit) through their long-term and life affirmative work for the sustainable evolvement of intelligent life.

This paradigm makes a clear distinction between the micro dimension of life, where all humans' activities like studies, work, family, friends, religious affiliations, and personal interests are incorporated and the macro-dimension of life, where human activities focuse solely on our global, long-term, sustainable evolvement. Only by working on the macro-dimension can intelligent life attain real megalopsychia.

After reading it aloud, the Green Man nodded and uttered, "I knew you could do it!"

"Many people can write science fiction and formulate proclamations for a fancy society. It's not a big deal."

"Oh yes. Many people can write science fiction, but only few can write it in such a way that it can become a reality. There lies this little difference!" he muttered.

I sighed. "This is just a piece of paper which cannot enliven the fantasy of human beings. It demands immense sacrifices and a determined focus. And you know people—they will always choose a piece of cake or some other sweet or distraction when being faced with the choice of either grabbing it or shouldering such a daunting task."

"Yes, I know this all too well. Yet in the village of these feebleminded people, some people whom I know undergo the last stages of transforming into something entirely different from the people you have in mind. In their minds, they follow the same track sketched as guidelines on this paper. I am not going to press them to come out into the open. Somebody else has to utter the battle cry. They have all been through a discrete pruning process and wait for the right timing, when to come out into the open and how to do it without being trampled down. The time is soon ripe. The mounting crisis in global affairs is the sign."

"There is nothing new about our crisis. Since the beginning of this century, we have been running into crisis, be it the dot com crisis, the bursting real estate bubble, the financial crisis, the economic crunch, virus crisis, or now the food and water shortage in many parts of the world, the climate, and our numbers. There is nothing new under the sun . . . So why should they rise?"

"You play stupid now, Abraham. There is growing intensity in these crises. They are stages in the death qualms of an outdated paradigm and reckless civilization. They are signs of what is awaiting humanity already from the middle of this century. When it hits, it will be like an unimaginable tsunami sweeping away almost everything in its way. I do not wish to scare you, but this is what is on the menu."

I shook my head. "I do not believe in all these cataclysms and doomsdays. We have the capacity to survive and adapt . . ."

"You are like an old gramophone, playing the same melody on and on with the psychotic energy of delusional hope, Abraham. This time there is no light in the tunnel! This is why you and other people like you must come into the open and transform humanity. *Homo sapiens* are doomed because of their short sight. Mene, Mene, Tekel. Their days are numbered, and they have been weighed and found wanting." He rudely handed me the paper and said, "Remember Jacob and his struggle with the angel! Please call Akram as he is to be engaged in the process. And start devising a viable plan. You do not have time to waste. I will keep you company once in a while, Abraham." He clapped my shoulder and disappeared in his usual manner.

CHAPTER 14

Roma locuta est. Causa finita est. Rome has spoken. The cause is finished. In those days, when we worked hard on making the first steps of our exodus, the evolver was assisting me with both advice and instructions, not to talk of a few dictations, which resulted in some flare-ups on my part. It turned out that he was right about the potential mutants all around the world who were just waiting for the "whistleblower." So I did it through many channels, including the Internet, presenting both the outlines of a program and the practical steps needed to create our own viable society. It surprised me to realize that lots of families—mostly of young people— were willing to take the risk of starting a new society.

There were also those who were willing to leave their families behind to join us. It was obvious that among the countless who contacted our representatives abroad, there were both loonies and unsuitable people. Three years after broadcasting my ideas, we had both the capital and the expertise to start screening the volunteers. Once we finished this task of sorting them out, we started the next stage of fine-tuning. In this respect, the evolver (the Green Man) and I worked as a perfect team. But when it came to the matters of building up a military force to deter potential enemies from derailing our project, I preferred the first stage, the meek approach, where we did not provoke our mighty hosts and neighbors. The evolver insisted on a real exodus, where from the start we projected a military might. He insisted on building up a deterring force, which would keep our enemies at bay and, when needed, could be used to cement our growing influence. I objected, saying that we would just be repeating what HS had been compulsively doing throughout their history. He responded that we would differ from them in many respects, but we had to have a deterring force to reach detente with potential enemies. Once we had reached supremacy on the planet, we could start to disarm. I was not pleased.

It all started when I asked the evolver what I was to do if my family did not wish to follow me to the new colonies which we had purchased. Could I, in such a case, stay behind with them as an "embassy representative" for our movement?

"When will you stop being sickly sentimental about your family and about this decaying race?"

"I have the right. My family is essential to me, and these frail and treacherous human beings are my brothers and sisters. They have given me and us all what we have. They made it all. They built this precious civilization, and our knowledge and comfort and medicine and even my dreams. They protected me. It was a hard battle, and it was a struggle, a bloody fight all the way. Can't you understand that? And you want me to be Judas? Of all creatures on this planet, you want me to betray the most important things for me: my integrity, my family, and humanity?" My face was contorted as I screamed this infamous name right into his face.

"Not Judas, never Judas, but an illuminating, reluctant Abraham! That is what I want you to become. What have you imagined all these years when you wished me to grant you a Bustan? I told you about the price. I told you about the weeding up, of rooting up old trees. What have you imagined? Do you expect a pleasurable, free-ticket trip with no costs at all? Why did I wait so long to call on you? I thought that slowly, you would become the right man to carry forward this mission, yet here I stand in front of a frightful man who knows the odds yet dares not sacrifice!" and he pushed me hard on my chest with his fist. "Think it over, Abraham! You can be as reluctant as Moses was, but you cannot hide your cowardice under family ties, justice, and fairness. You know as well as I how brutal humans can be while pretending to be loving and compassionate. You are not going to achieve any of your goals without being strong, determined, and using your force. Everything gets much more difficult when the premises for solving the problems of humanity create the problem instead of the solutions."

"What does that mean?" I said stubbornly.

"It means that without enforcing sustainable demography, economy, and ecology on this world, nothing will work, and I think you know it, as

205

well as if your family will reject to resettle, you will have to leave them. This is the reason you need both brtual force and determination."

"I am not so sure," I muttered.

"I will come back, and we will settle this matter once and for all." He turned around and spat on the floor before leaving the room.

CHAPTER 15

Many years had gone by since we took the first initiatives to branch off from humanity. It is not appropriate for me to expose the strategies and tactics we applied to accomplish this daunting and finely balanced task. I can only disclose here some of the outlines for our comprehensive actions to gain our place in the new history of advanced intelligent beings.

We had to have capital to buy areas where we could settle down and build up our colonies without conflict. We got lots of money to finance our projects by using arrays of persuasive and coercive methods. It was surprising and encouraging to see how many people wanted to support this project. We did not say no to money contributions, but we had to select among the volunteers who wanted to join our ranks. We had to equip the colonies with all the needed hardware and software to survive and quickly become sustainable, self-sufficient, and capable of resisting minor military incursions and assaults. The idea was to make them self-sufficient in food, water supply, infrastructure, clothing, and housing within a period of five years from their establishment. This idea was copied from "transition towns," which had flourished just before the end of the oil era. We went further by building up in every new territory a military capacity enough to deter gangs and even small states from invading or meddling in our affairs. We trained our populations in guerrilla warfare, and in city combat, we equipped them with first-class weapons, capable combat officers, offensive swarm like bots, communication gear, and devised effective mobilization procedures. Most transition towns in the old world had lacked military might, and therefore, many of them were invaded by gangs and burned down in the period of the global turmoil, but with our weapons well-equipped colonies it could not be done.

Our colonies also had the advantage of backing each other up through our connections, which included commerce, political coordination, and a highly trained` and mobile military force-including swarm like bots- which could be sent in wherever colonies risked being run over by an enemy. We made some projections regarding the time it would take for the old order to crumble down. Our need for a deterrent force in this preliminary period was obvious. We made some projections and reached the conclusion that up to the end of the twenty-fourth century, we would keep our capabilities and would begin to disarm in the beginning of the twenty fifth century so as to move into the next stage of our evolvement—peace on Earth.

Akram pushed hard as the chief of staff the programs of cyber sophisticated weaponry and of some smart and miniature weaponry, which for a long time we dubbed as the *sand corns* and the *buttons*. By developing them and deploying them in every strategic place in the old world, we slowly reached a kind of acceptance of our parallel existence with the old powers. We acquired first-class scientists in all vital areas to develop our projects. We also bribed our way through with money and by promising goods and services to various governments and officials, like our life-extending regimen, which proved to be highly effective and with a minimum of ill effects. These years required a great deal of skilled diplomacy to negotiate our rights for some territorial integrity in various lands under the status of "social genome experimental areas" and to build up our institutions and infrastructure, including the military deterrence systems just under their noses. We knew so much about the *Homo sapiens* state, and times were so hard that it was rather easy to corrupt their resolve and decency in those days. We did all this, and I was proud of this achievement, even though we came to accomplish certain things by some obscure means.

CHAPTER 16

Slowly, the political conditions became favorable for our project. The decline of the West was already apparent. The rise of China and India was accompanied by lot of political tension, skirmishes, and growing global chaos, which we exploited to the maximum. As the tension in the world rose because of adverse climate change, shortages in drinking water, cheap oil, and essential metals used to keep up a modern society, lots of conflicts flared up, confirming our conviction that Homo stupidligence were on a spree of self-destruction. In this period, when many countries looked for strong alliances and a safe food supply, we could buy or lease areas for settlements, which were less favorable. From 2040, we gathered in operational groups, which had different goals, like recruiting wealthy people who would finance our projects, recruiting the elite of medical scientists, and buying the best-equipped laboratories for them. We even got into our ranks space and rocket scientists and experts in the production of weapons. They built, in the '50s, the weapon factories underneath our settlements and devised some of our best deterrent devices in these years. We came to command some very advanced technologies in the fields of robotics, nanotechnology, cyber warfare, bots warfare and high explosives and bought often, through straw men, the brand-new technologies. We had friends among the powerful nations who supported our experiment and were promised "a ticket" if the earth started burning under their feet.

In the period of 2035–2045, we bought some more areas around the mother colonies, thereby extending them. In 2045, we numbered some eight million creators but with a center connecting them all into a well-functioning web. As the political conditions in the world worsened, the big powers were preoccupied by holding one another in check and were therefore reluctant to intervene in their neighbors' affairs unless their interests were threatened. We became the "darlings" of certain regimes, keen to see where this "social genetic experiment" could lead, and thereby we slowly gained rights for self-determination and autonomy. These agreements were confidential and signed with governments, which benefited by these relations. They were also keen on seeing how we could develop, away from warmongering, imperial dreams and develop good neighborhood relations.

In these years, while building our force, we projected a meek political line. In 2040, all twelve colonies and six settlements had achieved a vibrant and strong economy with a well-functioning, prudent financial policy. The colonies became self-sufficient and could survive for a long time on their own except when they had to defend their territorial integrity, which we resolved by building up a mobile task force in each of them and a centralized offensive force, which could be sent into action on short notice.

There were also the silent heroes among us, the "missionary" units, whose main operations were to motivate, squeeze, and coerce rich men and corporations in the old world to help finance our projects. We were not interested in bloodshed or in getting involved in conflicts, although I gave permission to silence some "long tongues" who brought our vital interests into danger. We had also built a police force whose main goals were fighting criminality in the colonies and hunting down illegal immigrants. As we had very little of both compared with the old world, they used much of their time to educate the citizens in our colonies in the art of good citizenship. Of course, we ran into some difficulties and were even exposed to some attempts to invade us and assassinate our leaders, including me. I preached for restraint because, as I stated, while getting stronger, we had to play meek. I believed, too, in a Samson who was strong without unnecessarily threatening or intimidating his neighbors. My view of not projecting too much of our growing might was not shared by the evolver.

When I figured out that some atrocities in the old world were committed and financed by some covert agencies linked to us, I decided to start an investigation, which pointed toward Akram and his officers. I intended to stop him, but then the evolver intervened and told me that Akram's actions were in accordance with the grand plan, and I should let Akram do what he was good at. He told me to work on the political and ideational lines.

"You served your role as the creator and leader of this new movement.

Now it is time for others to readjust your vision in this world of mud," he said.

"Why should the bloodshed of the past repeat itself?" I asked him.

"It is because it is a tool which must be used as long as you are in this stage of your creation. Once you come to the stage of mastery, without mortal threat for your existence, the rules will change."

"What will happen afterward, when our glorious generals leave behind them floods of blood?"

"None of your concern," he said bluntly. "Stick to what your domain is, and do not recreate past problems!"

"Did I hear you right?" I mumbled. "Are you a kind of demigod, trying to start it all over again and use me as an instrument to avoid certain problems?"

"I am the evolver, and I have no last say unless the two others, Moria and you, will move in my direction, and for this to happen, the fourth force has to accommodate, complement, and oppose all three . . ."

"Is the erection of the evolving Bustan dependent also on the fourth force?—"

"Yes. It is. Without the fourth force which can relate to us three in an accommodating, complementing, and opposing manner all at the same time."

"I do not understand a bit of what you are talking about!"

"Do you remember the last ultimate hymn?"

"Yes, and I still do not understand what this last ultimate hymn is all about," I said. The evolver looked at me.

"The last ultimate hymn is to be found there on the fringes of chaos and farsighted creativity . . . in this very spot, where chaos, annihilation, and creation collide, the Bustan will come to life and further evolve. There, if you balance well, the Bustan will become the hymn. There will intelligence life transcend, no more *Homo sapiens*, only ever evolving creators," he said.

I was dumbfounded. "How is it supposed to happen?" I stammered.

"In due time, you will know it, Abraham!"

"So what am I supposed to do from now on?"

"I have encouraged you to become a moral prophet and a pathfinder who knows the difficulties of the way ahead and how to motivate your people to follow."

"So I failed?"

"Not a bit," he said, giggling. "You have done it, but you are not supposed to go into the Promised Land and fight the dirty war, which is necessary in order to win the war!" I fell silent.

"So my time has run out," I whispered.

"Not yet! You can watch from the sideline the military campaign and tower up as the moral authority as to heal frictions and divisions."

His words made me thoughtful. He truly followed the story of Exodus but at the same time wanted me to oppose him. In true hero fashion, old Joshua defeated all enemies because of his superior personal cunning and valor. The Canaanites, though formidable enemies with their war chariots and walled cities, were not a united group of loosely federated city-states, each ruled by a petty king. As the Canaanite resistance died, the first rough boundaries of what eventually became Israel were formed. Our Akram created the backbone of the armed forces; equipped it with the best arms, both stolen and purchased; and developed the stratagem of "one hand with the olive branch while the other hand undermines the order of the alien, greedy civilization." It was not a dirty war because it was not a real war, but it was a dirty stratagem to create sustainable and connected territories for our growing populations. I was assigned the role of holding our people together with my moral authority and leadership while Akram fought for achieving the military supremacy, which would open up our spiritual supremacy as creators. It was a clever plan, but too much bloodshed could confound our direction.

CHAPTER 17

I once had a remarkable moment of revelation in the desert. It was Arif, the pathfinder, Akram's father, who had presented it to me, but I could not comprehend its significance at the time. We were in his camp, and night had fallen on the desert when we took a walk toward a hidden place, where sweet water sprang out of the cliff. He wanted to show me where water came a long way from the mountains, to tell the insightful truth about the course of the grand journey. We sat in the darkness and watched silently. All of a sudden, I could see a chain of people appearing in the dark. The one in the front held a blazing torch in his hand and then passed it to the next one behind him, and so did the next until they disappeared in the night shade.

"What was this?" I asked.

"So you saw it!" said Arif.

"The water told you . . ."

"What did the water tell me?" I asked, intrigued by the scene and by his cryptically worded sentence.

"You saw the grand journey of intelligent life. You saw them pass on the torch when they died. The torch you saw was the Barakah (blessing), and those who see it are blessed by it."

I thought at that time, *Fine. I am lucky and hopefully will keep being a lucky fellow.* But as I learned later on, this Barakah was meant to encourage me to attain knowledge on a much greater scale than my own life. This was something I learned after the evolver came back. And I could see the way of this awesome journey, and I knew that my mind children would inherit the earth and space, yes, space too, and they would reign for a long time until the day they could not pursue their mission any longer. My mind children would become the seekers and voyagers of space, and their reign would last long after the gruesome crunch, which would destroy mankind. After coming to terms with my Barakah, I also learned to avoid my own vanity for fame and status, which was such a relief once achieved because I knew by then that I was really free from my old bonds to human folly.

CHAPTER 18

After the short yet brutal nuclear war in the old world in 2045, which resulted in more than a hundred million casualties within one week, lots of disease outbreaks took place in the old world, and countless sick people came wandering to our no-man zone, where we had established a permanent makeshift hospital. I was asked by high-ranking officials from the central government to lead this humanitarian project. Not surprisingly, I was accused by some military folk for lack of political consequence in relation to HS. I defended my view, referring to the magnitude of the disaster and to the fact that helping them did not compromise our project. In less than a day, the massive nuclear devastations had plunged millions of people from the twenty-first century back to the Middle Ages in the Middle East alone. The large number of huge weapons detonating simultaneously at first blew immense quantities of dust into the air and then created draughts that drew it upward, where it mingled with particles created in the fission phase of the explosions. They knew absolutely nothing of what was happening beyond the borders of their own towns. So they went toward the sources of communication, which were the cities. But most big cities were in flames.

The city survivors, on the other hand, were streaming into the countryside and toward our borders. There were large numbers of people with hearing loss due to blast pressure. Others suffered not only from burns but also of toxic reactions to "synthetic"-fibred clothing that had melted into their skin. Radiation sickness was virtually an epidemic and was followed shortly by all the diseases we have come to associate with large groups of undernourished, debilitated people. Our military spy flights over their territories indicated extensive damage in many areas in the Middle East, South Asia, and North America and in some parts of Europe, where the populations were in a state of confusion or upheaval, and the local authorities were not able to cope with the pressure of feeding so many people who had lost their homes. There was a massive migration from these areas all throughout the summer—more than three million individuals banged on our ports, virtually all of them starving. Many of these people who arrived at the no-zone suffered of starvation and radiation sickness, and others were infected by cholera and corona infections, and they could spread it to our population. We encouraged the relocation of individuals out of the uninhabitable zones and had to leave those who refused to move to their destiny. Most of the children who were brought to our clinics suffered brain damage from radiation or other poisoning and infections. We found numerous cases of mental breakdown. Paranoia, schizophrenia, and mental withdrawal were all present in this population. We were not able to treat the mentally ill who were unable to function. They were left to their families. Many chose to end up their lives by using the cyanide capsules, which we made available. We faced countless cases of radiation sickness. These individuals were usually covered with sores from secondary infections and were in great agony. We had a large number of burn sore cases, scarred to the point of crippling: refugees from firestorm, some of them profoundly crippled.

Upon being told of the hopelessness of their situation, most of them accepted a painless and dignified death. Our doctors and nurses spent days living out tragedies with the victims, and then at night, in dreams of indescribable horror, they heard the agonized people calling from their graves. Among the problems with which we could not cope were the various parasitic diseases and killer virus pandemics. We simply failed to anticipate their presence in the no-man zone. Hookworm, tapeworm, giardiasis, and a new mutated corona virus were the most serious of these. These diseases were, in adults, unattractive and debilitating, but in children, they were devastating. We instructed them on the use of saline enemas as a means of temporarily reducing the infestation, especially in the cases of hookworm and tapeworm. But the only real relief, namely, proper medication and a good, clean source of food and water, simply was not available on this scope at the time.

We realized that parts of the old world were dying in front of our eyes. There were only twenty babies under the age of six months in our camps. Some had been blinded, and the others were suffering from a severe systemic infection. We were burying, each day in the first four weeks of this crisis, five or six hundred people a day, generally in shallow graves in fields in the old world. The local priests, imams, and rabies officiated at the brief ceremonies. Our most overwhelming wish was to get great loads of food and clothing and, above all, medicines for these people. But it was but wishful thinking. We offered, though, to send what supplies we could muster to them if they went back home, but we couldn't provide much. The situation was stark. If they stayed, all these people were going to die. We certainly met with some hostility while doing our duty. Our personnel had to make decisions that shortened life. When they isolated populations to prevent the spread of disease and sometimes even withdrew medical assistance to allocate it to areas where help would still matter, it was hard, but there, they also fully understood the obligations that followed by becoming creators.

On the other hand, we had been able to help countless people. I was a part of the committee that decided to allocate sufficient social resources to these people so as to prevent them from dying of starvation or neglect and to house them in makeshift public facilities. We did make decisions in favor of life whenever we could.

CHAPTER 19

I was back to where my life had started. This land between the River Jordan and the Mediterranean Sea generated great sunsets as it had done once with sunrises. The other day, the sky turned from deep blue to pink, and then orange and flaming red before the sun, a glowing red ball, descended into the sea. The fading light glowed on the roofs of our expanding settlement, which looked like little fortresses along the area between the sea around Ashkelon and where my kibbutz had once existed. We were the masters of this piece of land and deep into the Negev desert and Sinai. The political entities in this region have either withdrawn from this area or were too weak to control it after the devastating wars, which had taken place in this region and in the Persian Gulf.

No superpower had been able to deliver peace to this region after the war of annihilation in 2045. How sad and prophetic it was because it was here I had been granted my first troubling insight on *Homo sapiens'* propensity to destroy himself, no matter the price. It was also here where I had come to dub this species as Homo stupidligence. In the Middle East and in the Persian Gulf, where the strength of a leader had been measured in an old-fashioned way, human vanity came to destroy them. Now we were here, projecting a military might to reckon with. And they who survived were all scared of us. The landscape has changed, though, since I was child here. Many areas have become almost uninhabited and arid due to climate changes, chemical poisoning, radiation, and political disintegration after the Big War, the war that wiped out most of old Iran, Syria, and Lebanon, with extensive damage to the other regional countries, including Israel.

Because of this political vacuum and chaos, we could lease certain areas up for ninety-nine years. We have adopted some surviving groups as a part of our worldwide program to "re-socialize *Homo sapiens*." That was the name of the program, and since it was financed solely by us, the very weak governments in these areas considered it a kind of humanitarian help. But in fact, we worked here on reprogramming *Homo sapiens* to become more decent guests on this planet and to follow our example. This "reforming them to follow our ways" was our second most prestigious project as creators. I became the leader of this project because of my psychological background and experience. We worked with isolated groups of up to one hundred people, and I can say so far that being creators for them is the most rewarding and exhilarating task I have ever engaged in.

The preliminary results of changing the stubborn characteristics of *Homo sapiens* have been published in science for HR last year, with my pseudonym. When I tried to recall those vile abominations of that barbarous life in the old world around us in the past years, I found myself asking the question "Is it worthwhile recording them?" And with ever stronger conviction, I found the answer was affirmative because that was the real loathsome truth about the shameful life of HS in the first half of the century, and we had to remember it so it would never repeat itself. I had seen unimaginable suffering, both spiritual and physical. I had seen the bestial, animal-like existence of countless *Homo sapiens* begging in the streets, taking their pickings from refuse heaps. I had seen the rampage caused by criminal bands as the social order collapsed in their societies and the eruption of the beast in them. All these terrifying scenes should be a stark warning for us.

Young scientists from our largest colony came to visit me once in a while and always found some good reasons to interview me. In fact, they downloaded me. They took stem cells and other DNA samples from me. They asked me about every aspect of importance in my life before and after my mental mutation and videotaped me. They asked about my childhood, my parents, my kibbutz, the Bustan, meeting with the Green Mand and Moria, and the revelation of the last ultimate hymn, and they probed me about my feelings for my family, Smadar, Gili, Arif, and even Akram, who became our general—all dead by now. I answered them willingly. They asked me how I had come to invent the new paradigm, the covenant of the creators. They registered my brainwaves and measured my body and skull and my mental agility. I was sure these scientists had been given an order to recreate me as a cyborg of some kind once I was gone.

But when they asked me about my wife, my daughter, and my youngest son, I retreated into myself, and they apologized. I knew I had not acted like Judas, but I felt like this whenever they talked about my wife and my children. They measured me day and night, and at last, I asked them, "What for?" The other day, they told me that they were on the verge of a technological breakthrough in which they would make me into the first ultimate cyborg, in mind, spirit, and body, of the new civilization. So I was right! Was I supposed to be content with this practical arrangement, with this cult of my person, my retouched personage, which was supposed to serve as a model for all their youth and children hundreds years from now? Was I content? Maybe a bit, when my human vanity gained the upper hand, but only for a while because most of the time, I thought about my family members whom I deserted when I had decided to branch off from humanity. And I cried sometimes and waited eagerly for the moment when I would be freed of this unbearable burden.

CHAPTER 20

I really do not know whether the guards securing my safety in this barren, arid, and obscure region are also my prison guards. I tend to think so, but we do not talk about such things, only about news coming from the old territories and from our colonies. We have much to celebrate as the colonies become slowly more powerful and influential in the affairs of this bruised world, and six of the big colonies have merged together in Asia to create a new territorial integrity, which would become the heartland state of the creators. There is no bitterness in my mind against those who continue my work in this muddy world. They do it with the utmost conviction, diplomatic and military skills, and deception, morality, brutality, and flattery, all these things I had taught them to prevail.

I am soon to become 104 years old. I keep writing every morning, although my heart is tired of all that I had to live through, and at twilight, when the sun descends over the desert and casts its multitudes of colors, my heart aches and my soul sobs when my dear ones come to see me. Soon, they are rising in the darkening sky as the stars they have become, and I watch them all, and we talk sometimes, and they tell me that they will be with me once I am gone, and I believe them. Some humane part in me is still throbbing in my heart. And I cry and try to persuade my stubborn mind that they are in me, all these voices, including the three with whom I fused to start this evolution. I am not happy but not unhappy either in my loneliness. I have been away for almost thirty years from human beings, and from this distance of time, although their destiny pains me, I know for sure that being so vain and shortsighted as they had been for such a long time, I had no choice. I had to do it. I know that in their dying world, they must put the blame for their demise on somebody else but themselves as they always have been doing.

But I also remember fondly my childhood among them, my life as an adolescent in my kibbutz, the most dedicated friends in the wars we were thrown into, meeting my wife, watching my children grow up, and having so many rich and kind contacts with the people of this cursed race. And all this time, the knowledge that was planted in me grew slowly so as to reach a painful fruition as the world of humans became self-destructive and destroyed my trust in their wisdom. I had wished my innocence could keep my eyes closed, but instead, my life brought me to this human Babylon, where they all talked different languages until their tower of civilization collapsed. Sometimes I feel that I am evil because I could have helped some of them, when the crunch hit them for the first time. I could have given them some shelter and bread, some solace, but I did not do it because they were doomed, and I had to be resolute and hard.

I did not write all this, my children, to get sympathy or justification but to convey to you the understanding that although we are a new emerging species, they still live partly in us, and there is no reason to keep denying it. They had some qualities I am proud to bear in me. Even this vanity, which has driven them to their end, has driven me. I wanted to make a difference, to change the tide of history, to become immortal, sacrificing my life to this mission, and without some vanity, I would not have survived my trials. So remember, my mind children, that they had brought the torch of intelligent life as far as they could, and we must pay attribute to their endeavors, although they were not wise enough to keep on track. I, Abraham, who started my life as a human being and have lived much of my life as a human being, with human tears and cheer, with human sorrow and fear, with evil and goodness, with justice and injustice, with weakness and strength, will soon depart from this world as a transcendent as the first one to transcend the oblivion of the world of humans. I have shown the way to the stars; I have shown them the outlines for our grand journey, so I am not afraid of anything, least of all, death, because I have transcended their world, and if at the end of this way, my dear ones await me, I will feel truly happy.

CHAPTER 21

How sad is the world at twilight and how mysterious the mists over the arid soil. You will know it when you have wandered in those mists, when you have suffered greatly before leaving it, when you have walked through the world carrying my burden. You will know it, too, when you are weary and ready to leave this earth without regret, ready to give yourself into the arms of the last fusion, knowing that you have created forever the fluid, mutable permanence for intelligent life by fusing with the three. There is a secret that had burdened me for quite some time, and I kept it away even from my cherished family and friends, so terrible and awesome it was. I have been bearing it with me, and it slowly sapped my energy. But now that I can see the end of my mission and calling on this destitute planet, and I clearly see the ultimate meaning of the strange and unexplainable things that happened to me throughout my life, the time has come to tell this very secret, which is what had made me into what I had become. Right now, when you read this document, you will not understand what this secret is all about, but later on, if you think of the realm that opened up for me, you may know it, and it will become you too.

A disturbing event keeps popping up in my mind on these walks. I experience it as vividly as if it were yesterday, but more than thirty-five years have passed by since it took place. I was on my way to the new colonies. I failed to convince my wife and my children and their children to follow me. And I was broken.

My wife and my two sons, with their families, refused to move away on the grounds that it was enough with one person in the family who had turned his back on humanity in its worst trial. So came the day when we had our last talk, which became imprinted in my memory. Stepping out of the car, leaving my wife crying in the back, I felt I was entering the world of shadows where nothing was clear or defined any longer. "That is a pretty thing to do," she said in a toneless voice, "to leave us after these many years…" "Stop it!" I said. "Of course you have planned it for quite a long time," she said.

"Stop it!" I said. "Don't worry," she said. "We will manage while you split up humanity." "Listen," I said. "We show a new way, and you can be a part of it!" "What is your new way? Your monstrous global vision, whose strength is its focus on the long-term well-being of all of humanity, when you actually create sub-groups among us, which will develop or decay in different tempi? Here we have the comfort of knowing what we have, which most people prefer than following you to an uncertain experiment." "You have twisted my intentions. What you just named is the human condition that has become the main problem. I had realized that humanity was not capable moving into a sustainable and evolving direction in the same pace because it was infected by the Babel-tower mortal disease; they talk different languages and insist on their short sighted interests. Your many tongues are not compatible. From this recognition, I had developed the strategy of different paces for different groups where we try to be the torch or model to follow if you wish…" "Regardless the price, that countless lives will perish in this process?" "They will perish anyway due to humans' own folly and short sight. We just show a way out of the madhouse of self-destructive, collective behavior." "Is this what you meant by 'leaving a mark behind?' Letting people die and building your own little alternative world?" "I follow the track which was granted me," I said stubbornly. "I follow the script of intelligent life!" "What is this script that you are the only one to see?" she cried. "I am not the only one to see. There are many like me although they differ in creed and gender. When Adam had tasted the fruits of knowledge, God asked him: Where are you Adam?' Of course, God knew where Adam hid, and therefore the meaning of the question was Adam, now that you know who you are and your world as well, are you going to shoulder your responsibilities toward your world?'

"Man is the creator of all things and all ideas and can accomplish miracles. Nevertheless, man shows himself to be bedeviled by his opposites, torn by fears of failures, and too prone to self-deception, and I cannot help them all. We too face a mortal danger, but we fight to make the difference for the forthcoming generations, and you can be a part of it!" I tried to caress her, but she shoved my hand off. "There's a lot which could be done without splitting up families and humanity," she sobbed. "Why didn't you poison me instead?" "Stop it. Stop it. Stop it!" I said. She looked at me, with her fine blue eyes full of tears. "I'm through now," she cried. "I just wish I could believe in our and your sacrifice...and now, I'll stop."

My wife helped me pack my things, and her face was ashen. We had spent many years together, ever since she was twenty. She looked at me with these tear-swollen eyes as if she mourned me, and I knew what was on her mind: Why do you not feel responsibility to your own family and leave them behind to pursue this inhuman course? She looked at me as if she did not recognize me any longer. She looked at me for quite a long time, pleading and trying to find the man she once had known, and then she started sobbing, covering her face with her hands, and I tried to comfort her, but she got up to her feet, stumbling out of the café where we had met for the last time. And there I stood, watching her disappear, for the last time, out of my life.

Sometimes in the long evenings, we sing as we did in my youth in my kibbutz. And this is how we begin to sing: one of us will sigh deeply in the midst of our daily chores, and then we will begin one of those songs whose gentle melody seems always to ease the burden on our hearts, the burden of them who had to leave the home of mankind. At first, one sings to himself, and we others sit in silence, listening to his solitary song on a dry, smoldering night, when the gray heaven hangs like a leaden roof over the earth. Then another will join in with the singer, and sad voices will break into song on the porch of my house, not so far from the sea. My bodyguards will join in, and the song will surge up like a wave, will swell upward, until it would seem as though our constricted hearts were widening out and opening. Then all of us will be singing our loud harmonious songs, which I have taught them. Our songs will wander beyond the houses and the camp's parameter and the seashore, in moaning, moving our hearts with a soft, tantalizing ache; tearing open in me old wounds; and awakening these bittersweet longings. And sometimes I see a dusty road in front of me—a sunlit, broad road in the distance, which I, in my mind, wander toward. And I wink in my heart to my faithful tunnel of light, which has guided me all these many years and has given me determination and courage to accomplish my mission and to suffer as only a human being can. I hope that the new generations of creators will not know what some of us have been through. We sing out our grief, the grief of prevailing and of giving intelligent life a new start, of weary hearts of warriors who have borne the burden of the heartache of the new creators.

Sometimes I sing to myself a song from my childhood, a song from a time long forgotten, when I was still a human and had a loving family. It is a sorrowful song, but I allow myself to sing it now and then, after I have accomplished my mission. It was written by the poet Rachel and sounds like this:

> *Listen to my voice, faraway friend! I am calling you as I reach the end! My sorrowful voice cries in the deep stillness, as lonely child who silently weeps. Yet beyond our lifetime's veil, blessings it grants and yields.*
>
> *The world is immense, with its multitude ways. For a moment, we meet then forever sway away. Like a longing man, with his bursting heart, I looked after you in vain, you— my missing part . . .*
>
> *My last day is closing near. Yet it is a day without tears. For I will wait for you until my life has gone as Rachel had waited for her only one . . .*

But we have something else besides the singing, something I love that brings some sunshine into my vanishing life. In the second story of my house live two of my great-grandchildren, Serene, who is sixteen years old, and Laura, who is twenty years old. Every morning, they peep in through the glass door with their rosy, sweet faces, with merry blue eyes while a ringing, tender voice calls out to me, "Good morning, Great-Grand!" This is how they have nicknamed me. And I gaze at these two lovely girls who decided, on their own, to leave the old territories and to stay with me as long as they wished. Their families approved of it, and now and then, some members of my scattered family in the old world get a permit and come to visit me in my exile. I turn around and gaze at these two good-natured girls, with their joy and pure girlish faces that smile at me so sweetly. The sight of their noses pressed against the windowpane and of the small white teeth gleaming between the half-open lips has become for me a daily pleasure. I rise from my chair and limp toward the door to open it, and they step in, bright and cheerful, holding out their hands in a ballet motion, with their heads bent to one side and a smile on their lips. And I, ugly and misshapen by age, feel as though my heart becomes warmer. And it does because regardless of our tribulations, the youth from the old world seem to accept us as the extended family of evolving intelligence, not as traitors but as saviors. Sometimes tears fill my eyes when they enter my room.

"Why do you cry, Great-Grand?" they ask, hugging me.

"Because I am so happy at last . . ."

CHAPTER 22

Rain is falling. Actually, it is tumbling down, columns, stripes of rain moving over the arid soil to the camp, and nothing can be seen through the wet veil. I almost forgot when it last rained so generously in this area. Thunder and other noises rumble outside my window; the camp has grown silent, it shudders, the rain and the wind push it about, and it seems as though my house glides on a soapy surface and rolls down the slope toward the sea, its roaring waves splashing on the shore. And as for me, I feel a premonition of some kind as if somebody is awaiting me. It's growing dark. What more shall I write about? Two men or more have lived inside me. But how could they, one being *Homo sapiens* and the other a creator? That is all that I can tell. Perhaps it is not so. Whatever it is, it is too late to regret. Done is done, and anyhow, I was one of just a few others who had fought to grant a new chance to intelligent life.

This is how I hope they would remember my legacy, and it is too dark to write now. Now that I am frail and unoccupied, I often daydream about the two horsemen—the Evolver and Moria—who will appear one day when twilight has fallen on the small sand dunes surrounding my hiding. I will see them coming, but the commando units and the combat force that keep the place safe against intrusions and attacks will sense nothing. I will be going toward these two horsemen. I will walk toward them, unassisted, and they will embrace me, and the whirling ring of extreme beautiful fire will roll over the skyline slowly until it ebbs out. Once it disappears, I will be gone, leaving no trace, just some burning signs on the sand.

CHAPTER 23

I haven't slept the whole night. The air is stifling. After the rain, the sun has scorched the earth so severely that a moist heat, as from a steam bath, poured through the window of my bedroom. In the sky, some clouds were floating. They reminded me of all the people I have loved and missed. They kept walking up in the sky in a long procession, and my lips moved silently, blessing them, while my mind rejected the scene. All through the night, I kept looking back at my life. What else is there for me to do? It is like peering into a chink, and behind the chink is a mirror in which my past is congealed, reflected. Maybe it is time I should let it come and take me away.

Book 2

Beyond Sapiens' Wisdom,
Ultimate Meaning,
and Fixed Destiny

CONTENTS

INTRODUCTION

My head is filled up with mental pollution.
Religion feeds it with delusions,
Politics—with stupidity and illusions
and modern life—with confusion.
  —BK, 2019When to our upgrading you say `yes`,
      our further evolvement you bless

and global sustainability-you grace,
you accept my vision` essence!

—BK, 2020

This book describes and argues why we have to escape our mental slavery by upgrading ourselves to become wise creators who keep on creating ever-evolving realities while avoiding self-destruction and destruction so characteristic for *Homo sapiens*.

We know for sure that humans as well as animals live as far from being just, fair, and merciful seen from humanistic perspectives. I have seen and witnessed overwhelming bloody indifference and cruelty in this world as to believe in the reign of benevolent God on earth (some people believe, though, in different, less proactive gods). I don't believe either that we, potential megalomaniacs, have created the best world of all worlds. Look at the global mess a virulent virus like corona had caused to our civilization in 2020 and think why it has spread like bonfire.

This virus has taught us some grave lessons on our "best of all worlds" and lifestyle: that we have become an invasive species, a vermin; that we live too densely and often under terrible conditions; that we travel around in total crazy manner spreading diseases; that we have become obese (they die over proportionally of the corona); and that we don't live sustainably and healthy lives.

Are we going to learn of these lessons? I don't think so. Only much harsher beatings in the future and badly needed upgrading of us (or some of us)—to gain far sight and reduce the greedy urge for self-interest—will teach us this lesson. A few have had this realization but, for most, will return to a frantic pace of activity, overconsumption, and crazy mobility in the usual style; business as usual, is invetibale as they are hooked on this lifestyle.

Yet people losing their aspirations to change a dysfunctioning human world and themselves to the better make their lives and humanity future existence both miserable nad redundant.

The reality of the human world when I write these lines (2020) is that we constructed and maintain a very complex, fragile, unsustainable, and self-destructive civilization, which a lethal virus—corona—by its global spreading brought to halt. It hit us in our Achilles' heel—overpopulation, dense concentrations of people in mega cities often in slums, overproduction, overconsumption of everything including meat(which makes the spread of virus from huge animal farms to humans very likely), massive pollution, and crazy-frenzy worldwide mobility (which makes it possible for pathogens to spread very quickly). Corona is just the first "script on the wall," and in the future, the likelihood of much more virulent viruses and cataclysms hitting our bloated, vulnerable humanity is huge.

In this book, I describe why we must change the name of our civilization/species' game (including new rules and new participants) and how by following a new, sustainable and evolving paradigm/ vision, we will develop a much wiser, farsighted, and evolving civilization than ours.

In this book, I don't only challenge all the three major cornerstones regarding our life like; *what is wisdom, what is our ultimate meaning with life, and what should be our destiny*, but I also place them in new contexts with new ideas, which are meant to save ourselves from our self-destructive tendencies.

My vision is based on the following facts:

1) Life is basically harsh and unjust (which raises the question of the relevance of a benevolent God). Lots of innocent children, youngsters, grown-ups, and animals never get a chance to grow up to maturity or get a chance for decent life because they are being killed, maimed, or become severely or chronically sick. This is life on earth. If there is a God involved directly in the affairs of humans (as most religious people believe), he can't do much to reduce our terrible sufferings. I was working with people, both as psychologist and in other contexts, for more than forty years and can tell you that the minds of many people are flawed, pained, and sick in many respects. Just look at the little country where I live, with around 5.6 million people. There are 50,000 suffering of dementia, 300,000 of drug and alcohol abuse, 40,000 of schizophrenia, 200,000 of depression, 250,000 of anxiety, 100,000 of compulsion problems, 100,000 of eating problems, and 100,000 of borderline problems, not to talk about the sociopaths, autistics, and other people hit by problems that diminish their mental capacity as Parkinson's and sclerosis. And there are a lot of dumb people too, being born so. If this is the design of God, this God is far from being a good engineer.

Such God can at the best be a source of comfort and (false) hope for the many.

2) *Homo sapiens* are fundamentally advanced social animals for good and bad. We contain noble and generous sides but also sinister and vicious sides because of the fact that we are evolved animals on a low level of development and awareness, equipped with old-fashioned brains. Many people contest these limitations of our brains by claiming that it is not a matter of brain power but that we lack right guidance in using it. Philosophical schools and religions have tried to put guidelines but so far in vain regarding altering the populace behavior.

3) Making false impression—pretending—is a human specialty. In the academic world, for example, most of the published papers are written for this sole purpose, which is, namely, deception to get funds and grants. Human beings behave also often as herd followers who follow leaders with the capacity to play on their emotions/impulses. Here, too, deception plays a major role.

4) Most sapiens suffer of three inherent "S" defects that make our future bleak—short sight, self-interest, and self-deception. Short sight, greed (self-interest), *Mundus vult decipi* (self-deception), unchallenged collective convictions, and faith undermine the perceptions of what are facts and what should be considered as farsighted wisdom.

5) In the human world, everything is temporary, including our religions, values, and ourselves as species, a fact that most humans are inclined to ignore.

6) Sapiens is but a unit in the potential evolving process of advanced intelligent life, not the crown or the glorious end of it.

7) The potential ultimate meaning with our existence is to further evolve as to become masters of our lives and death and expand to far away environments in the universe and to steer this process of our further evolution.

You may by now get a notion why in this book,I describe sapiens' mental shortcomings, which endanger our future survival, while suggesting how to develop alternative, greater and deeper wisdom, consciousness/awareness, and ultimate meaning in our descendants as to eliminate these shortcomings.

Why did I feel compelled to undertake such immense task as writing a vision for future advanced human beings? Am I a megalomaniac?

No. I am not megalomaniac at all. It was as simple as this: the task was there and had to be addressed immediately, so I decided to take up this challenge and devise a viable future vision for our further evolvement. Shouldering such a taks has much to do with my background and life story.

Growing up on a kibbutz, which had been established six years before my birthday, and living in Israel, which was established two years after my birth, I was exposed simultaneously for two great and historical visions and missions in operation, where both were historically extraordinary and with almost all odds against them. The destiny of me, my family and my people (Jews), changed dramatically because of these two forces unleashed by fervent, almost zealous Jews enacting on the human history arena in the right time and right place. So I grew up in a reality with both great visions and missions, where the self-sacrificing efforts exerted by lots of people, who could not see another solution to their existential threats, were their driving force.

After fighting two wars in the armed forces of Israel, I moved to Denmark and got a family and established a fine professional career. Life in Denmark demanded knowledge of language, adjustment to pacifistic mentality, so for years, the fighting, visionary parts in my mind were dozing because of these demands of adaptation.

At around 1988, I realized that we, *Homo sapiens*, were in big shit regarding our global, environmental conduct, and by 2000, I drew a painful, almost unbearable for me, conclusion that sapiens as a species were not wise enough as to take care of our planet in the future.

Now when I write these lines, it is obvious that we manage it catastrophically, if not suicidal. In 2020, when I write these lines, democracies all around the world are on the ropes, and the value of human life is being degraded quickly. The global politics seems to go nuts.

What I see now is the wearisome ennui of doing the same over and over and covering over our shortcomings and faults by endless pep talk.

All of a sudden, there was a great cause, leading to a creation of a new vision and dedicated mission. My visionary/warrior being was brought back into the struggle against the new tyranny of our time, our excesses (overconsumption, overproduction, overpopulation, and massive pollution).

My struggle for liberty from this tyranny demanded transcending our minds' debilitating constraints.

Right now, 2020, we experience hard times because of the pandemics of corona and economic crisis, yet this hard time becomes also ripe for a great vision/mission aimed at transforming and upgrading ourselves as a wiser global civilization. So let it be light!

CHAPTER 1

Human Nature/Nurture

A) Humans' positive virtues and limitations
B) Humans' compulsions, delusions, free will, and God

A) Humans' positive virtues and limitations

There are three not always distinct rather solid mind-sets abound in the human world:

1) Realistic: hopeful, expecting, and proactive as to realize both reality and the human state as they are and to improve them to the better
2) Illusion prone: excessively and unrealistically hopeful, daydreaming, and wishful thinking prone without any viable strategy or purposeful actions
3) Delusional: where contact with reality and what it can bear is broken/nonexistent

I wrote once to a friend of mine about the difference between seeing reality through different glasses and seeing it without glasses:

> *From my humble opinion, most people focus more on the glasses—their convictions—than on facts on the ground.*

239

You have an optimistic approach to us and life, which means that you believe that we can find solutions for all our self-created problems. This conviction stems basically from the instinctive hope inbuilt in most human brains/soul; Never lose hope regardless how absurd it is (The story on Pandora's box is a vivid illustration). You ignore the fact that all human civilizations had collapsed at some historical point, and as societies become more complex and ignore the need to take into account the limitations nature defines for all living beings, the closer it comes to its demise. Living in the wilderness in the future and growing food in the air or on water—without using soil—for a population of billions of people as a solution to future civilization is absurd and I think that on a further thought you will see the absurdity in breaking the limits of nature in the belief that we can keep exploiting it. As a thinking man, try to find out why you would rather watch reality through glasses—convictions and overblown hopes—than facts. Since I started writing my gloomy predictions for our future, they have—so far—come true. So maybe it's not because of glasses I predicted right, but rather because of the factual analysis of closed systems interactions that we're stupid to ignore because we wear omnipotent convictions' glasses.

Believe it or not, although most human beings claim to grasp reality as it is, most humans cannot discern among true facts, false facts, and speculative assertions.

It is a dangerous shortcoming as their judgment is at least partly built upon speculative foundation, and their actions are influenced by this twisted view of reality. Let me demonstrate this:

Is it true that we are all going to die, and many can reach old age, losing vitality in this process of aging? Yes! It is undeniably true!

Is it true there is life after our physical body is exterminated? This is a speculative and unproven claim!

Is it true that we are amid global crises caused by our excessive overproduction, overconsumption, pollution, and overpopulation? Yes, it is true!

Is it true that our current climate change is due to the sun pulsations? It is a false fact/speculative assertion.

Is it true that human life from our general/accepted humanistic point of view is unjust? It is true, for otherwise, why so many young innocent lives are being terminated cruelly? Life is, in fact, a pretty brutal affair.

Is it true that God in our human world is benevolent and almighty? It is a speculative assertion as it is obvious that God can't be almighty, allowing these terrible things to happen to us and other living things all the time.

When I grew up, I figured out this interrelation between constructs on the one hand and reality on the other hand and also how constructs can change reality. But still, I held that to keep up the basic functions of living going on, there was no need for constructs, and they could not replace the need for water, food, sleep, breathing, secreting, and keeping our body safe. These facts and others were to serve as the foundation to the human mind to avoid too much and dangerous distorting of reality. *Unrefuted facts were unnegotiable, while perceptions were negotiable.*

We were taught that the Jews who served as the founders of Israel and my kibbutz were mental giants. This was part of the ideological narrative but not facts. They had a chance to change history, and they rose to the challenge, still being faulty human beings. In the neighboring village, people and their children believed in God, while we believed in socialism.

Our different faiths were, of course, self-confirming and promoted in both groups a sense of identity through their religious and ideological narratives.

It took me time, though, to realize that humans' constructs of reality and human aspirations do shape reality to the point of self-destruction, as the Jews under Second World War practiced, waiting for God to save them from the Nazis or as our world practices right now, being unsustainable.

When you live in a world with finite resources, you can't live the way we currently live on earth with greedy and relentless consumption without destroying our life conditions on the same time. This self-destructive behavior is promoted by the narrative of liberal capitalism with proponents like Yuval Harari claiming in his book from 2015 that the near future would be free of hunger, epidemics, and wars, a stupid prediction due to his ideology blindness and lack of knowledge of human nature. When the defining narrative was based on prudence and impulse control before our time, moderate progress was achieved with less global self-destructive outcome as the underlying idea was partly sustainability.

What does cloud our brains/minds to such an extent as to make us turn against our long-term interest and survival chances or to judge our future prospects so stupidly as Harari did?

Is it the fact that we, being greedy, self-deceptive, and shortsighted, make it impossible to improve ourselves by means of education, socialization, and training? Yes, it is this fact!

We can control our whims to a certain degree in times of hardships and shortage, but abundance destroys it all as the narrative of cognitive capitalism has proven so vividly, giving free run for our greed and short sight.

As long as people has a vision/mission to fight for, they may keep these shortcomings under control, but if they don't, they surface us as the following saying expresses vividly: *the first generation establishes something new, the second builds up upon it, and the third destroys it by friction, indulgence, pettiness, and hatred.*

How does our attachment to people and ideas can impair our thinking and reality perception?

We start our emotional attachment by the process of imprinting, like many other animals. Imprinting is a rapid learning process by which a newborn or very young animal, inclusive human babies, establishes a behavior pattern of recognition and attraction toward other animals of its own kind as well as to specific individuals of its species, such as its parents, or to a substitute for these.

Then comes long nurturing, which implies model learning and socialization for most toddlers, and in this phase, most children internalize, without reflecting, systems of convictions and faith, including views of the world and beyond. Once the system is established, it is very unlikely that the person who internalized it will be able to erase it since it is attached to lots of memories, feelings, and experiences. This becomes both the base of one's identity and a faith system. Lots of people, if not all, are, in fact, bearers of such systems and can't get rid of them or defy them simply by their will power as their strong emotions/memories define for them who they are. The system of faith, bound together with the notion of one's identity, gives little place to revolt against it or to critical thinking aimed at it; thus, it fixates the mind of the bearer, distorts reality, and dumbs the person down since he cannot see clearly and think free and contextually.

Most people don't even know that our brain is a pretty fragile, gullible, and receptive organ in the forming years of childhood, and manipulators can form its reality in accordance with their convictions/illusions/goals.

This brain hallucinates, grasps reality as it suits it in accordance with its fear, anxieties, compulsions, values, and convictions.

It is, in fact, a mental slavery to seduce/force small children to think through premises of faith systems, convictions, and narratives supporting them.

Billions of children have been taught, like parrots, to follow a religious faith or other ideologies or self-made convictions without a shred of doubt and challenge to their validity. Children all around the world are exposed for this kind of enslavement of their minds, which undermines badly their reality sense. Some do break away from the spell of their childhood faith system, but most stay fixated.

There was a woman who had to attend a Greek Orthodox indoctrination as a child, and she didn't want her daughter subjected to the same formal religion. The priest had attempted to molest her. Trusting authority was no longer credible to her.

Great power is exerted over the vulnerable/children in all societies. The mystique of religion can cloak sinister motives. It can also inhibit natural curiosity, which can lead to mental stagnation as we often observe.

Our worst collective delusion is that we believe that our brain gives us a trustworthy picture of reality, while it often shows us what we expect/wish or taught, like parrots, to see. It is therefore reasonable to challenge our view of wisdom as such as it is partly based on hallucinations, compulsions, obsessions, and wishful thinking.

Our capacity of reasoning and self-reflection compared with other animals

Many *people* think that the main *differences between humans and* other *animal* species is our ability *of* complex reasoning, our use *of* complex language, our ability to solve difficult problems, and introspection. (This means describing your own thoughts and feelings.) But animals don't, as we know, do self-reflection, and if they come to multiply excessively, nature regulates this so they don't destroy their own life conditions on earth as we do. Are we wiser than them when we try to push nature's limits to a point of no return for us?

Self-reflection has being promoted as the most defining difference between humans and animals. It is the capacity to self-reflect. Although chimpanzees, our closest genetic relative, can be taught to do almost everything humans can, albeit at a more primitive level, they cannot self-reflect. They cannot take that mental leap of stepping outside themselves and studying themselves from an alternate perspective, even having a relationship with themselves—of dialoguing with their internal self that they are alive, that their heart is beating, that their life has purpose and meaning, that they will die someday, and, ultimately, that they can make creative, conscious changes in their internal and external environment based on what they learn on their life's journey. This is the realm of humanity—and perhaps of dolphins and whales too to a certain degree.

Yet most humans do so little self-reflecting, which results in changes in their attitudes and behavior. This includes many of the most intellectually sophisticated people. They work in complex jobs, have profound memories, learn numerous languages, but rarely stop to contemplate on their existence in any different way than their social groupthink dictates them. They live as highly intelligent animals—smart and functional in their pursuit of private goals—but not very wise socially or globally. This observation also applies to *Homo sapiens* a masse: as a species, we are certainly not very self-reflective—we are ruining our habitats and driving ourselves down mentally and physically and bring both intentionally and unintentionally a lot of animal and insects species to the point of extinction. Yes, there are global movements regarding all from climate issue to social injustice, etc., but they have not had any significant impact on the global, most burning problems as overpopulation, overconsumption, growth economy, and adverse climate change. In this way, we are the least wise animal, perhaps supremely self-destructive parasites.

Although as individuals many of us are created with the capacity to develop into beings who know in varying degrees ourselves and our minds intimately, this process seems to go astray for many people often because of groupthink's immense influence on people's minds.

Groupthink plays a great role both in collective violence and in practicing self-destruction

Groupthink describes a psychological phenomenon where peer pressure prevents critical thought. Eight symptoms characterize groupthink: (1) illusion of invincibility, (2) stereotypes ("us and them"), (3) rationalization ("We can always explain our failings and shortcomings."), (4) belief in moral superiority, (5) censoring thought, (6) illusion of unanimity, (7) pressure on deviants, and (8) fear of exclusion, keeping disruptive ideas out.

Groupthink makes it impossible for most people to reflect on themselves and their life and reality as it colors their view and hamper their critical and independent mind. Groupthink plays a dominating role in unresolved relational/national/social/religious/ideological conflicts and wars. It clouds our inward-looking lens and even crushes our self-reflective capacity entirely.

On the other hand, modern-styled individualism can bring about the opposite extreme of the debilitating thinking emerging from groupthink.

Many people may sense that the gift of too much self-reflection in their personal spheres can get out of control, topple their self-deception defense mechanism, and force them to wake up to all their existing pain—and to the ugly reality of how far they have strayed from their buried potential humanness (to think independently and critically), so they try to snuff it out.

Yet in some rare few souls, self-reflection is strong and is accompanied by reflection on the state of humanity and world affairs, also regarding the human potential capacity. These people, children even, refuse to give up that which is most special in them and nurture it despite all odds. As a result, they grow internally stronger and better able to see the naked truth about humans and reality as it is and how they can be reformed and they can come up with some enduring solutions for the dilemma of man, who wishes to do good without being destructive and self-destructive. I see these few as our future leaders and guides, who may help us evolve into a higher level of intelligent beings.

But the odds are not promising right now unless a dedicated long-termed vision/mission to promote this future potential will take over the old, obsolete ideologies. Who will win in this coming combat? The greedy, shortsighted, and self-deceptive and self-destructive sapiens or those who will help us branch away from sapiens' beastlike attribute and toward a much wiser and noble beings? We are split up between these two extreme poles with a slight weight right now toward the beastly endgame.

More on the human brain, our Trojan horse

Modern humans are slaves of not less than four gods—God, greed, self-deception, and short sight. As long as they don't rebel against them and weaken their influence on their minds, they will keep being what they are until their bitter end.

The human brain is basically lazy/conform/uncritical and convenience/comfort-oriented. Mental inertia hits it not just as the outcome of getting mentally lazy but also as the consequence of being uncurious and defocused.

Rejection of dire aspects regarding our reality is common for this brain. The human brain can encompass particulars, the construct of Gods, and even some strategic capacity, but it is blind for its own inbuilt limitations. It is not aware as to see its limitations.

The brain prefers quick satisfactions/fixes, even though they are self-damaging than waiting for the fruits of long-term efforts (think of the countless people destroying themselves because of their lack of control over their impulses and lusts).

Their brain is fixated on nurturing hopes, often groundless. 'In the land of hope, the sun shines always` is its unconscious motto.

Hope is the last thing that humans desert, which means that many of them react psychotic like, promoting delusional and infantile humans instead of responsible grown-ups.

Our hopes should have been bound to our long-term wise actions to realize them but are often bound to the magic/speculation that things will change to the better by God or other outer forces, not by our hard, longstanding, and wise enterprises.

Our brain runs into great difficulties, dealing with scopes larger than a society. When it comes to global affairs and resolving self-created global problems, it fails miserably to deal with the challenge. (It explains why we can't deal effectively with our self-created global problems). The core problems that we face with deteriorating global state and worsening mental state/physical state of people worldwide have mostly to do with our brains limited capacity.

Our brain can hamper our clear-sighted thinking in varied manners

Many, if not most, people decide very quickly who they like or dislike without knowing the persons.

Attractiveness, as bias, may depend on familiarity with one's own tribe such as racial characteristics, color, shape, etc. Anything perceived as exotic or too different can be threatening. The same bias exists with personality characteristics. Our brain will not accept people on this ground without checking them closely. Yet not everyone is biased to this degree, where they openly discriminate, but it does determine their social choices to a high degree.

Most people reject new ideas on the base of instinctive like–dislike base, not knowing them at all. They do so especially if the ideas constitute a threat to their belief system, which they may or may not realize.

When I seldom indicate for boastful people who have it all in their mouths (and none in their deeds) this discrepancy, they get offended and reject my idea that the best, most useful knowledge is in action, not in theory, although it is very obvious.

The poisonous seeds of intolerant fundamentalism are to be found in closed, rigid, black-white categorizing minds nurtured by ideologists, religious teacher, and well-meaning humanistic and progressive people. Right now, when I write these lines (2020), a dramatic process undermining our universal humanism is taking place as the EU rejects by force the entrance of immigrants and refugees into its territory and in Italy because of the epidemic of corona, the doctors decide who will die, and who will live. Within one week after the outbreak of the corona, our cherished humanistic idea of the holiness of human life has been devaluated and our rights curtailed by decrees. Ergo, people change much faster when fear of death and anxiety to their security and life is on their minds. Fear combined by immense suffering is an even stronger motivator for great change in our behavior and mind-sets.

The fundamentalist humanism is thus being undermined by grim realities on the ground.

That human beings are extremely prone to follow Mundus vult decipi. Our crucial failing is that we often blow our significance, competence, and godly prowess up while living just ordinary and temporary lives. There is no question that this propensity is in built in our brain.

We may think that the higher our intellect and understanding, the further we remove ourselves from our animal origin. Unfortunately, it is not so. This is also one of our brains "make believe" self-compliments. When it comes right down to survival, our brain is geared to cooperation (as long as there is an authority keeping order), total senseless and sensual getting loose (as one is doomed to die), or beastly self-survival struggle on dwindling /scarce resources (as the Black Death in Europe in 1348 and other places had shown.

This is the state of our brain that guides us in daily day life.

This has a huge consequence on our behavior, which the most devastating of them all is human stupidity.

Definition of a stupid person: knowing the truth, seeing the evidence of the truth, but still believing the lie
   There are four main reasons for human stupidity:

1) genetic/organic
2) stupidity borne by groupthink and its common convictions, which very often surpass facts and distort reality, thus harming people
3) current global stupidity due to our brain capacity, creating huge global problems, is being demonstrated by our global incapacity to attain global overview and far sight as to reverse our global unsustainable lifestyle, numbers, and deteriorating climate change. Economists project a growth of 50 percent in our economic output by 2050 compared with 2020 and population growth by 26 percent (1*: BBC: 23.3.2020). These projected figures tell you about how the human brain is out of its fucking mind
4) humanism-prone stupidity caused by us was to bring to halt natural selection and thereby bringing into the world many mentally/physically handicapped babies, which have to be taken care of, reducing the number of smart children

All four forms of stupidity are being nourished by our illusions and convictions, demonstrating clearly why self- deception is so rife among us
   The most alarming thing about human stupidity is that it can infect more and more people, further evolve as a virus in human populations, and extend its reach as it is borne by epigenetics.

More about stupidity that is caused by the process of epigenetic
   As I pointed out, the mere fact that we almost annulled the natural selection regarding our procreation meant adding many more people with mental deficiencies than before. If we will continue like this, it will result in reducing human intelligence significantly by the process of epigenetic.
   Unlike most inherited conditions, there are some conditions not caused by mutations to the genetic code itself. Instead, a much more obscure type of inheritance is taking place: events in someone's lifetime can change the way their DNA is expressed, and that change can be passed on to the next generation.
   This is the process of epigenetics where the readability, or expression, of genes is modified without changing the DNA code itself. Tiny chemical

tags are added to or removed from our DNA in response to changes in the environment in which we are living. These tags turn genes on or off, offering a way of adapting to changing conditions without inflicting a more permanent shift in our genomes.

The effects of trauma may echo down several generations, from a grandfather to their son and then to their grandson.

But if these epigenetic changes acquired during life can indeed also be passed on to later generations, the implications would be huge. Your experiences during your lifetime, particularly traumatic ones, would have a very real impact on your family for generations to come. There are a growing number of studies that support the idea that the effects of trauma can reverberate down the generations through epigenetics, which opens the hell gates for human stupidity because of lack of natural selection and life-saving procedures.

Stupid humans ignore a growing harsh reality on earth. Fantasy and diversion play a large part in these people's lives, and humanity is caught up in the trap, which the poet T. S. Eliot expressed rightly: "Humankind cannot bear very much reality."

The core problem with human stupidity is that it is incurable with the means we have to our disposition as its bearers are not aware of it dwelling in their minds. It is invisible for them and sometimes makes them think that they are wise.

So the nature of human stupidity is- among other reasons- by nurturing of social/ideological and religious pressure and control through groupthink, and it is much more devastating than we generally are willing to acknowledge. It takes a strong ego and special talent/capacity to accomplish more than ordinary lives as the pressure to conform is ceaseless. Weaker ego persons, and probably less talented, sometimes disparage exceptional people out of their own insecurity and jealousy. Megalomania is a flight and domination, separate from great achievements.

It is also nurtured by our brain's programs

Humans as a totality (with rare exceptions) have been unable to emerge successfully from their animalistic evolutionary past. The base qualities still persist—greed, self-indulgence, selfishness, egocentrism, vanity, aggressiveness, envy, gluttony, jealousy, territoriality, pride, covetousness, and short sight. Our brain's capacity is sandwiched between its innate capacity on the one hand and its gullible weakness for brainwashing and indoctrination.

Our free will is due to the abovenamed factors—pretty limited, indeed. We have, though, the potential for greater free will, but that implies removing/reducing the influence of the above mentioned factors, which enslave our minds.

Liberalism, socialism, religions, spiritualism, and humanism are unable to change fundamentally human nature beyond its limitations. This may sound as a postulate, yet watching mankind's poor evolutionary position after a longtime acquaintance with these factors lend credibility to this assertion.

They have failed miserably this mission time and again as the core problem for our stupidity seems to be our brain`capacity/structure.

"Oh, this human pain, with our split-up brain,

with our free will-lame, thus our life direction-insane!"(B.K)

B) Humans' compulsions, delusions, free will, and God

The almighty, benevolent and boundless, wise God, the moral free nature and human boundless self-deception had a heated discussion regarding who of them was the most powerful in human affairs.

"I created them and granted them the potential to discern between right and wrong and to evolve further. I am their designer and animator!" boasted God shamelessly.

"It might be right or not! I am not to judge if it was you or me," retorted nature, "but in my kingdom, they are submitted to my laws, which are, admittedly, both harsh and morally nonbenevolent. Ergo, I dictate the limitations for their behavior and excesses. If they don't obey, I can, with my arsenal of plagues and disasters, send them all back to the state before you supposedly turned them for nonliving dust into living organisms!"

"You are both mighty and exert huge influence on their lives as well as their potential demise," whispered human self-deception. "But I am the invisible, not acknowledged twin of all their brain/mind processes. I can make—and do make—their

frontal lobes believe that they possess free will. They confabulate on why they do things and believe in it, not realizing that more often than not, they act semiautomated. I am their real fatal virus, and they don't know it. I still wonder who of you two granted me such invincible power on their lives, but as you two can't stop me, I must be the strongest of us at least as to form their destiny!" said self-deception. As the three of them are very pretentious, the discussion keeps going on and on, like as ours humans . . .

—BK

Why do people believe in something that cannot be confirmed/verified by observations and scientific methods?

There are many reasons for why people believe in God. Faith in God is imprinted into the minds of small children and into our social fabrics in different forms: customs, habits, tales, rites, comforting phrases, and traditions. They all give a sense of security, community, and transcending meaning. Aesthetic expressions may also play a role for many. But for most, the underlying reason is to assuage anxiety, meaninglessness, and loneliness. Lots of families—dissolved or intact—do not provide a sense of belonging and forms of religion can offer sheltering warmth. Depending on the individual's intelligence and emotional needs, it can serve a good purpose or feed delusions and result in evil deeds. It is a dangerous force for many and dredged in patriarchal power politics.

When faith in God is used as a cover for lack of intelligent action or as a substitute for self-improvement, it is a psychological crutch rather than a spiritual exercise. Depending on the place of worship, it can be a source of education or a delusion. A community of worshippers usually contains both. It is sometimes easy for uneducated/gullible or wounded people to come under the spell of a charismatic leader who is neither wise nor spiritual but who masquerades as a person of "God." Many examples came up lately, in recent years, the large number of Catholic priests who were charged with abuse allegations. The priest caste, usually male, holds the key to knowledge of God. Those followers must obey him. He is supposed to be wise, to be trusted. In many Muslim countries, religion practices hold women down as second rate and accept honor murdering of them. If one rebels against their traditions and power structure, one is ostracized or literally killed.

———

Societies reinforce conformity, and we need cooperation to survive; hence, religious faith can glue us together even if it means social stagnation or regress, when the power element becomes distorted. It has almost always been so.

Religion did develop man to the higher level within the areas of arts such as music, paintings, architecture as well as philosophy but not anymore. The misuse of religion is, of course, a human fault, not the dogma, which man always corrupts.

God and our painful reality

If God was to exist in our harsh reality, he could not be almighty because in such, a suffering world God does visibly a terrible, incompetent job taking care of his believers. Judging God on his performance, he is mostly suited to serve as comforting and soothing source for the multitude of his suffering believers.

Could sufferings be a godly tool to provoke evolving action? We know that too comfortable life conditions can make people passive, the deeper one "sleeps," the lesser one sees a need for change. Only if these sufferings gave people, as individuals and social beings, a fair chance to learn of their sufferings and mistakes as to reduce them could God be credited for that, but reality does not show such effect.

Faith does not give place for free will. "Either you believe or you are out in the social wilderness" has been the dominating theme of many religions. The only "choice" has been to follow your faith, not challenge it.

These contradictions in our minds show how impossible it is for people to reconcile between their faith, which demands surrender on the one hand and their insistence of commanding free will on the other hand. My assertion is that if we could take faith in God away from believing people, most of them would mentally crumble down, losing their very sense of meaning with their lives. How can we define these people then? Free-willing creatures or compulsion-driven creatures?

Homo sapiens are mostly—let's admit it—driven more by compulsions regarding the role of God and faith than by free will. Facing a life as meaningless journey is something most people cannot endure, and as they cannot inject into their lives another bearing meaning, they are virtually trapped. Therefore, they need God to shed meaning into their short, ordinary, and often painful lives. Can this dependency on God to grant this meaning dumb them down? It is very likely as evidence from groupthink indicates that unreflective, semiautomatic thinking is forced upon the masses can make people dumber. If most members of a group tend to make certain errors, then most people will as the case is vividly demonstrated with our lack of living up to demands of global sustainability.

We know that knowledge may promote pain/doubt and struggle, sometimes to achieve great goals, and wisdom, which is based on extensive and varied knowledge, which can help us out of our tribulations and delusions. But wisdom demands critical—contextual—challenging and flexible thinking and acting, which religious faiths don't promote any longer.

We face therefore two critical contradictory choices between:

1) Submitting to God's supremacy over our lives or
2) Challenging God by fighting to change mankind's limitations, including their self-defeating mind-sets. The latter grants much better potentials to our further betterment and survival chances. The big question in this relation is whether there is any other viable way to the divine in us without submitting our faculties to dogmatic faith or whether the way is by exerting our full free will to ascend our physical/mental/cognitive limitations, including the notion of God's supremacy.

Human addictions and obsessions driven by inner compulsions

Human addiction is overwhelmingly widespread, and it is driven by mental compulsions, probably the same force that makes most people believe in God. There are over 1.1 billion people smoking, and countless people are abusing alcohol, drugs of all sorts, medications, food, and sex and engaging in regular violent and self-mutilating behavior. Human addiction is strongly connected to the mechanisms in our brains promoting obsession/compulsion, be it in connection with pleasure feelings, excitement, and euphoria, trying to gestalt meaning with life and reach release from tensions, insecurity, and lack of safety and low self-worth.

Human addiction is not limited only to the abovementioned afflictions/expressions. It is overwhelmingly present—the compulsive/obsessive behavior exposes them—in our species, uncompromising binding to greed, self-interest, deception, and self-deception. It is present in our struggle for status, power, riches, groupthink, hedonism, gossip, scoops, sensations, banality, triviality, daydreams, all resulting in real massive waste of our life time (endless repetitions and rituals).

Summing it up, can we become wiser at all with all these shortcomings ingrained in and shoved into our minds/brains?
Yes, but only if we transcend them by upgrading our selves!

What is wisdom as evolutionary phenomenon?

The current definition of wisdom is the quality of having experience, knowledge, and good judgment and the quality or state of being wise, knowledge of what is true or right, coupled with just judgment as to action—sagacity, discernment, or insight. The *Webster's Unabridged Dictionary* defines wisdom as "knowledge and the capacity to make due use of it."

I add to it my condensed version of wisdom: *Wisdom is composed of sustainability in all crucial aspect for our long-term survival, far sight, oversight, problem solving, and further evolving.*

Defined as such, it is tempting to draw the conclusion that we haven't, as a civilization, lived up to these wisdom criteria, with our overconsumption, deadly pollution, overpopulation, and alarmingly growing numbers of useless humans.

The gap between the scarcity of this wisdom among humans brings up the questions, Why is it that regardless of our acquired experience/knowledge, we behave often unwisely? Are we basically self-conscious/aware, or are we basically automated/instinctive?

I will elaborate more on this alarming fact—the lack of wisdom in the global human affairs—in chapter 2 on our current global state.

CHAPTER 2

Modern Babel Tower's Era, the Deteriorating State of the Human World

The human cicadas of today will soon fade away,
as they in their conduct and minds go astray.
Carrying on their Babel Tower's cacophony,
will they prepare their own death ceremony.

—BK

What is wrong with this sapiens,
from immortal stuff he was made,
living his life as a fleeting shade
as he was destined away to fade?
Why doesn't he himself upgrade?

—BK

Producing a kilo of cow meat is more polluting than a kilo
of pig or a chicken meat, but most polluting is a kilo of human
flesh, especially in our obese overpopulated human world.

—BK

Our obvious and fatal shortcomings

Do you remember what the corona virus did to us in 2020? It showed us how fragile our civilization is and how quickly a lethal virus can topple it. It showed a gullible, crazy, overpopulated, economically overheated, and growth compulsory civilization, which brings upon itself these disasters by invading more and more natural habitats and consuming recklessly.

In BBC, the following was to read: (2*: By Lindsey Galloway 23 March 2020)

> *Brexit, coronavirus, and trade tiffs may be making economic headwinds, but despite immediate challenges, the world economy is projected to keep growing at a rapid pace over the next few decades. In fact, by 2050, the global market is projected to double its current size, even as the UN forecasts the world's population will only grow by a modest 26%.*

This growth will bring with it plenty of changes. Though it can be challenging to predict exactly how the future will unfold, many sensible people agree on one thing: our civilization will be in even deeper ecological shit, reaching catastrophic dimensions.

First, we create the conditions for such global epidemics with stupid convictions (unstoppable global population growth and greedy consumption), and then when we are inevitably being hit by our own discarded boomerang (lack of prudence/sustainability), we react like a flock of panicked chicken.

Covid-19 reminds us that infectious diseases haven't vanished. In fact, there are more new ones now than ever: the number of new infectious diseases like SARS, HIV, and Covid-19 has increased by nearly fourfold over the past century. Since 1980 alone, the number of outbreaks per year has more than tripled.

There are several reasons for this uptick. For one, over the past fifty years, we've more than doubled the number of people on the planet. This means more human beings to get infected and, in turn, to infect others, especially in densely populated cities. We also have more livestock now than we did over the last ten thousand years of domestication up to 1960 combined, and viruses can leap from those animals to us.

As Covid-19 is painfully demonstrating, our interconnected global economy both helps spread new infectious diseases and, with its long supply chains, is uniquely vulnerable to the disruption that they can cause. The ability to get to nearly any spot in the world in twenty hours or fewer, and pack a virus along with our carry-on luggage, allows new diseases to emerge and to grow when they might have died out in the past.

For all the advances we've made against infectious disease, our very growth has made us more vulnerable, not less, to microbes that evolve forty million times faster than humans do.

What is happening now is just a prelude to the future. New viruses will come to us and require us to rethink, on a world-class level, about human dominance of nature.

The viruses are not new. What's new is the fact that we expose ourselves to them constantly by invading forests and jungles. We invite this terrible fate by our reckless multiplication and by our invasion of new habitats all the time.

What did it look like, our amazing world, before the virus's arrival?

Denmark experienced the warmest January ever. February was the wettest with flooded fields all over and an agricultural crisis that needs to consider a dramatic reordering of the crops. The Australian continent was in flames, and it is estimated that a billion animals were killed. The days of the Greenland inland ice are here. The seas rise while they are acidified. We are in the midst of what science calls the sixth mass extinction, in which biological species die out with dizzying pace.

The planet is at once too small and too big. The Western way of life, which now also extends to China and India's middle class, requires not one but four planets. Is the planet too big? Yes, it is too big for local solutions. Global warming requires common ground, but man does not seem to be wise enough as to coordinate such global efforts.

Climate change is upon us, and it is accelerating faster than any scientist had predicted. The doomsday clock stands at two minutes before twelve, and we don't seem to stop it only to talk about it in endless public debates.

Other shortcomings of current human beings

Humans suffer rather often of chronic lack of viable, new, and unifying ideas that can make them work together.

This seemingly chronic impotence regarding defining and practicing a new unifying global vision that will save us is painful to watch as it is what we need mostly (and what I have done in my writings). There are some visible signs that this lack of comprehensive viable vision hits us on all levels. Look around you, and what do you see in 2020? The model of EU in resolving problems has brought this block to standstill and paralysis. This liberal-, dialogue-, and debate-minded model is but a political anachronism. Nothing worthwhile and longstanding comes out of this political model, only too late adaptations to changing reality.

USA, China, Russia, and other nations nurture their own interests and don't care much regarding the deteriorating global order. For most countries, their influence and interests play the major role.

This human world is a metaphorical Babel Tower indeed. So here we go around the bush, discuss, argue, pour out lots of words and phrases (verbiage), feeling important and wise while not being able to find a common ground for both regional and global comprehensive actions.

Human beings in our time and their compulsions

As we are contradictory, shortsighted and don't know ourselves very well, we often get in the long run what we didn't wish to get or to be.

—BK

About half of the people on earth are by now obese or overweight. The number of people suffering from mental problems, due to our inhuman lifestyle, is on a sharp rise. The scores of intelligence tests show worldwide decline in the population intelligence, and health problems related to both stressful life and pollution like asthma, autoimmune ailments, and even heart problems and cancer are on a sharp rise. Manipulating agencies and people, like as the case was with cigarettes and alcohol, try to tell us a false story that the reason for this alarming rise of problems (including decline of intelligence) is that we have become better to detect these malaises. It is bull!

It is our compulsions camouflaged as greed and short sight that brought about these huge problems.

More of the same

The numbers of useless, isolated, and lonely people in the modern world is growing rapidly too.

People are social animals and much of their self-worth is derived from being useful in different ways for the common good. Yet more and more people are either considered being useless or consider themselves to be useless. Useless people can be shared in the following two categories:

1) People who don't contribute anything worthwhile for the common well partly because they can't or they don't wish to do so.
2) People who feel that they are both worthless and useless.

A poll among British people (3*:12.4.2017) revealed that as many as 37 percent Brits think they have a job that is utterly useless. They had what anthropologist David Graeber refers to as "bullshit jobs."

The notion of being useless has become much stronger among many people in modern mass societies as many of them don't have the family, community, and a sense of purpose that bonds people together in many cases. An illness, age, or adverse life situation of any kind can leave a person feeling helpless. The healthy, young, and prosperous have resources, but once lost, it can be hard to rebuild. Human interest and caring can help, but inner motivation, once lost, can be difficult to recapture for mentally fragile modern man. Cumulative loss and trauma can trigger depression, and from depression, which has exploded in the modern world, to a feeling of worthlessness and uselessness, it is a short way.

There is a loneliness epidemic in modern world

Nearly one out of three older Americans now lives alone, and the health effects are mounting, experts say. Two in five Americans report that they sometimes or always feel their social relationships are not meaningful, and one in five say they feel lonely or socially isolated (4*:17.1.2019).

More than a fifth of adults in the United States (22 percent) and the United Kingdom (23 percent) as well as one in ten adults (9 percent) in Japan say they often or always feel lonely, feel that they lack companionship, feel left out, or feel isolated from others (5*: 30.8.2018).

Higher levels of loneliness are associated with higher levels of social interaction anxiety, less social interaction, poorer psychological well-being, and poorer quality of life, the *Australian Loneliness Report* found. Loneliness increases the likelihood of mortality by 26 percent, research has found (6*: 15.11. 2018).

Social isolation impacts approximately 24 percent of older adults in the United States, approximately 9 million people.

The problem of drug addiction

In 2017, an estimated 271 million people, or 5.5 percent of the global population aged fifteen to sixty-four had used drugs in the previous year. While this is similar to the 2016 estimate, a longer-term view reveals that the number of people who use drugs is now 30 percent higher than it was in 2009 (7*: a survey from 26.6.2019).

Alcohol abuse

About 2 billion people worldwide consume alcoholic drinks, which can have immediate and long-term consequences to their health and social life. Over 76 million people are currently affected by alcohol use disorders, such as alcohol dependence and abuse.

Apropos drugs and alcohol

There are many young people in the West growing up in our consumer impulse free culture who cannot distinguish between reasonable self-control and compulsion.

Insomnia

Various studies worldwide have shown the prevalence of insomnia in 10 percent to 30 percent of the population, some even as high as 50 percent to 60 percent. It is common in older adults, females, and people with medical and mental ill health.

About 25 percent of Americans experience acute insomnia each year, but about 75 percent of these individuals recover without developing persistent poor sleep or chronic insomnia, according to a new study (8*: 5.6.2018).

According to the National Sleep Foundation, 30–40 percent of American adults report that they have had symptoms of insomnia within the last twelve months, and 10–15 percent of adults claim to have chronic insomnia (9*: 28.5.2009).

Depression

While there are more and more treatments for depression, the problem is rising, not falling.

In the period of 2005 cases of depressive illness increased by nearly a fifth. People born after 1945 are ten times more likely to have depression.

This reflects both population growth and a proportional increase in the rate of depression among the most at-risk ages, the WHO said (10*).

A key reason for the continuing rise in depressive illness is lifestyle, which predisposes people for stress, depression, and anxiety.

Other reasons given for the continuing rise in depressive illness include an aging population (sixty- to seventy-four-year-olds are more likely to suffer than other age groups) and rising stress and isolation.

Dementia is on a rise and its more hidden trigger

Long-term stress > anxiety > depression > huge risk for suffering of dementia= a formula of modern life.

Lots of people are constantly stressed/anxious in our times. Too much stress in your life can ultimately lead to depression and dementia, scientists have warned. A major review of published research suggests that chronic stress and anxiety can damage areas of the brain involved in emotional responses, thinking, and memory, leading to depression and even Alzheimer's disease.

The straining bluff of being unique

A Western culture claim that all people are unique deprives them from the drive to become unique, making them complacent/self-sufficient. You need a mental suspension/exertion of enduring effort for the long-term common well, bound to social rewards/prestige to become a unique, better, and wiser human being.

The commercialized bluff of making us unique has infected and inflated billions of ordinary people minds.

Our individual so-called uniqueness has become, through the commercialization of our minds, our collective trap as it is bound basically to overconsuming and Maj fly` seductive lifestyle.

The falling scores of intelligence measurements

Why are there so many dumb-witted people in the world, a fact that makes life hard both for them and the rest of us?

What percent of people are below average intelligence?

Most people (about 68 percent) have an IQ between 85 and 115. A small fraction of people have a very low IQ (below 70.16 percent) or a very high IQ (above 130. 16 percent) (11*: 10.4.2018). This distribution of intelligence, that so many people are not bright, creates a lot of visible and invisible problems in human existence on all levels, mostly devastating on a global level, as many of them cannot perceive the consequences of their personal and collective deeds impacting our environment.

Useful and beneficial self-reflection for most people; How common is it?

Without realizing our inbuilt limitations and shortcomings, self-reflection is but a bad joke.

It is also hard to be honestly self-reflective being wrapped up by cognitive conspicuous capitalism, which its admirers stupidly promised to bring paradise on Earth. Just thirty years ago, it was their declared goal. A long term, beneficial/sustainable self-reflection is therefore not always a matter within your private sphere and thoughts.

Growing number of psychiatric patients

Many people are affected by severe mental problems. According to Kommunernes Landsforening (12*: Denmark) 14.9 percent of children under eighteen years in Denmark had in 2019 one or more psychiatric diagnose. In 2012, the figures were 11.2 percent.

This figure (almost 15 percent of the children with psychiatric diagnosis) indicates strongly that something is wrong/rotten in the Kingdom of Denmark and the rest of the modern world.

One in four people in the world will be affected by mental or neurological disorders at some point in their lives. Around 450 million people currently suffer from such conditions, placing mental disorders among the leading causes of ill health and disability worldwide (13*: 4.10.2019).

Physical faltering health

What percentage of the world is physically unhealthy?

Overall, just 4.3 percent of people had no health problems, a researchers found. The likelihood of having any disease or condition increase with age. In developed countries, about 64 percent of kids under age five had a health problem in 2013 compared with 99.97 percent of adults ages eighty and older (14*: 8.6.2015).

How many people in the world have an incurable disease?

Generally, incurable and ongoing chronic diseases affect approximately 133 million Americans, representing more than 40 percent of the total population of this country projected to grow to an estimated 157 million, with 81 million having multiple conditions.

We are warmongers

On top of all these human terrible frailties and shortcomings, we are still vicious warmongers.

Global defense spending was on the rise in 2019 in an unstable world. There were also growing numbers of sites around the world, where low-scale yet vicious wars and fighting were going on and on.

In 2019, global defense spending rose by some 4 percent compared to 2018, the highest year-on-year increase in a decade.

This is a reflection of a changing world and the return of state-on-state competition/rivalry.

So as you may realize by now, there is ample evidence proving that we, sapiens, are far away from being well constructed and assembled. Too many defects and frailties invalidates the claim that we were formed in the image of God, and that we have created the best world for humans.

All in all, these many defects result in what we see today: global stupidity expressed by both worsening of the physical and mental health of people in this world and the climate crisis leading to growing global anarchy.

Why than most people reject the idea of improving ourselves mentally and physically by further evolvement /upgrading, when it is self- evident, that we suffer of essential frailties and deficiencies? The sole explanation to this is; Human stupidity.

"The global human stupidity" marching plague

> *The most rejected and invisible mirror for humans shows*
> *our fundamental stupidity.*
>
> —BK

In 1976, a professor of economic history at the University of California, Berkeley, published an essay outlining the fundamental laws of a force he perceived as humanity's greatest existential threat: Stupidity(15*).

Stupid people, Carlo M. Cipolla explained, share several identifying traits: they are abundant, they are irrational, and they cause problems for others without apparent benefit to themselves, thereby lowering society's total well-being. A stupid person is a person who causes losses to another person or to a group of persons while deriving no gain to oneself and even possibly incurring losses.

There are no defenses against stupidity, argued the Italian-born professor. The only way a society can avoid being crushed by the burden of its idiots is if the none stupid work even harder to offset the losses of their stupid brethren.

I must admit that it will be hard, according to his definition of stupidity, to find sane enough people to achieve his goal.

His second law regarding stupidity seems now out of touch with modern reality.

Law 2: The probability that a certain person becomes stupid is independent on any other characteristic of that person. I don't agree as I contend that it can be reduced through upgrading of sapiens.

Cipolla claimed that stupidity is a variable that remains constant across all populations. Every category one can imagine—gender, race, nationality, education level, income—possesses a fixed percentage of stupid people. There are stupid college professors. There are stupid people at Davos and at the UN General Assembly. There are stupid people in every nation on Earth. How numerous are the stupid among us? It's impossible to say. And any guess would almost certainly violate the first law anyway.

Academic excellence and high intelligence may promote your cleverness but not your wisdom.

Why is it that you have lots of people who are successfully intelligent, but they are unwise, he asks? He had studied IQ and analytical intelligence and had seen people who had high IQs had high test scores and degrees, but if you put them in a job or a relationship, they made a mess of it.

One answer to these questions, he argues, is that in the pursuit of high academic goals, common sense and self-knowledge are lost. You get people who are so smart and who are so highly rewarded by school and university and society for being smart that they see the world as their tool, and they only see consequences for themselves, he argued. Then they start to think they know everything. Academics are particularly prone to this.

To prevent clever people falling into the fallacies of their own egocentrism, omniscience, omnipotence, and invulnerability—all of which he lists as stages of stupidity—they must be taught by experience on how to practice knowledge by action.

The values that should be offered also to the elite must include compassion, but how should a man as semi automated be reprogrammed to gain a function that he does not possess?

As I pointed out in chapter 1, on human stupidity, it is caused by genetics and organic defects, by massive indoctrinations, and by epigenetics. Annulling the natural selection regarding our procreation and giving birth to lots of babies with severe defects on top of them these causes makes human stupidity becomes more infectious and widespread in modern times.

Though he is wrong regarding the immutability of stupidity and of the number of stupid people in the world, we can resolve this immense problem by upgrading and evolving further away from sapiens mental limitations, constructions, and bloated humanism.

At least seven more specific aspects in our lives contribute to dumb people down in our time:

1) The consuming/individual-centered ideology (cognitive capitalism) dumb people down by turning them into obsessive, nonreflective consumers.

2) The resurgent fundamentalist religions and ideologies turn billions of people into unreflective worshippers, lacking the capacity to think beyond the boxes of their doctrines. I reckon that most religious people do reflect within their box; some are extreme in their opinions and certain needs, which lead them directly toward fundamentalism, but are they a majority? I don't know for sure.

3) Overweight and obesity are associated with many ailments and also with mental decline. As nearly half of humanity is overweight, it is a probable source for slowly dumbing us down.

4) Massive pollution in our cities and countries destroys our health and dumbs us down (especially children and youngster in the process of growing up). I don't know for sure if it is increasing, decreasing or stable.

5) The rise of CO_2 in the air seems also to impair our mental capacities, making us dumber. New research shows that as the human-caused climate crisis worsens, one of the symptoms of our increasingly sick planet may be dumber and dumber humans. The new research paper, written by a team of scientists from the University of Colorado Boulder, the Colorado School of Public Health, and the University of Pennsylvania (16*), suggests that the gradual rise of CO_2 levels in Earth's atmosphere could cause cognitive decline in humans as a whole. Studies have shown that too much CO_2 in the air can trigger cognitive issues, decreasing the ability of a person to focus and hinder learning.

This research indicates that if temperature will rise in the end of this century by 4 degrees Celsius, which is very likely, it may effect up to 50 percent of our mental capacity because of huge concentrations of CO_2 in the air.

6) Growing mental problems and fragility worldwide because of our stressful and straining lifestyle, including alarmingly growing loneliness, do effect our mental agility and capacity. Modern societies are characterized by booming loneliness, which is strongly connected with high risk for being plagued by dementia. Participants in a research who reported greater feelings of loneliness were more likely to develop dementia over the next ten years. Individuals who feel lonely are likely to have several risk factors as dementia, diabetes, hypertension, and depression and are less likely to be physically active (17*: 29.10.2018).

Mental-burdened people don't think very well and almost always lack overview regarding their lives and reality. They tend to doubt, ruminate, and think in circles as they are tied down mentally by their unresolved problems.

7) Our annulling of the natural selection in our own procreation and the massive saving of life of many babies with severe mental and physical defects add also its heavy toll to the global growing stupidity.

If you add on top of these causes, the probable fact that due to growing overpopulation in a future world and the need to cut down on eating meat, big contributor of CO_2 and methane, people will eat mainly vegetarian and vegan diets, which is associated with reduced mental capacity. These diets are known to dumb humans down in the long run. It seems as we are ending up in a trap, which we can only come out of by cutting drastically on our consumption, production, and population and upgrading ourselves beyond our debilitating shortcomings.

Have we got a better alternative? Can you imagine the impact of even dumber humans than we are in future civilization, while we didn't act to prevent this catastrophe?

What have we done wrongly against humans' dignity?

1) Humans were seduced to become greedy in a compulsory/sickly manner.

2) Humans were manipulated to believe that they were unique and special without contributing anything of enduring value for the long term common good; hence, many became complacent and self-focused. This

amounted to both grand cheating promotion, where ordinariness and political/ideational passivity got new shiny names.

3) Humans were manipulated to believe that happiness and pleasure were the ultimate goals with their lives as the following tale illustrates:

The Pursuit of Happiness

An old man lived in the village. He was one of the most unfortunate people in the world. The whole village was tired of him; he was always gloomy, he constantly complained, and he was always in a bad mood. The longer he lived, the more bile he was becoming and the more poisonous were his words. People avoided him because his misfortune became contagious. It was even unnatural and insulting to be happy next to him. He created the feeling of unhappiness in others.But one day, when he turned eighty years old, an incredible thing happened. Instantly, everyone started hearing the rumor:

"An old man is happy today. He doesn't complain about anything, smiles, and even his face is freshened up."

The whole village gathered together. The old man was asked, "What happened to you?"

"Nothing special. Eighty years I've been chasing happiness, and it was useless. And then I decided to live without happiness and just enjoy life. That's why I'm happy now."

4) Humans were persuaded to become ego-centered and self-focused regarding their excessive needs and whims as the bearing meaning in their lives, forgetting their commitments to keep Mother Nature sustainable and healthy for their own and the coming generations' sake.

5) Humans were seduced to become addicts of food, drugs, booze, sex, and other harmful perversions, which destroy themselves and others.

6) Humans were seduced to be dumbed down by the mass media and religious and ideological propaganda, including the seductive and harmful liberal capitalism. Much of the mass media is tendentious, hysterical/sensationalist, neurotic, lacking long-term perspectives, and thus nurturing anxiety and narrow self-focus.

7) Humans were led to believe—falsely—that we have become much more enlightened, wiser, almost omnipotent semi gods, compared with our predecessors as to be able to resolve and solve all our self-created problems and entanglements.

So what are the inevitable conclusions you, the reader, can draw from this current global deteriorating mental and physical state of humans?

'I will say it very plainly:
You may be a bit saintly,
yet devoid of an evolving vision
you're still seated in your prison!'(B.K)

1) The major question current people ask today is, who is to decide the limit for our unfolding and multiplications, and how shall our future look like? In 2020, it became very obvious for lots of insightful people that nature decides this absolutely, and its rules override ours. A virus named corona made our governments tremble and remove for a while most of our rights. This scene will take place with growing intensity and ferocity and will end up costing humanity its future. So our principles can only go up hand in hand with the limitations nature puts upon us and other living things combined with our own evolving vision. We ignored this very obvious reality of sustainability, and payback time followed. Regulating and reducing our population, consumption, pollution, and economical activities via global political measures, even by enforcement, is in accordance with what nature will accept and accommodate .

2) It is right to place responsibility on man himself. Seduction cannot take place unless a receptive individual is on the other end of line. The reason behind people's senseless behavior should be found both in their mental makeup and in basic needs/motives that are not being answered by modern thought and lifestyle.

3) Fin-de-siecle, that something new, a new order, must come up backed up by a viable and evolving vision/mission for new humanity. "Business as usual" and "More of the same" can no longer change our self-destructive global course.

CHAPTER 3

Is There an Ultimate Purpose
for Intelligent Life as Us?

What is the essence of being sapiens?

Homo sapiens wish to transcend their fixed, ordinary lives.

Can this aspiration, to transcend and evolve beyond our inbuilt limitations, be the ultimate purpose with *Homo sapiens'* lives?

In his book *Menneskets vej*, Martin Buber tells of a Chassidic rabbi who was imprisoned for suspicion of conspiracy against the regime. The commander of the prison visits him and wishes to catch him in religious contradictions. He asks the old sage, "How come God asked Adam where he hid himself after eating from the Tree of Knowledge, 'Where are you, Adam?' If this God knows all, as you Jews present Him, why does God ask this question?" The rabbi told the commander that God was all-knowing, and the question should be understood as God's inquiry to all Adams who have existed since the first one: "Where are you in your life? Are you hiding from yourself and me? How are you shouldering your responsibility to your world as to find the way of meaning within your life?" And the rabbi ended the discussion, telling the commander, "And you are forty-six years old. Where are you, Adam?" Adam tells God, "I am hiding," so he knows he is hiding, ignoring his responsibility to his world.

This attitude, which the rabbi expresses in this story, is called *Tikun Olam, the mending of the human world,* and was considered by some Jewish groups as the ultimate meaning with life. But when you try to qualify this meaning—what it means repairing the world and from what to what—it becomes much harder to find a common ground for people to agree upon as humans' love to split up and differ almost compulsively.

I have devised a very simple, universal question to discern whether you are globally wise or outright stupid. (Remember that a stupid person can be intelligent and academic.)

The question is, "Do nature's rules and limitations overrule all other rules, principles, and values when it comes to conflict?"

If you reply the following question honestly, you may get a clear-cut result of your mental habitus on the spot.

Supplemented question to verify your state of mind is, "Do you believe in, and practice, the principles of global/nature sustainability and accept that in the end of the day, nature is the BOSS, or do you believe in, and practice, ceaseless economic growth, the right of people to get as many children as they wish and to live and consume as they wish?"

There is no way you can escape the outcome of being stupid if you back up our current practice and policies, regardless your arguments, but by changing your mind-set and practice, you can still become much wiser.

Without being very down to earth, detailed, with clear outlines and defined goals, it seems that *Tikun Olam* is a blocked way in the human antagonistic and sometimes xenophobic world.

Tikun Olam is, in my view, as far as it aims at making people better humans, an illusion as long as we keep having the same mental/cognitive capacity. The idea that we can improve and perfect human nature as to make us more benevolent, amiable, less brutal, and greedy through example and learning has not materialized in our history. It sure can be done for some but not for the great majority of people. The illusion is promoted by another illusion that saint like people, like Gandhi, Dalai Lama, and Nelson Mandela, can change our psych and behavior for good. Many people may be inspired by people like them but cannot change themselves fundamentally as to transcend the collective human nature and behavior. All these saints like people could not avert wars and atrocities in their own societies. India is split up this very day between Muslims and Hindus as it was in Gandhi's period. Tibet is occupied by the Chinese, and Dalai Lama can do nothing about it, and Mandela's South Africa is the most dangerous place on Earth regarding violent criminality.

Besides, the idea of serving humans and humanity is only qualified good as long as it is based on global sustainability and farsighted and enduring goals as our further evolving. Serving humans on a short-term base and thereby gaining some satisfactions and joy is worthwhile, but it cannot change sapiens as to become a higher and better beings and therefore cannot be the bearing meaning with our lives.

Most people have got hands full dealing with their private lives. This is the capacity/life situations granted to them. Many humans with some awareness have faced the doubt of their insignificance and looked for an escape gate from this insight. Religion has offered them this escape gate by making them believe that they are personally loved and cared for by God. Western humanism has offered them this escape by making them believe that they are unique when they are in fact mediocre/ordinary.

But are they working in reality as to change people to the better? Not at all as I see it.

So is there an ultimate purpose for intelligent life like us beyond our personal/social/religious horizons? Can breaking away from our mental and physical constraints and becoming masters of our own body, mind, and fate by evolving further be this ultimate meaning?

Because of my life experience, I can clearly state that

- There is an ultimate meaning with advanced intelligent life beyond God and other human ideologies, and this meaning is the ever evolving of us to attain greater mastery and power and to go for the stars. I call it to become creators due to our own merit.

- We must upgrade many of us as to become wiser and more farsighted so we will be able to pursue our ultimate meaning/mission and avoid derailing it as we do right now.

Paul Eluard, a French writer/poet (1895–1952), wrote the following: "Hope raises no dust. The faith that stands on authority is not faith. Who so would be a man must be nonconformist. A foolish consistency is the hobgoblin of little minds, adored by little statesmen and philosophers and divines. With consistency a great soul has simply nothing to do. Hitch your wagon to a star" (18*).

This meaning offers by continuously evolving enduring survival chances for our progenies and their growing mastery and control of life and death and to reach accessible parts of the universe, without which, our lives so far is but an episode doomed to oblivion.

CHAPTER 4

A Sustainable Long-Term Evolving Vision for Saving the Best in Us

The humanistic blubber on changing our course and human nature by free will and benign means is but a daydream. Fear, anxiety, and suffering are much better to do this job! A lethal corona virus scares people to death, forcing them to halt their wild consumption for a while anyway!

—BK

Goodness is not real goodness without being long-termed life affirming, sustainable, and evolving.

—BK

Be truly humble. Don't consider sapiens as the crown of creation, just one, important though, unit in our further evolvement.

—BK

Many people use a lot of energy "running away from home," be it their family, social background, native country, personal petty lives, or from being mortal sapiens and difficult reality. But they bump into an invisible barrier within themselves, which keeps them bound to an unfinished conflict. They try to run away from their original home to a new landscape/home but cannot accomplish this fully. Why? It is because they can't completely free themselves from their own conditioning, meaning all the experiences and teachings that have molded and influenced them as children and members of groups and of our species. On the other hand, a complete rejection of one's own past to start a new and evolving journey is impossible without containing the best part of the old one in the new molding.

Therefore, if a species like us does not carry with it the necessary and useful substances from "its old home" into the "new home," which it intends to move into, it won't make it.

So how may a future civilization differ from and resemble ours?

The future civilization, which I envision hundreds of years from now, may look, albeit me, as following:

1) A new grand narrative for humanity, free of superimposing God and the lust for mammon and greed, is the backbone of this paradigm. It is designed to focus on grand, farsighted, and longstanding goals, a long-term mission and ultimate meaning that serve intelligent life's survival and evolvement.

2) Micro- and macro-dimensions in our lives: The micro reality encompasses our personal, interpersonal, social, occupational, political, and religious-spiritual spheres of existence. Macro reality encompasses our long-term, sustainable existence on the planet and our evolving journey as an intelligent species. By acting in relation to the macro level of our reality, people will find much more gratifying and enduring life meaning than any other ideology or religion can possibly grant them in the long run.

3) *Homo sapiens* must be upgraded because they are characterized by (a) behavior of "short-term gain, long-term pain; short-term resurrection, long-term self-destruction" and by (b) possessing a troublesome and unstable combination of intelligence and mind-clouding stupidity. He is also characterized by (c) defective self-knowledge since it does not encompass the macro-dimension of his existence, by (d) a strong propensity for self-deception and wishful thinking, by (e) a strong propensity for greed and profit, by (f) excessive behavior, a lack of "everything in moderation,"

and addictions of all kinds. The inevitable impact of these "characteristics" can become his endgame.

4) The creators are a new species, wiser and more farsighted than HS, and therefore lead the evolving journey of intelligent life. The creator is supposed to clean up the mess after *Homo sapiens*. His ultimate goals are (a) transcending the mental limitations of both *Homo sapiens* and those enforced by nature and resetting the global climate back to preindustrial era, (b) creating a sustainable and evolving civilization, and (c) "to the stars with difficulties."

5) *Life value* will be for such civilization (a) the value granted human life only when people live in a sustainable manner and in accordance with the planet's capacity to renew itself and regenerate its life-giving resources and (b) the measure of their usefulness in a stable and enduring manner, to the long-term survival and evolving prospects of future generations and civilization. The maxim dynamic "The first generation establishes something new, the second builds up upon it, and the third destroys it by friction and hatred" will not happen as the project of evolving, struggling to create something new and better will be the very essence of this civilization.

6) Global governance with dictatorial powers over essential issues like economy, ecology, demography, production, traffic, and defence. On regional level, democracy will be a part of the political fabric.

7) Hypotension regarding lifestyle, consumption, production, and transport/traffic. Free movement will be reduced strongly.

8) Borders will still be useful and will be enforced. Borders will be a necessity as to regulate the movements of people and goodies. As free travel over long distances and from continent to continent will be strongly reduced to reduce epidemics, pollution, and waste of resources, borders will be a necessity.

9) All production, including food, will take place-where it can be practiced- close to where people live as to save the cost of expensive transportation and increase independence of the local societies.

10) Mega cities' numbers will be reduced and towns and cities will not exceed one hundred thousand humans. The measures are meant as to reduce loneliness and estrangement and encourage cooperation and solidarity among people.

11) Human commitments regarding the long-term common good of evolving humanity will precede human rights. Human rights will be dependent on fulfilling one's public duties.

12) Global population will be, over hundreds of years, reduced to upgraded humans of three to four billion on Earth altogether and some millions common sapiens.

13) Global sustainability in all essential areas will be the iron rule.

14) Fairness and justice will be the iron rule, and social or financial privileges/speculations/elites will be curtailed.

15) Prudence, humbleness, impulse control, and long-term common needs will precede the individual needs.

16) Aspiration for megalopsychia (the greatness of the soul) via one's contributing deeds for the common well will be their cherished focus, and they will be rewarded and respected for this.

I had some heated discussions with friends regarding the idea of evolving and transcending beyond sapiens, and some of them reminded me of Plato's allegory of the cave. Everyone thinks that THEY are outside this `cave` watching the others, that is, they are knowledgeable free people while all the others are the people chained to the wall of the cave, facing the blank wall, watching shadows projected on the wall.

To get out of the cave, you have to design and follow a route beyond sapiens' constraints and limitations; otherwise, you are in "the cave" regardless of what you think/ imagine.Plato allegory is not a destiny. Knowing in the first place that you are in the cave and identifying its contours makes it possible to escape it. But you have to know the dynamics between you and your cave, its spell on your mind, and what it hides from you on you. A person who knows that the only way to escape our "cave" is to evolve beyond sapiens limitations has definitely found an escape route out of it—the human mental traps, shortcomings, and blindness.

In the last twenty years, many people contested my global vision regarding our inevitable upgrading, but none of them came up with another viable alternative vision on how to curb our self-destructive excesses.

This aspiration/focus on evolving and upgrading is a part of the advanced evolving wisdom of tomorrow. The current view of wisdom is that it is the outcome of accumulative knowledge on oneself, the others, and our world/reality in life-affirming manner performed by the mentally balanced, flexible-minded, and experienced human.

Future evolving wisdom is based on the same premises, but the knowledge in action here is long termed, life affirming, evolving, and sustainable, and the subject practicing this wisdom is ever-evolving intelligent creature, far beyond sapiens' limitations. The future wise, upgraded beings will know the truth regarding sapiens, lucidly conveyed in the following lines:

> *Basically, you are still but Universal Maj fly,*
> *Noisily you buzz, pretending to ascend high.*
> *Before your day long life is gone and you die*
> *You'll reject this truth with delusions and lies.*
> *Silly Maj fly; stop your self-delusions' cries!*
> *Your only escape from this destiny is a try*
> *to evolve far beyond your encased Maj fly.*

—BK

What can be achieved by upgrading humans already from the middle of this century?

> *As we engineer hardened sorts of wheat, corn, and rice, we will have to engineer stupidity-resistant human beings for the future civilization!*

—BK

On a personal/social level, future upgraded humans will be equipped with much better brains than ours. They will receive obligatory and lengthy education and practice in the following disciplines: cooperation, equality, and fair chances to compete in a fair and sustainable manner, decency, empathy, toughness, far sight, tactical/strategic thinking and planning, sustainable life attitude, prudence, focus on and determination regarding long-termed goals, freedom from depression—anxiety, stress, and psychiatric conditions. They will be free of the physical problems sapiens' excessive lifestyle results in like obesity, self-destruction through alcohol and substances, etc.

Regarding their view and practice of freedom

Their point of view of freedom, whatever it is today, being consumption minded, self-realizing, deceptive oriented, will be bound to responsibilities for a sustainable and evolving world. In an overpopulated world, lacking sustainability and slowly running down as ours, freedom cannot stand as a sacred principle. It is bound to responsibility. If it is not going to be so, as the case is often demonstrated in our perverted times, freedom leads to pervasive human stupidity with severe consequences for all of us, with great risk to our downfall.

The big challenge will be how to form and support the development of individual thinking based on these values. Once I came across the way that some small societies practiced so-called monitored education. A youngster would be introduced to so-called impossible images—in our world would be a car with square wheels, etc.—as a way to introduce an alternative world view. Shock and surprise has been used as well in monitored portion. Somehow our identity and tendencies will be formed in a direction that creates a wondering soul, a person who questions, verifies, and practices life in a different way than today.

Rebellion against our brains/mind conditioning is the key word in upgrading us. One should not be rebellious against the limitations of nature, but as nature allows evolutionary potentiality, we can engineer a much better human brain. Nature has left possibility for evolvement from lower being to higher being, and this possibility we should exploit.

This vision holds up the flag of transformation of our biological or godly destined fate and limitations, where a further evolvement is possible.

It includes a brand-new ultimate meaning for advanced intelligent life, a new ultimate purpose for the future citizens (becoming creators and mastering the process of life/death and the chaos in the universe), and a new destiny for us beyond sapiens.

All together this vision presents new life perspectives and direction.

Let start with *our destiny*. How can we devise a new destiny to creatures like us who are doomed to die out rather quickly? It seems sealed-decay, demise, and disappearance of two reasons. The obvious one is our self-destructive drives. The second seems to be an absolute truth: everything in nature is temporary, including us.

But if we want to escape this bitter fate, we must view ourselves, lives, purposes, and meaning from entirely different points of view. One point of view is challenging and defying, and changing, the fact of us being shortsighted, greedy, and self-destructive. The second point of view is challenging and changing our biological and mental limitations/blueprints, forced upon us by nature. The third point of view is challenging, defying, and altering the role of God in our lives. God wants us, from this point of view, to challenge him by evolving further and becoming masters of our own destiny, including control over the process of life and death and expansion into the outer space.

From this altered destiny, the *ultimate meaning* with our life becomes obvious: the ultimate meaning for advanced intelligent life is to ever evolve to higher level and to master the biological process of life and death and to expand our reach out into space and to learn how to control/avoid/deflect the dangers the universe presents.

The ultimate purpose for each member of such sustainable and evolving civilization is to free himself/herself from the shackles of their mental/biological slavery.

First, when we rebel against this mental/biological slavery, we will become advanced humans, ergo creators.

There are, of course, secondary purposes and aspirations for these members, which encompass their ordinary lives, including individual, social, religious and political aspirations, wants, rights, and duties.

An upgraded man may sound to some readers, wrongly thought, as a kind of Nietzsche's super being/über menschen, so they may ask, who will do the less intellectual/sophisticated requiring work as service functions etc.? As we know, people regard promotion/advancing as getting to a less physically demanding job as a goal to strive for.

Much of the manual jobs will be done and managed by intelligent robots, and a part of them will be managed by the upgraded people in rotation and as a way to keep them "down to earth and appreciative of all kinds of contributions to the common well!"

Without weakening the mental programs of God, greed, Mundus vult decipi, and short sight and building up new life attitudes, the project of evolving will fail, and advanced intelligence life will end up in blind alley while sapiens will die out anyway.

What are the prospects regarding such an evolving future?
In short, humanity's future can take one of several routes:

Stasis leading to extinction - We largely stay as we are now, with minor tweaks, mainly as races merge, which eventually will result in extinction.

Speciation - A new human species evolves on either this planet or another, which is what this vision goes for.

Symbiosis with machines - Integration of machines and human brains produces a collective intelligence that may or may not retain the qualities we now recognize as human, which is also what this vision goes only partly for.

Transcending our sapiens limitations is our ultimate cure against sapiens short sight and fixed destiny. It will be done by advanced technologies stemming from CRISPER, robotics, and artificial intelligence.

What is Crisper

I have lived through eventful times. I have seen a world in flux, but when I try to peer into the future, I come to the conclusion that the story of humankind's ability to understand life on its most intimate level and be able to tinker with it for our benefit or detriment is likely to be the biggest one of them all setting us on evolving course away from the self-destructive sapiens.

We are living in one of the greatest epochs of human exploration, and it reshaped our world so profoundly as to force us either to transform ourselves into wiser beings (creators) or to disappear altogether.

This brings me to a term that has become a big part of my life over the last seven years: Crisper. I now know it's an extremely powerful tool for editing genes in seemingly any organism on Earth, including humans. Scientists doing basic research have been uncovering the mechanisms of life for decades. They have been creating tools for modifying individual genes, but Crisper is one of those revolutions where what researchers thought might be possible in the distant horizon is suddenly available now. It's cheap, it's relatively simple, and it's remarkably precise.

There is something you need to know about it. If you are worried about your health, mental capacity, or the health of your children, if you are concerned about how we might need to engineer our planet in the face of the climate crisis, Crisper is likely the answer for these challenges. To start with, it will cure genetic diseases such as sickle cell and Huntington's. It is being tested against cancers and HIV. It will elevate people's intelligence and mental health. It could also potentially be used to make crops more drought-resistant or food more nutritious. But not so far in the future, it will make the first generation of wiser upgraded humans, whom we need badly to take over our further evolvement and future journey.

Directed evolution

We have directed the evolution of so many animal and plant species. Why not direct our own? Why wait for natural selection to do the job when we can do it faster and in ways beneficial to ourselves? In the area of human behavior, for example, geneticists are tracking down the genetic components not just of problems and disorders but also of overall disposition and various aspects of sexuality and competitiveness, many of which may be at least partially heritable. Over time, elaborate screening for genetic makeup may become commonplace, and people will be offered drugs based on the results.

The next step will be to actually change people's genes.

Assuming that it will become practical to change our genes, how will that affect the future evolution of humanity? It will probably affect it a great deal. Suppose parents alter their unborn children to enhance their intelligence, looks, and longevity. If the kids are as smart as they are long-lived—an IQ of 150 and a life span of 150 years—they could have more children and do better and contribute more than the rest of us. Socially, they will probably be drawn to others of their kind. With some kind of self-imposed geographical or social segregation, their genes might drift and eventually differentiate as a new species. One day then, we will have it in our power to bring a new human species into this world. Whether we choose to follow such a path is for our descendants to decide and they will probably go for it as the best long termed way of surviving/prevailing.

Even less predictable than our use of genetic manipulation is our manipulation of machines—or they of us. Is the ultimate evolution of our species one of symbiosis with machines, a human machine synthesis? Many writers have predicted that we might link our bodies with robots or upload our minds into computers. In fact, we are already dependent on machines. As much as we build them to meet human needs, we have structured our own lives and behavior to meet theirs. As machines become ever more complex and interconnected, we will be forced to try to accommodate them. This view was starkly enunciated by George Dyson in his 1998 book *Darwin among the Machines*. He claimed that everything that human beings are doing to make it easier to operate computer networks is at the same time, but for different reasons, making it easier for computer networks to operate human beings. Darwinian evolution, in one of those paradoxes with which life abounds, may be a victim of its own success, unable to keep up with non-Darwinian processes that it has spawned.

This vision is against such a direction, where smart computers may take over biological intelligence. The smart machines will serve this advanced humanity only to a degree that it will be under their control, even while enhancing their capabilities.

CHAPTER 5

How Will the Future Upgraded Human Beings Differ From Us Regarding Their Qualities?

How did you contribute to the long-term welfare/progress
of humanity beyond your own self-interest is the real, ultimate
question regarding your longstanding value.

—Bk

My mind children, the creators, will differ from our sapiens' mind-sets as the camel in the following tale differs in its outlook from the donkey (Sufi story):

A donkey and a camel were walking along together. The camel moved with long strides, and the donkey moved impatiently, stumbling every now and then. At last, the donkey said to his companion, "How is it that I am always in trouble, falling and grazing my legs, in spite of the fact that I look carefully downwards as I walk, when you, who never seem to be aware of what surrounds you, with your eyes fixed upon the horizon, keep going so fast and yet seemingly at such leisure?"

The camel answered, "Your problem is that your steps are too short, and by the time you have seen something, it is too late to correct your movements. You look all around and do not assess what you see. You think that haste is speed. You imagine that by looking, you can see. You think that seeing near is the same as seeing far.

"You guess that I look at the horizon. In fact, I am merely gazing ahead so as to work out what to do when the far becomes near. I also remember what has gone before and do not need to look back at it and stumble once again. In this way, what seems to you baffling or difficult becomes clear and easy."

Similarly, donkey-minded people are those who believe that they can learn enough to improve themselves or their lot by shortsighted means. This includes not looking toward the future or even into it. It includes demanding a certain pace without realizing whether it is counterproductive. The ass is the ordinary sapiens, while the camel is the wise, evolving human.

Unfortunately, the state of humanity right now is characterized by few camels surrounded by too many stampeding donkeys.

But this ratio will change dramatically in the coming three to four centuries.

The upgraded humans slowly will separate themselves as a new race from sapiens. They will be much wiser than an average sapiens, equipped with both stronger raw intelligence and wisdom, which will be farsighted, prudent, contextual, proactive, and ever evolving. Being farsighted and more mentally balanced, they are going to be less war/power mongers than sapiens and more benign. They will suffer only a fraction of the mental problems and physical frailties, which plague humans on a large scale.

With individual ecological footprint quota implementation for them and stress on being useful for the long-term common good, they will save themselves from our vices.

They will be fully aware of that without acquiring far sight and sustainable life approach and eliminating sapiens' greed and blame game, they will be doomed.

They will be very flexible in their minds as to adapt to ever-changing circumstances.

There is the tale on the olive tree and a bush that lived side by side. The olive often mocks the bush. "See you, every little wind can bend you. I, on the other hand, am strong and unbreakable." Later on, a strong storm came and broke the olive. The bush, however, bent down, jerked in the wind, and finally returned to its place. Most of us think Darwin said the strong survives, but he basically said the flexible survives. Adapting to the newly created situations includes, among other things, postponing gratification, reducing unnecessary expenses, and utilizing the time to go ahead in resolving the crisis, problems/challenges at hand. Crises are a great opportunity to challenge perceptions and conventions and will force the creators to changes in their lives that they probably wouldn't have made if it hadn't been for the crisis that was needed to be resolved.

Their humanism will be contextual as well. Humanism without regard to changing contexts, without regard to available resources or the consequences of excesses (see how many people become obese and sick and shorten their lives by indulging food, drugs, and alcohol) will be considered by them as vain and stupid.

Their humanism will consist of counter poles, commitments and obligations to the common well on one hand and rights depending on fulfilling these commitments on the other hand. Their humanism will be based on sustainability in all essential areas and the use of tough measures and sanctions aimed at stopping those who undermine the new vision goals.

They will work hard to achieve the great goals embedded in this vision/mission. They will live in relative enduring peace after their takeover from sapiens (tensions and some conflicts cannot be ruled out) compared with current sapiens' reality. They will suffer less diseases and ailments and will enjoy a much longer active life than us as aging will be restrained and eventually subdued, and prolonging life at will may become an option at a certain time out in the future.

Their global order will be much better and smoothly functioning compared with our dissolving and bloated global order. They will live a more natural life, in smaller structures like towns, and put stress on social cooperation. Mega cities will not be their living choice. Creative pursuits will be open to all of them, not an elite privilege. And they will behave with profound simplicity, fairness, and prudence. Lifelong learning will be offered to them as a secondary occupation. A new brave world, realized but revised.

They will be equipped with superior mental/moral attributes: context thinking and moral, noble-warrior-and-wise-life attitudes. They will become resistant over time to problems and deviations expressed in antisocial and criminal behavior and dependency on drugs, alcohol, and other forms of addictions, which take a heavy toll on human lives and health.

Pursuing great goals and struggling for a great cause will form a strong, proactive, and focused character in them, contrary to the self-focused, fragile character, which so many people are burdened by today.

And they will be long-term planners and executors with courage, stamina, and endurance.

They will follow the motto from a Jewish old song.

THE WHOLE WORLD
IS A NARROW BRIDGE
The whole world
is a very narrow bridge
a very narrow bridge
a very narrow bridge

The whole world
is a very narrow bridge
A very narrow bridge.

And the main thing to recall
is not to be afraid
not to be afraid at all.

And the main thing to recall
is not to be afraid at all.

They will weigh facts/verifiable knowledge much higher than unproved convictions, in sharp contradiction to current sapiens.

They will possess greatness of mind, which does not follow the paths of tutored humility, resignation, conformity, lust, greed, and pleasure seeking. Greatness of mind is shown by defying all kinds of tyranny and by suggesting and fighting for viable and life-affirming, evolving solutions.

Last words: Dialogue

> The moralistic persecutors of the world draw most of
> their energy and zeal from the boundless source of human
> envy/jealousy.
>
> —BK

It is hard to judge whether humility is needed when you promote a vision designed to save your own species from extinction. Fighting spirit is anyway a MUST!

It helps, though, to remember that life-affirming chance is scarce and time is a slashing sword. What I have tried in many different ways to convey in the last twenty years was that we are marching toward collective suicide, partly by assuming that we are wiser than we are, and I came up with a workable vision on how to survive sapiens' aftermath. Yes, some people do consider me to be boastful, embarking on such a project that will surpass sapiens, yet they don't offer any new and refreshing ideas, just more of the same and some small adaptation, which don't work any longer. They entrench themselves in the "more of the same" reservations and critique. So it is a struggle, a hard one, and I will keep on promoting my message till my last breath. I don't need to promote myself, just the vision. I live otherwise a very modest life, without any connections with celebrities, big money, show off, holy spirits or God, just me, a little human worm, with some friends who inspire me, my thoughts, and a great need to help our current stupid humanity out of its suicidal course. Nothing else!

Terms

Awareness: knowledge or perception of a situation or fact.

The quality or state of being aware: knowledge and understanding that something is happening or exists.

Awareness relates to being able to be, at all times, in connection with one self, aims, and objectives. Mostly, man can keep his attention toward a certain subject in a very limited amount and time.

Advanced, ever-evolving awareness means that we know that our long-term survival is dependent on us evolving beyond sapiens as to become master of our expanding worlds and of the process of prolonging life by will.

Wisdom: the quality of having experience, knowledge, and good judgment; the quality of being wise.

Sapience or sagacity is the ability to think and act using knowledge, experience, understanding, common sense, and insight. Wisdom is associated with attributes such as unbiased judgment, compassion, experiential self-knowledge, self-transcendence, and nonattachment and virtues such as ethics and benevolence.

Advanced, ever-evolving wisdom embraces both the definition of wisdom and the knowledge of how to upgrade ourselves, evolve further, and expand our horizons and capacities in the most constructive manner for the transcending beings.

The ultimate purpose/meaning with advanced intelligent life: to become a master of its own destiny. To free oneself from the shackles of the low-function state nature has attributed man. Being free of these biological/mental shackles opens for new possibilities for advanced, evolving intelligence.

BOOKS IN ENGLISH WRITTEN BY THE AUTHOR

Stupid Sapiens: Evolve or Become Extinct (2019)

365 Years of Solitude, Sufferings and the Rise of the Creators: 2020–2384 (2019)

Den forvandlende og forvandlede Bustan. Min sandfærdige, fiktive og magiske livhistorie (2018)

A Survival Kit for the Upcoming Creators (2017)

A Portrait of a Visionary Trans Human and His Work (2015)

The Inevitable Human and Godless Faith (2015)

A Paradigm for a New Civilization (2013)

I, the Reluctant Creator (2012)

Global Psychology: Solving Eddie's Dilemma (2008)

The Fifth Narrative: The Wiser Ascent of Icarus (2004)

A Journey of Enhancement (1999)

References

1. BBC: 23.3.2020.
2. BBC: By Lindsey Galloway, 23.3.2020.
3. A growing number of people think their job is useless. Time to rethink the meaning of work. Rutger Bregman Correspondent, De Correspondent, Netherlands. 12.4.2017.
4. The "Loneliness Epidemic". HRSA: Health Resources & Service Administration. 17.1.2019.
5. Loneliness and Social Isolation in the United States, the United Kingdom, and Japan: An International Survey. Prepared by Bianca DiJulio, Liz Hamel, Cailey Muñana, and Mollyann Brodie Kaiser Family Foundation. 30.8. 2018.
6. Stonegate: One Is the Loneliest Number: Combating Senior Isolation. *Part 1: Assessing the Epidemic.* 15.11.2018.
7. United Nations

World Drug Report 2019: 35 million people worldwide suffer from drug use disorders while only 1 in 7 people receive treatment. A survey from 2019

8. Penn Today: Health science one in four Americans develops insomnia each year. Greg Richter Media. 8.6.2018.
9. SleepFoundation.Org: Insomnia and sleep. 28.5.2009.
10. News: The Guardian; What is depression and why is it rising? 4.6.2018.
11. Health line: What Is the Average IQ? Medically reviewed by Timothy J. Legg, PhD, PsyD, CRNP, ACRN, CPH. Written by Jacquelyn Cafasso. 10.4.2018.

12. JAMA Psychiatry. 1;76(3):271–279. doi: 10.1001/jamapsychiatry.2018.3428.
A Nationwide Study in Denmark of the Association Between Treated Infections and the Subsequent Risk of Treated Mental Disorders in Children and Adolescents.

13. World health report: Mental disorders affect one in four people. 4.10.2019.

14. Livescience: Are You the 5 Percent? Small Minority Have No Health Problems. By Rachael Rettner. 8.6.2015.

15. The Basic Laws of Human Stupidity. Carlo M. Cipolla (1976) Publication date. Publisher Ebury Publishing. 24.10.2019.

16. Climate change is likely making us dumber, *New York Post*. *nypost.com › 2019/12/23*

17. Florida State University News: Massive study by FSU researchers confirms that loneliness increases risk of dementia: The Journal of Gerontology. Serie B. 29.10.2018.

Lightning Source UK Ltd.
Milton Keynes UK
UKHW041445101120
373146UK00008B/479/J